$1.50

THE GREAT COMPOSERS SERIES
EDITED BY ERIC BLOM AND J. A. WESTRUP

Handel

PERCY M. YOUNG

Revised Edition

A LETTER FROM ONE OF HANDEL'S CONTEMPORARIES

"Mr. Handel's head is more full of maggots than ever. I found yesterday in his room a very queer instrument which he calls carillon (Anglice, a bell) and says some call it a Tubalcain, I suppose because it is both in the make and tone like a set of Hammers striking upon anvils. 'Tis played upon with keys like a Harpsichord and with this Cyclopean instrument he designs to make poor Saul [of the Handel oratorio]. His second maggot is an organ of £500 price which (because he is overstocked with money) he has bespoke of one Moss of Barnet. This organ, he says, is so constructed that as he sits at it he has a better command of his performers than he used to have, and he is highly delighted to think with what exactness his Oratorio will be performed by the help of this organ; so that for the future instead of beating time at his oratorios, he is to sit at the organ all the time with his back to the Audience. His third maggot is a Hallelujah which he has trump'd up at the end of his oratorio since I went into the Country, because he thought the conclusion of the oratorio not Grand enough; tho' if that were the case 'twas his own fault, for the words would have bore as Grand Musick as he could have set 'em to; but this Hallelujah, Grand as it is, comes in very nonsensically, having no manner of relation to what goes before. And this is the more extraordinary, because he refused to set a Hallelujah at the end of the first Chorus in the Oratorio, where I had placed one and where it was to be introduced with the utmost propriety, upon a pretence that it would make the entertainment too long. I could tell you more of his maggots; but it grows late and I must defer the rest till I write next, by which time, I doubt not, more new ones will breed in his Brain."

—from Chapter 6, "The Transition"

GREAT COMPOSERS SERIES

Formerly edited by the late ERIC BLOM,
and now under the editorshop of SIR JACK WESTRUP

(Collier Books published or in preparation)

Studies of the lives and music of other
Great Composers will be forthcoming.

HANDEL

1354

PERCY M. YOUNG

NEW, REVISED EDITION

COLLIER BOOKS
NEW YORK, N.Y.

This Collier Books edition is published by arrangement with
Farrar, Straus & Cudahy

Collier Books is a division of The Crowell-Collier Publishing
Company

First Collier Books Edition   1963

Library of Congress Catalog Card Number: 62-21615
This title was originally part of the Master Musicians series
published in the United States and its dependencies by Farrar,
Straus & Cudahy, Inc., in Canada by J. M. Dent & Sons (Canada),
Ltd., and in the open market territories by J. M. Dent & Sons,
Ltd., London

First pubilshed 1947

Copyright (c) 1962 by Farrar, Straus & Cudahy, Inc.
Hecho en los E.E.U.U.
Printed in the United States of America

IN AFFECTIONATE MEMORY OF
GARETH BERNARD BANTING

Contents

Contents

"Handel was the Jupiter of music; . . . his hallelujahs open the heavens. He utters the word "Wonderful," as if all their trumpets spoke together. And then, when he comes to earth, to make love amidst nymphs and shepherds (for the beauties of all religions find room in his breast), his strains drop milk and honey, and his love is the youthfulness of the Golden Age."

LEIGH HUNT (*Table Talk*)

Introduction

BY A HAPPY accident this introduction is written on an auspicious day. Handel appreciated birthday offerings from his disciples, and the author who has lived with his subject for some time is grateful to count himself among their number. The infectious personality of Handel explains the biographical minutiae of this study. He was a "character," as were Samuel Johnson and Charles Lamb. An effort has been made, therefore, to relieve his memory of the fictitious estimates (which have accrued despite the devotion of Schoelcher, Chrysander, Streatfeild and Dent, whose labours must be the starting-point of any modern scholar) of pedants and moralists. The intention is to present him as an eighteenth-century citizen. Similarly, his music is treated, so far as is possible, in relation to the audiences for which it was created.

It is hoped that this endeavour to remove an institution —like all such institutions too frequently taken carelessly for granted—from isolated eminence will promote added enthusiasm for the neglected masterpieces. It is, after all, the music that ultimately matters. Here particular singers and players who have contributed something to this book by accompanying the author on various Handelian excursions must have grateful memorial.

The list of acknowledgments is heavy. If there are omissions they are regretted. The Foreign Office, the Bank of England, the National Library of Ireland, the North Devon Athenaeum, the Fitzwilliam Museum at Cambridge, the Watson Music Library at Manchester and the Birmingham Central Reference Library have been helpful in putting material at my disposal. For the letter,

printed for the first time, on page 54–5 I am indebted to
His Grace the Duke of Devonshire and to Mr. Francis
Thompson, librarian at Chatsworth. The facsimiles of
documents on pp. 15, 20, and 22 are reproduced by per-
mission of Herr Konrad Sasse, Director of the Händelhaus, and Herr Walter Danz.

Dorothy Lady Brabourne, Lady Hatherton, Mrs. Phyl-
lis Brown, Mr. Norman Ault, Mr. G. J. K. Little, Mr.
H. Wathall and Canon A. E. Farrow have assisted in
supplying detailed information on particular points. In
recent years a great change of climate has occurred in
respect of Handel, both in England and Germany. The
operas (in England at least, for the German opera-houses,
especially of Hamburg, Göttingen and Halle, have done
much pioneer work and put Handel into the standard
repertoire) are now performed again, and more authentic
styles of presenting the other works are generally preferred; while musicologists have tidied many biographical
details—without, however, altering the main outline. I
am particularly obliged to Professor O. E. Deutsch and
to Herr Konrad Sasse, Director of the Händelhaus, in
Halle, for making certain suggestions which I have now
been able to incorporate.

P. M. Y.

August 1962.

Chapter 1

Birth and Apprenticeship

In 1685 CHARLES II of England died, and with him the prospects of the house of Stuart. In the same year Louis XIV, foreshadowing events to come, revoked the Edict of Nantes and dispersed throughout Europe the skill, intelligence and integrity of unpalatable Huguenotism. In 1685 Handel was born.

An artist may be, and frequently is, oblivious of the vagaries of political machination; but his career, his opportunities and his environment are subject to vicissitudes whose author is the politician. Thus two significant historic events in the year of his birth had some part in the moulding of the future of George Frideric Handel.

The opportunism of Charles II might have staved off the Glorious Revolution, but the stubborn miscalculations of James II, coupled with a respect for the dictatorial technique of the French king, made revolution inevitable. The deposition of James left an ultimate way clear for the Hanoverian succession, the development of modern parliamentarianism, the military achievements of Marlborough, the predominance of Low Church doctrine and such individual qualities *in arte vivendi* as were to excite the later applause of Voltaire and Montesquieu. France, whose habits of depredation stimulated uneasiness throughout Europe in the latter part of the seventeenth century, provoked the enmity not only of princes, but also of peoples by her renewal of religious persecution. England, watchful as ever of the balance of power, viewed with no disfavour the rise of a new, potentially counteractive state: that of Prussia. Under the tutelage of the

Hohenzollerns Prussia was beginning to merge as a unity, and by the time the Great Elector and Frederick I had impressed their personalities on various scattered German domains which had languished in semi-feudal torpor since the Peace of Westphalia she was a great power, with the third army in Europe, an imposing list of achievement in the arts and the sciences, and the competent continental check to future French ambitions in the east. But all this was purchased at a cost. The lives and liberties of her subjects passed from the inert or inefficient control of local princes to that of a centralized and efficient bureaucracy.

It was for the very reason that England provided a tolerable life for a man of independent proclivities that Handel made this country for the greater part of his life his home. It is, however, wrong to consider him a German. He was neither, but rather a European, and as such a glory to his own age and an example to others.

The independence to be discerned in Handel's character was (*pace* scientific scepticism) a hereditary endowment. The Händels in general pursued life with a superb faith in their own destinies. And since they were successful they aroused envious respect. Valentin, the first who comes into our field, was born at Breslau in 1583. Thence, having learned his trade as a coppersmith, he migrated to the more prosperous town of Halle, of which he was enrolled as citizen early in 1609. As a tradesman —that is the signification of the family name—Valentin Händel contracted an advantageous marriage with Anna Beichling, daughter of a master coppersmith. Thereafter he prospered, his money went into property, and he nurtured a large family in the fear of God—the upbringing was Lutheran—in bourgeois respectability and in a sound belief in the efficacy of balanced budgets. In 1622 his fifth son, Georg, was born.

As the coppersmith business eventually passed to his elder brothers Georg was constrained to attempt new fields of endeavour. Influenced, no doubt, by the prevailing needs of the times and by the contemporary carnage of the Thirty Years War, he chose surgery (with its ancillary craft of barber). Left fatherless at the age of fourteen Georg Händel developed that degree of self-dependence which necessity so often mothers. He was first apprenticed to Andrew Beger, whose wife was daughter of the English musician William Brade. Next he assisted Christoph Oettinger. After his death, in 1643, Händel acquired both his practice and his widow, who thus became Frau Händel. Of this *mariage de convenance* six children were born, of whom two survived the perilous passage of infancy. With that ambition induced by paternity Händel progressed in dignity to appointment as surgeon to the suburb of Giebichenstein and as surgeon-in-ordinary and *valet de chambre* to the Duke Augustus of Saxony. Three years later an episode occurred to show that municipal and individual rights had their eighteenth-century champions. Händel purchased a house-cum-wineshop (a commendable departure in medical practice), the *Zum gelben Hirsch* in the Schlamm, but the civic authority refused to renew the wine-selling licence. Händel referred the matter to the elector, who referred it back to Halle. But the indomitable Händel refused to be reduced by his fellow townsmen and shuttlecocked his grievances back to the elector, who thereupon, exhausted by the strain of attempting decisions of such magnitude, settled the matter in the plaintiff's favour. The town council was promised military occupation and monetary penalties should the matter be raised again. Nor was this the only occasion on which Händel asserted his rights. In 1680, on the death of the duke and consequent political changes, attempts were made, unsuccessfully, to deprive him of his court appointments. Whether, as a matter of fact, this would have entailed much loss of emolument is doubtful. Princes and dukes were conspicuous for the splendour of their surroundings rather than for their capacity for adequately recompensing their *aides*. However, Händel intended to conserve his personal dignity and in so doing ensured his unborn son's first entry into romantic anecdote.

By the Peace of Westphalia Halle had been assigned from Saxony to Prussia, but this arrangement became operative only on the death of Augustus. The local effects of this change were that the court was transferred to Weissenfels, where the new duke, Johann Adolf, set up the customary pathetic illusion of a *petit Versailles,* and that Halle resumed its more stolid characteristics, changing, incidentally, the Ritter-Akademie—an establishment exclusively devoted to the propagation and preservation of aristocratic privilege—into a university. Halle-an-der-Saale was a pleasant town, anciently a member of the Hanseatic League, with a sturdy tradition documented in its principal buildings. These included a medieval Rathaus; the remains of the castle of Moritzburg, established in 1478 by the Archbishop of Magdeburg and largely destroyed by fire during the Thirty Years War; the Moritzkirche; the Liebfrauenkirche (church of Our Lady), conspicuous by its curious twin-spired and bridged façade; and the ancient but altered Dom, Calvinist since 1689. The natural situation of Halle, which was a centre of salt manufacture, gave trading advantages, a certain cultural independence and a dignity which its most distinguished alumnus recollected gracefully in later years.[1] But part of the price paid by the seventeenth and eighteenth centuries for such cultural blessings as excite the envy of later generations was plague, famine and sudden death. Georg Händel himself was given up for dead in 1681. His recovery possessed, so far as his kinsfolk were concerned, elements of the miraculous. His eldest son, Gottfried, perished in a general and alarming epidemic in the following year. His wife died in 1683.

Giebichenstein, where Händel worked, had as its Lutheran pastor Georg Taust, of Bohemian descent. He had two daughters. One, Dorothea, became Händel's second wife a few months after the passing of the first. The other, Anna, followed to the Schlamm when the onset of pregnancy demanded sisterly sympathy and domestic reinforcement. In 1684 a son was born to Dorothea. He died almost immediately.

On 23rd February 1685 a second child was born who

[1] *Vide* reference to the coat of arms of the Foundling Hospital on page 110.

Record of Handel's baptism.

did survive. He was christened on the following day at the Liebfrauenkirche. The names given to him were Georg Friedrich. Confusion with the old-style calendar (in which the year began on 25th March) impelled earlier authorities, including the engravers of the memorial inscription in Westminster Abbey, to place the date of Handel's birth in 1684.[2] A further digression may here be relevant. The family name was susceptible of various orthography: thus we meet Händel, Hendel, Händeler, Hendler, Hendtler, and the charming feminine form of Händelin (to Christiana Susanna Händelin Handel ultimately bequeathed £300). The commonest English usage was, and is, Handel. Hereafter the composer shall be called, as he styled himself in England, George Frideric Handel.

Those who, in the period under review, survived the hazards of infancy were, beyond doubt, hardy. Handel, who inherited a good deal from his father, received therefrom the benefit of a tough constitution. Old Händel mercifully survived his illness of 1681: at the same period of his own life his son recovered from a severe and paralytic disorder. They were, literally, a breed of diehards. In later years Handel's physique became one source of anecdote. More important than this is the fact that his bodily powers had particular reference to his creative activities, his capacity for hard work and his resilience in the face of misfortune being directly consequential. The bowed legs[3] of maturity may suggest a vitamin deficiency in childhood, otherwise the parents may be exonerated from any suspicion of early neglect.

The incidents of youth are germane to the later development of the biographic subject. Accordingly the Händel household needs to be set in proper perspective. Episodes imperfectly recollected from John Christopher Smith by the gullible Mainwaring have furnished material for romantic screeds of significance only to the unmusical.

[2] The Gregorian or new-style calendar was introduced in England in 1752. It was welcomed with the reserve accorded to all innovations.

[3] Hawkins, v. 142.

A not unnatural affection for an estimable mother and a later aversion from the bonds of holy matrimony have been construed into psychological jargon as "mother-fixation," while a fatherly inclination to suggest a career other than that of music has had the elder Händel arraigned for tyranny. Such facts as are available suggest that Georg Händel had excellent good sense, pride in his son's potentialities, and a willingness to provide for educational opportunity. His surviving portrait adds to these qualities a grave, patrician dignity. If the percussion instruments of the nursery really were incinerated and the clavichord acquired only against interdict the natural desire of an elderly surgeon for a quiet home may be held responsible. The lusty presence of George Frideric's younger sisters[4] provided distraction enough.

Somewhere about his seventh or eighth year George Frideric accompanied his father to the court of Weissenfels. There, with a precocity not uncommon to the children of elderly parents, he proposed to the duke his intention of becoming a musician. The duke sensibly advised that self-expression should find its natural outlet under competent guidance. Handel was put, therefore, under that of Zachau, organist of the Liebfrauenkirche. At the same time his general education proceeded classically and conservatively at the Lutheran Gymnasium, a grammar school. An incident of these years which appropriately stuck in the mind was the operation which his father performed in 1692 on Andreas Rudloff, the "Halle Sword-swallower." The incident may be quoted as demonstrating either the incredible surgical gifts with which Händel was endowed or the mythical propensities of many Handeliana.

Halle had enjoyed that sort of musical reputation which would now promote complacency in a similarly placed English provincial town. Before the reign of Zachau it had possessed two notable organists in Wolff Heintz, a friend of Luther's, and Samuel Scheidt, the son of a saltworks manager and a father of German music.[5] In the

---

[4] Dorothea Sophie and Johanne Christiane.

[5] For his knowledge of English music see Appendix C.

palmy days before pietism stepped on such displays Halle had gone some way in the inauguration of the *Singspiel* as opposed to the infiltrating Italian opera. Zachau himself combined competence with sobriety, was painstaking and friendly, and had a good collection of Italian and German music.[6] Young Handel learned the organ, the harpsichord, the violin, the hautboy, composition and common sense. The contemporary attitude to music was utilitarian. Much was required for ceremonies of church and state and, library facilities being non-existent, had to be composed *ad hoc*. The embryonic organist was early initiated into the mysteries of ecclesiastical tradition, and Handel, as a matter of course, wrote a weekly cantata as exercise. But sacred music was hardly his first love. "I used to write like the devil in those days, but chiefly for the hautbois, which was my favourite instrument,"[7] he is reported to have said. A set of sonatas, written at the age of ten, were discovered by Lord Polwarth later in Handel's life in Germany, but have since disappeared again. Another loss to the biographer is the exercise book which was compiled under Zachau's direction. This contained copied extracts from such models as Froberger, Krieger, Kerl, Ebner and Strungk. As a historic figure Strungk is worth momentary consideration. He was a conspicuous composer, a member of the German resistance party fighting at Hamburg the cause of native opera, who left a large catalogue of works which quickly passed into the limbo of forgotten achievement. Some of his titles have a familiar ring, *Nero* (1693) and *Agrippina* (1699) in particular. Handel no doubt spent the impressionable years of his youth reflecting on the splendour of their associations. His own copies of Strungk were probably made from *Ein hundert auserlesene Arien zweyer Hamburgischen Operen, Semiramis und Esther. Mit beigefügten Ritornellen* (1689).

Three or four years of Zachau's able tuition, absorbed together with the nearby schooling of the Gymnasium, qualified Handel for inclusion among the ranks of the

[6] Mainwaring, p. 14.

[7] Burney, *Commem.*, p. 3 n.

prodigies. In this capacity he visited Berlin in 1696.[8] There Frederick,[9] later to become by imperial grace King of Prussia, held court. While he continued his father's work of Prussian organization and diplomatic opportunism—he had previously supported the claims of William III to the English throne and was later to aid the allied cause in the War of Spanish Succession—his second wife, Sophia Charlotte, occupied herself with the department of *Kultur*. Lest, however, it should be thought that the elector himself was a Philistine, it should be recorded that he was responsible for the foundation of the University of Halle and of the Academy of Science in Berlin, that he appreciated French culture despite political antagonism and that he welcomed (*autres temps, autres mœurs*) to Berlin victims of political and religious discrimination. Across this scene Handel flitted meteorically. He impressed the court, the electress, herself a practising musician, and the elector. The latter made an offer not unusual for a period in which crowned heads felt easier with a maximum *entourage* of sycophantic retainers. He suggested a further course in musical education, inevitably in Italy. Old Händel, however, was not enthusiastic. Still supporting the conventional thesis that the precarious possibilities of music offered improbable avenues of worldly success, he emphasized the advantages of a legal career. It may be urged that, as a matter of fact, jurisprudence formed a better training for musicians than music: among German musicians Schütz, Walther, Mattheson, Kuhnau, Telemann, Emanuel Bach, as well as Handel, were "spoiled" lawyers. Georg Händel died on 11th February 1697. The melancholy event was commemorated by his son in a poetic effusion duly published.

[8] It was not on this visit that Handel met Ariosti and Buononcini, as neither was in Berlin in 1696. Ariosti arrived in 1697 and Buononcini in 1702. Mainwaring was probably right in recording a meeting between Handel and these musicians, but, as usual, he gets his dates wrong. Mainwaring may be credited with the invention of the bed-time story about the youthful Handel sitting on Ariosti's knee.

[9] As Elector of Brandenburg this ruler was Frederick III, as King of Prussia, Frederick I.

Poem by Handel on the death of his father.

Georg Händel was something of Horace's *justus et tenax vir,* and the value of independence, a quality which dictated his reaction to the electoral offer, he impressed on his son. The University of Halle, under the progressive leadership of Thomasius, further stimulated intellectual adventure, and the pietistic teaching of Francke, head of the theological faculty, laid stress on the necessity for freedom in spiritual experience. Handel entered the university in 1702 and, while his academic attainments may have been slight, he could hardly have remained impervious to the new liberalism of thought which characterized the foundation. Music was simultaneously pursued with added zeal. In the same year as entering the university Handel became organist of the Dom, in succession to the intemperate Leporin.

The composition of ecclesiastical music being an organist's necessary duty, Handel produced the proper sequence of cantatas for the Dom. The sole authentic survivor is a *Laudate pueri*. These Halle activities created a reputation that was not merely local. So that Georg Philipp Telemann, a young man of varied abilities, called on Handel round about the year 1700. Telemann was four years older than Handel, a native of Magdeburg, a nominal student of law and an undergraduate of the University of Leipzig.

A capacity for loyal friendship was a characteristic of Handel, and that with Telemann was lifelong. Forty years on they were still in amicable correspondence with each other. These early days were days of serious intent and, whereas the latest letters were devoted to horticulture, between 1701 and 1703 they engaged their pens technically on the "working-out of melodious compositions."[10] At that time melody was the *fons et origo* of all music. Personal intercourse also took place, and if this was not at Halle then it was at Weissenfels, for which court Telemann wrote a number of operas. The reciprocity of musical thought in the eighteenth century is indicated by the extent of Telemann's studies. Being as fluent in literature as in music—and Handel commented that he "could write a motet for eight voices more quickly than one could write a letter"—Telemann left valuable evidence in this respect. His recorded models were Kuhnau's fugues, the French overtures of Lully and Campra, "the true and barbaric beauty" of such Polish music as he came across while sojourning in Upper Silesia and the ubiquitous productions of Italy.

10 Mattheson, *Grundlage einer Ehren-Pforte.*

Notice of Handel's appointment as Cathedral organist in Halle.

But experience of foreign schools could only come to the home-staying student fortuitously. The proper way to learn was to travel, and this, influenced by Telemann's example and irked by the monotony of the Calvinistic round at the *Dom,* Handel proposed to do. He finished his year's probation as organist in the spring of 1703, leaving his place to Johann Kolhart, disconnected himself from the university, took leave of his family and started on the first stage of his Odyssey.

Chapter 2

"Il caro Sassone"

THE MAGNETIC TOWN of northern Germany was Hamburg, handsomely prosperous and culturally progressive. There would be met travellers from overseas and ample opportunities for intellectual exercise. By 1703 the onslaught of Italy was biting into the inner defences of German opera, despite the vigorous protective measures undertaken in Scholt's opera house. But this fact was an inducement to the young. Artistic theories worried Handel little. His career, law being now finally rejected, was to be that of a musician, which then implied craftsman. Music was required and therefore must be written, and if a particular style was in vogue then it must be obeyed; although later on Handel sometimes indulged in antipopular stylistic dictation. The Italian manner was favoured because it exalted melody. Therefore throughout the century we find great stress being laid on "air." In view of the later genius of the age it cannot on the whole be complained that public taste miscalculated in its postulations. Handel arrived at Hamburg with a provincial reputation and with provincial deficiencies. From a metropolitan point of view his achievement was thus summarized: "He was strong in the organ, stronger than Kuhnau in fugue and counterpoint, especially *extempore,* but he knew very little about melody until he came to the Hamburg operas."[1]

Thus the first stage in Handel's emancipation from German influence opened. Over the period with which this chapter is concerned presides the benign influence of

[1] Mattheson, *Grundlage einer Ehren-Pforte.*

24

one of the most remarkable of eighteenth-century worthies: the abbate Steffani. Born in 1654 in obscurity, carried off to the Bavarian court as a promising choirboy, tutored by Johann Caspar Kerl and Carissimi, Steffani acquired a high musical reputation by his twentieth year. But in addition to music he studied theology, mathematics and philosophy with equal success. He became a priest in 1680, after which he left Munich for Hanover, where an appointment as *Kapellmeister* awaited him. There he wrote operas for Giusti's new and elegant theatre, and in so doing increased the artistic reputation of Hanover. His operas were also performed at Brunswick and Hamburg. For the latter town, significantly, they were translated into German.

But this was only one side of Steffani's life. In 1698 he became the elector's ambassador at Brussels, and thenceforth his duties as plenipotentiary overshadowed his artistic activity. But not so much as to prevent the continuance of his enthusiasm therein. If there was one figure in Europe whose acquaintance and encouragement were worth a young man's acquisition it was Steffani. Handel was fortunate.

Precisely when he first met the abbate is doubtful. His own statement, as recorded by Hawkins,[2] reads:

> When I first arrived in Hanover as a young man, under twenty, I was acquainted with the merits of Steffani, and he had heard of me. I understood something of music, and could play pretty well on the organ; he received me with great kindness, and took an early opportunity to introduce me to the princess Sophia and the elector's son, giving them to understand that I was what he was pleased to call a virtuoso in music; he obliged me with instructions for my conduct and behaviour during my residence at Hanover; and being called from the city to attend to matters of a public concern, he left me in possession of that favour and patronage which himself had enjoyed for a number of years.

2 Hawkins, v. 267.

The latter part of this statement applies to 1709, in which year Handel attached himself to the Hanoverians. But the first part refers to an earlier period: prior, in fact, to 1705. Remembering that Handel had left Germany at least thirty years before Hawkins obtained this statement, it is reasonable to assume that what were two separate events had unified in mental coalescence. By emending Hawkins's punctuation[3] the antithesis becomes quite clear. Brenet suggests that Handel called at Hanover *en route* for Hamburg in 1703 and that then he made the acquaintance of Steffani. Such a meeting, resulting in mutual respect, would have been profitable. Steffani's good opinion would help to explain the trail of glory which Handel blazed at Hamburg and, to a greater degree, in Italy. And the later offer of the Hanoverian *Kapellmeister* post is more comprehensible if understood as the result of a more or less prolonged interest on the part of Steffani.

Arrived at Hamburg during the summer of 1703 Handel quickly made the acquaintance of Johann Mattheson, an aspiring singer, composer, author and man of the world. In the latter capacity he was serviceable to Handel: as an author to posterity. He left sufficient information in his encyclopaedic *Grundlage einer Ehren-Pforte* for a full-size portrait of the young Handel (an individual too seldom considered) to be re-created.

In this we discern a youth as much characterized by industry as by brilliance. Handel wrote arias, which were apparently interminable, and cantatas, visited organs, did the round of choirs, operas and concerts, became domesticated "at a certain house, in which music was practised with the utmost devotion," absorbed the correct dramatic style from Mattheson, to whom—after sociable meals at the expense of Mattheson's father—in return he gave contrapuntal assistance. "I learned from him as he learned from me. *Docendo enim discimus*."[4] In his capacity as second violin (perhaps after this example it will no more be regarded as undignified to sit at a second violin desk) in the theatre orchestra he "behaved as if he couldn't

[3] e.g. ". . . a virtuoso in music. He obliged me . . ."
[4] Mattheson, op. cit.

count five, being naturally inclined to a dry humour." His manner was engagingly modest, it being only with difficulty that he was induced to substitute for an absent harpsichordist. But life was punctuated by such pleasant trivialities as river excursions. And Mattheson, writing in 1740, looked back wistfully and whimsically on the occasion which brought them together at the Maria Magdalen church, where the organ-blower was a pastry-cook's son. "I know well enough," he says of Handel, "that he will laugh heartily when he reads this, though as a rule he laughs but little." And then there was the August expedition to Lübeck, in the pigeon-fancier's company. At Lübeck the bait was the prospect of succeeding the great Buxtehude. And this was made additionally attractive by the municipality who, alive as always to the possibility of rate reduction, offered not only an organ stool but also a marriage bed to the successful applicant. The intended pensioner was Buxtehude's daughter, whose lack in allurement and wealth in years recommended a quick return to Hamburg. What was refused by Handel and Mattheson, and three years later by Sebastian Bach, came eventually to one of Keiser's juniors—Johann Christian Schieferdecker.

The later months of 1703 passed less excitingly but more profitably. Handel became music tutor to the family of the English resident—John Wich.[5] This dignitary was an amiable soul, whose wine a few months previously had filled Addison with satisfaction and whose swollen legs with concern.[6] In addition to his tutorial activities Handel was composing a Passion (according to St. John), for next Holy Week, at the behest of Postel, an old librettist now turned Pietist. More time for composition was afforded by Mattheson's absence in Holland. Handel, however, missed his companionship and wrote accordingly on 18th March 1704. He finishes his letter: "I therefore beg you to notify me of your departure so that I may have the opportunity of fulfilling my duty, and come

[5] John Wich continued in office until 1713, in which year he was succeeded by Cyril (afterwards Sir Cyril) Wich.
[6] Letter from Addison to Wich, May 1703.

and meet you with Mlle Sbulens."[7] The lady has this solitary entry in history. Whether she came, as has been suggested, from Halle is a matter for speculation, as is the possibility of her having exercised particular claims on the affections of Handel. It may be suspected that some good reason prompted a joint welcome home for the nomadic Mattheson. However that may be, he deferred his return until after the production of the Passion. This work, relatively inconspicuous as it was, disturbed the *amour-propre* of Keiser, an older man prone to dissipation and jealousy, and spurred him to the composition of a similar work: *Der blutige und sterbende Jesus*. Mattheson thought little of Handel's Passion and indulged in its critical anatomy in his *Critica Musica* of 1725.

The Handel-Mattheson friendship went through rather rough waters in 1714. First Mattheson usurped his friend's place in the Wich household and then brawled with him in the theatre. The circumstances leading to this much publicized incident are peculiar, and one suspects more than meets the eye. On 20th October Mattheson produced his *Cleopatra,* in which he sang the part of Antonius. His custom was, having (dramatically speaking) expired, to descend to the orchestra and to supplant Handel at the harpsichord. The opera ran smoothly, with this curious arrangement not apparently disapproved, until 5th December. On that night Handel suddenly refused to resign his place at the harpsichord, and the irate composer took the opportunity, when outside the theatre, of slapping his colleague on the face. Anticipating Hawkins's bloodthirsty charge[8] at a later date Mattheson archly commented that a "dry slap on the face was no assassination, but rather a friendly hint, to put him on his guard." He further described Handel as "tall, strong, broad-shouldered and muscular; consequently well able to defend himself." The sequel was a Sheridanesque duel in which

---

[7] A Mr. Sbuelen is twice mentioned in letters from Handel to Michaelsen (10th August 1731 and 28th August 1736). On the second occasion we learn that wedding presents to Handel's niece were sent to Sbuelen at Hamburg.

[8] Hawkins, v. 265.

tradition assigns Handel's deliverance to a fortunately placed button or score,[9] which broke Mattheson's sword. The spectators must have repined at so anticlimactic a dénouement. A happy ending was effected by a dinner of reconciliation on 30th December engineered by a pacifically minded town councillor who also held shares in the theatre. Brawls, bloodshed and hot emotion were part of the eighteenth-century mode of life, and Handel was not immune from their incidence.

Tranquillity again prevailing, Handel and Mattheson turned to the business of wage-earning. This centred round Handel's first opera *Almira,* to a libretto by Feustking in mixed German and Italian. Fourteen songs had belonged to an earlier play by Lope de Vega. Mattheson was the *primo uomo.* After *Almira,* which ran from 8th January 1705 to 25th February, came *Die durch Blut und Mord erlangte Liebe, oder* (less sensationally) *Nero.* This had a run of three nights, and then came off. But Handel had achieved two things. First the opportunity of demonstrating to himself and to Hamburg in general that he was possessed of an exceptional dramatic flair; secondly and consequently the sour enmity of Keiser. Keiser was much annoyed and began work on new settings of both *Nero* and *Almira.* Neither was a success but, reading between the lines, Handel came to the conclusion that life would be more tolerable in another place. His mind turned to the prospects of an Italian journey. Steffani would have urged this; Ariosti and Buononcini,[10] whose acquaintance Handel had made in the days of his apprenticeship, would similarly have advised; and a new friend, Prince Giovanni Gastone de' Medici, still more importunately.

Gastone de' Medici was Micawber-like in impecuniosity, in good nature and in constant optimism. He had few grounds for optimism, which, doubtless, is why he was optimistic. His father was the despotic Cosimo III,

9 Mainwaring, p. 35.

10 It is probably correct to assume that Handel met Ariosti and Buononcini during his residence at Hamburg.

who handed Tuscany to the bondage of clerical task-masters; his wife, tied to him by statecraft and not by love, the stout, unrefined Anna Maria of Saxe-Lauenburg; his official home an isolated castle in the hinterland of Bohemia. Not surprisingly Gastone dedicated one half of himself to Venus and the other, less dangerously, to opera-going and flute-playing. It was these latter occupations which brought him into contact with Handel.

Thus encouraged to look south Handel took practical steps to implement his desires. He set to work on a third opera, an opera of such proportions that for practical purposes it needed dichotomy and became therefore *Florindo* and *Daphne*. Leaving behind him these scores and, according to Mainwaring, a good many other miscellaneous compositions, he packed his bag, counted his savings—200 ducats—and shook the dust of Hamburg off his feet. His travelling companion was an acquaintance named von Binitz who, if Mattheson's testimony is correct, subscribed the travelling expenses.

Italy in the eighteenth century was, like Greece at a more remote period of history, in process of conquering her conquerors. Fragmentated, Venice a nominally independent state of consequence to Europe in general as a pleasure resort, Lombardy and Naples subject to Spanish viceroys, Florence and Tuscany under Austrian attention, Savoy on uneasy terms with France, and the Papal States perpetuating reaction and obscurantism, she left practical affairs to the northern nations, setting herself the task of cultural diffusion. Which, in the realm of music, she did so inexorably that opposition was impossible. The schools of music were the courts, both lay and ecclesiastical, and the patrons-in-chief were such as Handel encountered.

His career in Italy was so unnaturally successful (for a Saxon to outshine the Italians on their own ground was surely unthinkable) that one is tempted to see behind it influence, then as now a surer guide to popular acclamation than ability. The influence, it might reasonably be surmised, was that of Steffani. First Handel went to Florence, where Gastone's brother Ferdinand, a patron of Alessandro Scarlatti, controlled the aesthetics ignored by his father. This was towards the end of 1706. A short sojourn at the Pratolino left time for some emendations to *Almira* and for the composition of some cantatas. But early in the new year[11] he was in Rome, where his arrival was thus noted in the Valesia Diary: "There has arrived in this city a Saxon, an excellent player on the cembalo and a composer of music, who has today [Jan. 14] displayed his ability in playing the organ in the Church of St. John Lateran to the amazement of everyone." Here he composed some psalm settings (*Dixit Dominus*[12], *Laudate pueri,* and *Nisi Dominus*), which, together with other Latin motets, have been shown to belong to the service of the vespers for Our Lady of Carmel. The protector of the Carmelites was the Cardinal Carlo Colonna, also a patron of Handel.[13] In July a new opera, probably begun when Handel first arrived at Florence, *Rodrigo,* was produced at the Florentine court. The reputed reward from Ferdinand, who had come to the recent conclusion that Scarlatti had deteriorated in amusement value, was a hundred sequins and a service of porcelain. Judging by the social assets which stood him in such good stead at this period an amorous interlude, detailed with customary factual inconsistency by Mainwaring, would not be out of place. Mainwaring's heroine —Vittoria Tesi—is ruled out by reason of immaturity: she was born in 1700. Although it may be that Mainwaring's lady was right, but his date wrong. Handel probably met her again in 1719. Vittoria Tarquini, the prima donna of *Rodrigo* (an alternative candidate to Tesi), was well ensconced in the good graces of the Prince Ferdinand, and therefore unlikely to have spent her energy in chasing an impecunious composer, however flashing his immediate reputation, all over Italy. Thus in uncertainty dies a promising anecdote.

[11] 14th January. Newman Flower, p. 62.

[12] Autograph note, 8th April.

[13] *Vide Handel among the Carmelites,* J. S. Hall, in *Dublin Review,* July 1959.

Venice was the next port of call. There Handel made the pleasant acquaintance of Domenico Scarlatti, who later reappeared in Handel's London life in 1720. An attractive trait was this capacity for remembering old friends with affection, and often with gratitude. Instances occur so frequently that the underlining of their incidence may be forgiven in that thus the conventionally drawn Handel is softened in outline. Handel also met Scarlatti's tutor Gasparini, Lotti and possibly (we may like to think) the young Canaletto.

There was also in Venice the Earl of Manchester.[14] The earl was an incompetent diplomat—he had previously failed in missions to Paris and Venice—but well-mannered: therefore, after normal convention in these matters, he was given full opportunity to continue in the wrecking of his own professional reputation and his country's interests. At this time he was negotiating the adherence of the Venetians to the Grand Alliance. They for their part were entertaining him with diversionary operations. Thus he came into contact with Handel and commenced an interest in his music which was maintained in later years. The advantage of the Grand Tour, whether for rich or poor, was a healthy diminution in chauvinistic intention. The intelligent were not over-conscious of nationality. The Earl of Manchester loved the Venetians, while deploring their policy of *attentisme,* and approved their opera in which the rising star was the German Handel. English lack of artistic perception, a deficiency more rare than is commonly believed, did not disgrace Her Majesty's representative. His lead was followed by another English resident. Joseph Smith, whose address Handel made use of on a later visit to Italy,[15] was beginning to lay the foundations of his bibliophilic reputation in 1707. And a final stimulus came to English affairs in Venice during Handel's visit, through the presence of Ernest of Hanover, brother to the future George I, who was basking in the glory attached to his house by the Act

[14] Created duke 1719.
[15] *Vide* letter from Handel to Michaelsen, 11th March 1729.

of Settlement (1701) and in the official satisfaction of diplomacy at its loyalty to the allied cause.

From Venice, having established useful contacts, Handel went with Domenico Scarlatti to Rome. Temporarily papal authority was frowning on opera and inferior princes of the church were compelled to divert their interest to a more godly form of recreation. Cardinal Pietro Ottoboni was the principal connoisseur of the arts and, being also a friend of Ferdinand of Tuscany, he welcomed Handel on his arrival. With the entrée to the cardinal's musical evenings Handel added to his growing list of acquaintances Corelli, in charge of the Ottoboni music, Pasquini and (if he had not previously met him) Alessandro Scarlatti. Handel was not only a musical but a social success. He proceeded from Ottoboni's to the favour of the Prince Ruspoli, prince by papal dispensation, and stayed in the luxury of his palace during March and April 1708. The Ruspoli archives are precise on this point, giving details of the hire and carriage of Handel's bed.

In the Palazzo Bonelli Handel wrote *La resurrezione*, which was performed in succession to Scarlatti's *Della Santissima Annunziata*. *La resurrezione* was received with satisfaction: the only discord was struck by the Holy Father, who sent a messenger to Ruspoli complaining of the employment in the oratorio of a female singer.[16] The next work was contrived with less care. It was a setting of Cardinal Pamfili's *Il trionfo del tempo e del disinganno*, fifty years later to be remodelled into *The Triumph of Time and Truth*. Although *Il trionfo* was a relative failure Handel felt sufficiently sure of his standing in Italy to remonstrate with Corelli for his inability to cope with the overture. "My dear Saxon," complained Corelli, "this music is in the French style, of which I have no knowledge." Nor was there any reason why he should have had in view of Italy's prerogative of supplying music to the rest of Europe. *Il trionfo,* performed for Ottoboni's Arcadians,[17]

[16] *Vide* letter quoted in *New Sources for Handel.* "La Resurrezione," Rudolf Ewerbert, *Music and Letters*, April 1960, p. 128.

was given under the shadow of political discontent and the imminence of yet another of the many sieges of Rome. Therefore Handel went south to compose *Aci, Galatea e Polifemo* for the marriage of the Duca d'Alvito, which was solemnized on 19th July at Naples. While in Naples Handel dallied with another lady, of whom no more is known than that her name was Donna Laura.[18] He also met the Viceroy of Naples, Cardinal Grimani, a friend of Lady Mary Wortley Montagu's, a connection of the family which built the San Giovanni Crisotomo theatre at Venice and a good librettist. Grimani prepared the libretto for Handel's next opera, *Agrippina*. This overshadowed all the other events of the Carnival season which opened at Venice on 26th December 1709, running for twenty-seven nights. Two of the singers later came to London. They were Margherita Durastanti, whose appearance in *Agrippina* at the age of fourteen or fifteen was less remarkable then than it would be now, and Giuseppe Boschi, the possessor of a Gostling-like voice of immense profundity.

Agrippina was Handel's greatest achievement to date, and he let it be his valediction to Italy. After the hysteria of "Viva il caro Sassone!" which punctuated every pause in each performance he determined to try his fortunes elsewhere. Invitations from Hanover were pressing, Prince Ernest had seen the success of *Agrippina,* and Steffani was pleased with the progress of his protégé. He had learned something of the favourable impression Handel had made when in Rome a year earlier. Steffani was too involved by now in affairs of church and state to continue his *Kapellmeister* office. Therefore he vacated it, applied himself to episcopal duties—he had been consecrated Bishop of Spiga, *in partibus infidelium*, and appointed

[17] The Academy of Arcadians was founded in 1690 "to further the cultivation of the sciences and to awake throughout Italy the taste for humane letters, and in particular for poetry in the vulgar tongue." In brief, the academy was an aristocratic institute for adult education, with stress laid on music and iced drinks.

[18] ". . . whether a Portugueze or a Spanish Princess I will not be certain."—Mainwaring, p. 66.

the pope's representative in Northern Germany—and deposited Handel at Hanover.

The three years in Italy were to Handel as a postgraduate course. He had previously learned the fundamentals of musicianship in good schools, those of Halle and Hamburg, but Italy provided the opportunity of absorbing, at first hand, the principles which were to dominate the eighteenth century. Stylistic considerations will be dealt with at a later juncture, but a sufficient guarantee of the value of this experience is denoted by the manuscripts collected of works by Alessandro Scarlatti, some of which eventually found their way into the library of Charles Jennens.[19] In Italy Handel was reminded of the welcome which would greet him in England, when he cared to make the journey. He left the country having gained in knowledge, in friendship and in reputation. The laity impulsively referred to him as "L'Orfeo del nostro secolo," which Germany subsequently thought of as "a rare honour, for no German is spoken of thus by an Italian or a Frenchman, these gentry being accustomed to scoffing at us";[20] the clergy with commendable zeal looked on him not only as a great musician, but as a worthy subject for proselytism. Handel reacted to this compliment by resolving "to die a member of that communion, whether true or false, in which he was born and bred."[21] At the same time he produced a large number of effectively opposite works, some of which, in the form of motets, are now preserved in the Santini collection at Münster (Westphalia).

[19] E. J. Dent, *Handel,* p. 37.

[20] Barthold Feind, 1715. *Vide* Romain Rolland, *A Musical Tour,* p. 84.

[21] Mainwaring, p. 64.

Chapter 3

English Patronage

LIKE OTHER EMPLOYERS of labour the eighteenth-century disciples of Maecenas had their faults. But Johnson's letter to the Earl of Chesterfield and Mozart's humiliation at the hands of the Archbishop of Salzburg have been allowed to overshadow the positive benefits accorded to numerous artists more fortunate in their selection of patron. The good and bad of the system will be evident from the progress of this book; with Handel's appointment to Hanover we enter upon a period in his life singular for its pleasant association with the great. It was in the middle of June 1710 that he took up his duties in place of Steffani. His emoluments amounted to 1,000 thaler per annum. Within a month or so he was, however, again peripatetic. First a dutiful call at Halle and then a visit to the electoral court at Düsseldorf. Here he already had contacts: the Electress Anna Maria was sister to Ferdinand and Gastone de' Medici; Steffani was a regular correspondent of the elector; and Corelli was *persona grata* there. For a short time the splendour of Düsseldorf, apparent in its opera and its picture galleries, beguiled Handel, but during the autumn he made his way to London. As a cultural demonstration this visit would have met with Hanoverian approval and Handel's success in London been regarded as of slightly more than artistic value. Handel did one important thing. He impressed many people of influence with what to them was a singular fact: that a foreigner, possessed of certain attributes, could override that insular prejudice which insisted that aliens were of necessity comic and/or offensive.

Heidegger, manager of the Opera, was both.[1] A Swiss by birth, he essayed various professions speculatively and graduated to opera by way of a privacy in Queen Anne's Life Guards. This he judiciously relinquished to invest his wits in the new potentialities of Italian opera. Thus he met Handel in 1710 with a view to establishing a fortune out of the latter's high reputation and the whims of the aristocracy. They, indignant at any suggestion that England (particularly after Blenheim and Ramillies) could be bettered in any department of life, but none the less slaves to continental fashion, were sympathetic to the newer form of operatic entertainment. The nearest contemporary parallel to the influence of Italian opera is that of the American domination of the film industry. If in some measure the reader understands the further implications of this parallel the difficulties of Handel's career will be better appreciated.

Had he lived, Purcell might have prevented the overwhelming success of foreign opera. But in the interregnum between his death in 1695 and Handel's arrival in 1710 developments had taken place which eased the way for Heidegger, Handel and the consequent combined operations of continental singers and composers. That Purcell went so soon was a permanent regret to the discriminating, and Henry Carey, a keen enough Handelian, was to voice the feelings of many who loved opera but had a shrewd idea that England, given a chance, could do it as well as anybody:

> Ev'n heaven-born Purcell now is held in scorn;
> Purcell, who did a brighter age adorn.[2]

It was not only, however, the dearth of composers which was responsible for a changed outlook. It was first

---

[1] Heidegger's appearance can be wondered at in Hogarth's "Cuzzoni, Farinelli and Heidegger" (1734) or in Pope's succinct
> "And lo! her bird (a monster of a fowl,
> Something betwixt a Heideggre and owl)."
> Dunciad, i. 289–90.

[2] "The Poet's Resentment," from Poems on Several Occasions, 1729.

such singers as Francesca de l'Épine and Francesco Tosi who demonstrated the histrionic possibilities of the Italian language. Superimposed was snobbery, which assumed that what was presented unintelligibly in a foreign tongue must be a symbol of high cultivation. Italian influence was insidious. *Arsinoe,* produced at Drury Lane in 1705, had English words and Italian music. A year later came Buononcini's *Camilla,* in translation. In 1707 the same work was done macaronically; l'Épine and Valentini sang in Italian, Mrs. Tofts, Mrs. Lindsey, Mrs. Turner, Leveridge and Ramondon in English. Addison's *Rosamund* did nothing to set the clock back. Addison had himself principally to blame. The text of *Rosamund* is a flaccid effort. In Italian the ridiculous would never have passed unnoticed, but in English verse Addison descends below banality with such lines as

> *Here will I stand*
> *With hat in hand*
> *Obsequiously to greet him.*

Nor was Thomas Clayton a composer who could get over the textual difficulties. The only interest of *Rosamund* is in its anticipation of romantic historiography and the revived balladry of Percy. Addison put his defeat down to stupidity on the part of others and upheld his dignity by poking through the chinks in the Italian armour. He had a prejudice, but his remarks on *Rinaldo* are very funny and not pointless. In 1709 Nicolini, "the first truly great singer who had ever sung in our theatre,"[3] arrived and took London by storm.[4] Early in 1710 the first three operas to be done entirely in Italian were given: *Almahide, L'Idaspe fedele,* in which Nicolini strangled a lion with great gallantry,[5] and *Etearco.* The conductor was Pepusch.

This new form of entertainment won the approval of society as a whole, but the intellectuals were against it

[3] Burney, *History,* iv. 208.

[4] For Nicolini's acting ability, *vide* Steele, *Tatler,* No. 115.

[5] Letter from Lady Mary Wortley Montagu to Mrs. Hewet, 1711.

from the start. Addison for obvious reasons, Tickell because he was a henchman of Addison. Elijah Fenton gave vent to England's latent Puritanism by recalling nostalgically in 1711 that

> There was an age, (its memory will last!)
> Before Italian Airs debauch'd our taste;[6]

Hogarth came later, and Pope with him, to protest that opera had damaged the true tradition of native drama. English singers ranged themselves, if not against Italian opera as such, at any rate against imported singers. Mrs. Tofts had expressed their point of view with some emphasis by employing a domestic to throw oranges at l'Épine during a Drury Lane performance as long ago as 1704.

> Effeminate in dress, in manners grown,
> We now despise whatever is our own.[7]

So Carey put forward the moral issue which was energetically thrashed during the years to come with particular regard to the exotic and repulsive race of *castrati*. All this being taken into consideration, Handel's success in opera is remarkable. But in these circumstances may be discerned the seeds of destruction.

Heidegger acted as Handel's cicerone in 1710. Among the quality to whom Handel was introduced was Sir John Stanley, a minor court official, to be precise a commissioner of customs, whose moderate Jacobitism ensured his subsequent rustication. With him lived his ward— Mary Granville. At this time she was a volatile child of ten, and her first impressions of Handel were later memorialized:

> I was struck with his playing, but struck as a child, not a judge, for the moment he was gone, I seated myself at the instrument, and played the best lesson I had then learnt: my uncle archly asked me whether I

[6] Elijah Fenton, "An Epistle to Mr. Southerne, from Kent, January 28, 1710–11."

[7] *Vide* Carey, "The Poet's Resentment."

thought I should ever play as well as Mr. Handel. "If I didn't think I should," cried I, "I would burn my instrument."[8]

So began a lifelong friendship.

Handel's first opera in England was *Rinaldo*,[9] commissioned by Aaron Hill for the company which he had a year or two earlier transferred from Drury Lane to Vanbrugh's new theatre in the Haymarket. The libretto was adapted by Giacomo Rossi from Tasso; Handel, with a characteristic burst of energy, wrote his music, much too fast for the unfortunate librettist, in a fortnight. The singers included Boschi, his wife, Vanini and Nicolini. The work was first produced on 24th February 1711. The *éclat* was terrific. For this the singers should claim as much responsibility as the composer: fashionable audiences at all times have a habit of paying devotion not to the quality of music so much as to its extraneous embellishments. It was Nicolini who carried the house away. Addison's trunk-maker "upon Nicolini's first appearance was said to have demolished three benches in the fury of his applause."[10] The absence of Nicolini two years later led to the failure of *Il pastor fido*. But in 1711 Handel could not foresee the possibility of failure. Nor could John Walsh, the music publisher, who began his long association with the composer by issuing five editions of the music from *Rinaldo*. Therein Handel was called either *Maestro di capella* or "Chapple Master" to the Elector of Hanover.

At that time Thomas Britton's musical evenings in Clerkenwell were one of the wonders of London, demonstrating how common interest could unite in amiability individuals of widely contrasted social status. Courtesy and intelligence intermingled at Britton's to form a pattern of democratic behaviour. Britton himself was a seller of small-coal: outside of business hours a bibliophile, rubbing shoulders at Bateman's bookshop by St. Paul's

[8] Mrs. Delany, *Life and Correspondence*, pp. 5 and 6.
[9] *Vide* Addison, *Spectator*, Nos. 5, 29 and 31.
[10] Addison, *Spectator*, No. 235.

and at the stalls in Little Britain with earls and dukes. He was also an amateur in chemistry, a Rosicrucian and a musician. "There goes the famous small-coal man," they used to cry after him, "who is a lover of learning, a performer in music, and a companion for gentlemen." Among his visitors in 1711 was Handel, who must have been surprised at the unconventional music-room over the coal-store, at the numerous quality who used to clamber shin-dangerously up the narrow stair, at the standard of amateur performance and at the sensitive understanding of contemporary music.

At Britton's Handel met, though he could hardly have missed meeting him before, Pepusch; Abiel Whichello and Philip Hart, organists and harpsichord players; Obadiah Shuttleworth,

> *Envy of foreigners, thy country's pride,*
> *Whose soul is harmony, nor ought beside,*
> *Oh! could Corelli hear thy charming lays,*
> *He'd hug thee in his arms, and give thee praise;*
> *For thou such justice to his works has done,*
> *He need not blush to call thee son.*[11]

Also John Banister, the younger, the leader of the opera orchestra, and the little prodigy Dubourg. Outside the ranks of professional musicians were Woolaston, a portrait painter; John Hughes,[12] poet and dramatist; and Henry Needler, recently appointed accountant for the candle duty at the excise office, who drank and fiddled by turns at the "Crown" in the Strand and rattled off Corelli to his boon companions at the Academy of Vocal Music. Add the bibulous Ned Ward, the eccentric Duchess of Queensberry and Justice Robe, and the gallery is reasonably complete. Such experience as this taught Handel that below the surface of English society ran an undercurrent of sympathy and understanding, and

[11] Henry Carey, *To Mr. Obadiah Shuttleworth. Made and Spoken Extempore, on hearing him perform a Solo of Corelli with great Propriety.*

[12] Hughes provided the text for Handel's first English cantata, *Venus and Adonis* (see p. 254).

that between posing nobility and crapulent rabble came a middle class of friendly philosophers with whom he could find much in common. This section of the community was strengthened by the progress of national tradition and without parallel in any other part of Europe. With such protagonists of independence Handel felt himself at home.

The passing of the season reminded Handel of his Hanoverian commitments. Therefore he returned, but by way of hospitable Düsseldorf, and with a sufficiently long stay there to concern both himself and the elector over his reception at Hanover. However, he eased his conscience by writing for the Princess Caroline acceptable duets and for the court chamber music. During the year he was in correspondence with his English friends. This correspondence, couched in the lingua franca of the time, demonstrates Handel's faculty for pertinent expression without too precise attention to orthographical detail. "Faites bien mes compliments à Mr. Hughes," he wrote to Andrew Roner in July.

> Je prendrai la liberté de lui écrire avec la prémiere occasion. S'il me veut cependant honorer de ses ordres, et d'y ajouter une de ses charmantes poésies en Anglois, il me fera la plus sensible grace. J'ai fait, depuis que je suis parti de vous, quelques progrés dans cette langue.

So another visit to England was in the wind. But before this was undertaken Halle called. Handel's sister Dorothea, married to a rising lawyer,[13] produced a daughter whose christening provided an opportunity for compassionate leave. Another year at Hanover followed, and then came the complete translation.

In the autumn of 1712 Handel was back in London. On 22nd November *Il pastor fido* disappointed him by its failure. Nicolini was away in Italy, and the new *castrato* Pellegrini, on his first visit, was too little known

---

[13] Dr. Michael Michaelsen, later a member of the Prussian Imperial Service and the War Council. Handel was always on the most cordial terms with him.

to attract a sufficiency of hero-worship. There was another reason why this opera failed. On 15th November the Duke of Hamilton had been murdered after a duel with Lord Mohun.[14] This was more sensational than a new opera, and the after-gossip precluded other activities. *Teseo,* produced on 10th January, restored Handel's prestige. This was dedicated by its librettist, Haym (who did little more than translate the text which Quinault had prepared for Lully in 1675), to the Earl of Burlington. An astute move, as Burlington was on the point of setting up as the general director of all the fine arts. His inherited wealth, his palace in Piccadilly, his acquaintance with Italy and his personal charm fitted him for this self-appointment. "He possessed every quality of a genius and artist except envy," said Horace Walpole. It was to Burlington that Handel owed the establishment of his reputation during the declining years of Queen Anne. Handel was a close friend of Henry Needler, a familiar drinking-companion, and a frequent caller at Needler's house in Clement's Lane. Needler was a useful friend. He was, as a gentleman, so qualified by his clerkship in excise, and a musician, on terms of friendship with many of the nobility, a frequent performer at the town houses, of the Duke of Rutland, Lords Burlington,[15] Essex and Percival. He had probably brought Handel into touch with Burlington. The concerts at which Needler played are worthy of mention as factors of importance in musical education. Uffenbach[16] describes one enthusiastically: "The famous Pepusch often gets up such a concert at the request of some noble lords. The orchestra was not very strong, consisting of not more than 16 persons [an average-size band in those days], but it was incomparable." L'Épine sang, but not so well as at the opera because "she sang whatever was put before her and did not take much trouble." The instrumental music, however, was

---

[14] Swift, *Journal to Stella,* Letter LV.

[15] Handel frequently had the direction of these concerts. Hawkins, v. 410.

[16] *London in 1710, from the travels of Zacharias von Uffenbach,* pp. 66–7.

very beautiful and the whole concert lasted for two hours. "I could have listened the whole night with the greatest pleasure."

Handel became a great citizen of London. In these early years of his residence therein we can visualize him as spending his off-duty hours at Britton's, until 1714, when Britton died, at the concerts at the "Swan" and at the "Crown," at Lœillet's séances in Hart Street and with the choirmen from Saint Paul's at the nearby "Queen's Arms." He was a frequent visitor to the cathedral, completely finished only in 1710, and pushing past the ballad-singers and vendors of nuts, apples and ginger-bread who shouted their wares at the west doors, would go in to hear the organ and the music of Purcell. In Italy Handel showed himself a master of Italian style; in England he paid like tribute to his hosts by taking as model the most brilliant (and how they lamented him at Britton's!) of recent composers. Purcell's *Te Deum* and *Jubilate* of 1694 encouraged the *Te Deum* and *Jubilate* which Handel wrote to celebrate the overdue Peace Treaty of Utrecht.[17] This, however, followed another work of particular significance, the *Birthday Ode* for the queen. This was done on 6th February (a very wet day), and the *Te Deum* at St. Paul's on 7th July. By this time Handel had progressed considerably in his English studies. We may presume friends at court to have engineered these occasional works, for it was unusual for alien musicians to write ceremonial music, and without proper influence being brought to bear we can hardly imagine an obstinate woman like Queen Anne, and no particular lover of the prospective Hanoverian succession, prejudicing herself in Handel's favour, and so far forgetting herself as to settle on him a pension of £200. Thus obviously in the good graces of the English, Handel had no particular desire

[17] With reference to this work the *Worcester Post Man* for February 27 reported that "the *Te Deum* (to be sung when the Peace is proclaimed) was rehears'd at the Banqueting House at Whitehall where abundance of the Nobility and Gentry were present."

to return to his somewhat less exhilarating duties at Hanover. He did not return.

He was intoxicated by social success and by the free-and-easy life of London. Prospects in the opera were generally good, the nobility was obliging, other people were generous in hospitality—Andrews of Barn Elms had given him house-room for a year—money was flowing in. In 1716 he started his investments by putting £500 into the South Sea Company.[18] And he was living well. He appreciated the gouty results of the Methuen Treaty of 1703, which brought port into the country almost duty free, and respected the enthusiasm of the English for the pleasures of the table. The times had altered less in some respects than might be imagined since the classic remark of Erasmus: "Britanni, praeter alia, formam, musicam, et lautas mensas proprie sibi vindicent."

The death of Queen Anne on 1st August 1714 involved Handel less than other notabilities. Bolingbroke, for instance, having been engaged in dictatorial aspirations and king-making negotiations, was caught most uncomfortably, and so were all the high Tories. The new king had more to do than to contemplate the caprices of an errant *Kapellmeister,* a minor official whose activities could have been of little consequence set against the panorama of politics. Hitherto Handel's desertion of Hanover has been rated too dramatically and the picture has been heightened by the legend of the *Water Music.* It is true that this was performed for the gratification of George I, that fifty players did add to the delights of a seductive evening spent with the Duchess of Bolton, Countess Godolphin, Madame Kielmansegge and Madame Ware, and that Kielmansegge arranged at considerable cost to himself the order of the evening. But that was long after George's accession; it was on 17th July 1717.[19]

The king's accession produced neither ode nor anthem. Handel was busy concocting with Heidegger another opera for the Haymarket. In the meantime *Rinaldo* was revived as a contribution to the coronation festivities.

[18] Letter from Handel to John G——, 29th June 1716.
[19] Newman Flower, p. 104 et seq.

The king came to *Rinaldo,* with one or other of his mistresses, and to *Amadigi,*[20] the new opera, on a number of occasions during 1715.

Handel had written no opera for three years, from *Teseo* to *Amadigi,* except for the miniature *Silla,* which, if performed at all, was done in privacy, possibly at Burlington House. This sabbatical period may be accounted for by the anarchic state of affairs, which reigned at the Haymarket after the Irishman MacSwiney, an able producer but, like so many of his countrymen, possessed of no financial acumen, had left his management of the theatre in haste and bankruptcy in the middle of the run of *Teseo.* Poor MacSwiney was more sinned against than sinning. He had left the army in 1705 in the optimistic belief that Rich would live up to his promise to provide "100 Guineas per annum Salary, a place at Court, and the Devil and all."[21] Only the last clause matured, and Mac-Swiney took his grievances and the contents of the box-office to Italy. After this episode Handel kept off the Haymarket, but occupied his time in consolidating his social bridge-heads.

Amadigi, so Heidegger tells us in his dedication, was composed by Handel at Burlington House. From 1715 to 1718 Handel lived there a good deal. He had rooms at the back of the house where, so nearly rural was Piccadilly, he enjoyed a pleasant prospect of open country. A fellow pensioner was the lively architect Kent, who came under the earl's wing in 1716. More distinguished beneficiaries were Pope and Gay. Another intimate was Dr. Arbuthnot, "a man of great comprehension, skilful in his profession, versed in the sciences, acquainted with antient literature, and able to animate his mass of knowledge by a bright and active imagination."[22] Arbuthnot was one of Handel's greatest friends.

Gay's *Trivia* (1716) has often been quoted for

[20] Produced 25th May.
[21] Grove, v.
[22] Johnson.

There Hendel *strikes the strings, the melting strain*
Transports the soul, and thrills through ev'ry vein;

but the whole poem should be read for the complete picture it affords of Handel's London. Splendour, squalor, misery, disease, vice and a little virtue all in proportion quietly blended. The *eheu fugaces* romanticists would do well to feel Gay's stabbing couplets on the seamy side. Heroic couplets is a misnomer. And those who over-estimate the comfort of Burlington House might be reminded of Lord Hervey's opinion that it was

> *Possessed of one great hall of state,*
> *Without a room to sleep or eat.*

But then Hervey was no lover of Burlington. Pope found Handel's fame and popularity perplexing. With a distaste for music, a heartier distaste for foreign musicians and a complete contempt for opera, he so far lacked confidence in his judgment as to apply to Arbuthnot on the score of Handel's reputation. Was all the rapture displayed by his audiences genuine or was it not?[23] "Conceive the highest you can of his abilities," said Arbuthnot, "and they are far beyond anything you can conceive." However, Pope interested himself in preparing libretti for Handel, and protested when in due course he learned that the composer was being traduced by those who were both fashionable and ignorant.[24] But Arbuthnot's good opinion was worth more than Pope's. Formerly physician-in-ordinary to Queen Anne, a political pamphleteer, an occasional poet and a shining light in the company of wit or wealth, he was capable of placing opportunities in the way of the young and ambitious.[25] Years later he proved the endurance of his loyalty by whipping Handel's detractors in *Harmony in an Uproar*.

Amadigi brought back to London Nicolini. With him in the cast was Anastasia Robinson. She was driven to a

[23] Warton's *Pope's Works*, v. 235 n.
[24] W. Coxe, *Anecdotes of Handel*, 1799, p. 40.
[25] "The doctor has great power with the queen."—Swift, op. cit., Letter XXXI.

profession by indigence and, having chosen singing, acquired her technique from Croft and Sandoni. At the time of the production of *Amadigi* she was little more than seventeen and at the outset of a career brief, glorious and not unprofitable. Gay rallied round with a somewhat commonplace compliment:

> *When Anastasia's voice commands the strain,*
> *The melting warble thrills through ev'ry vein;*
> *Thought stands suspense, and silence pleas'd attends,*
> *While in her notes the heav'nly Choir descends.*[26]

Success on the stage and a modest behaviour recommended Anastasia to the gallant and erratic Earl of Peterborough, Swift's hang-dog whom he loved dearly. Peterborough married Anastasia in 1722, but disallowed her the title of countess until 1735, when he assembled his friends, informed them of the lady's merits and announced his thirteen-year-old marriage. So ended with universal satisfaction the mystery of the virtuous lady who had apparently permitted herself the licence of noble concubinage.

By 1715 Handel was regarded as a great composer, but also as a great performer. As the best available harpsichord player he reentered the immediate entourage of the king. Geminiani, an old client of George I, brought himself to the notice of Kielmansegge and, having insinuated himself into that gentleman's graces and been invited to play at St. James's, insisted that he would play to no other accompaniment than Handel's. As a result of his renewed association with royalty Handel was granted a further £200 a year (titles and emoluments fell thick on German subjects in the king's English service), and this sum was added to, in like measure, by the Princess Caroline, who put the musical education of her daughters in his hands.

On 9th July 1716 George retired to his electorate as a respite from the responsibilities of constitutional mon-

---

[26] "To the Right Honourable William Pulteney Esq." (*Epistles on Several Occasions, 1720*).

archy imposed on him by an English parliament. Handel went with him. Here was an opportunity for him to air his English accent, a vile one according to his biographers but apparently effective enough for general purposes at Halle. For a visit to Halle formed part of this itinerary. Mother and aunt must have found it difficult to apportion their pride as between a relatively prodigal but clearly distinguished son and a wholly prosperous and respectable son-in-law. Old Zachau was dead, but Handel, with characteristic generosity, went out of his way to relieve the widow's straitened circumstances.

Correspondence was going on at this time between Mattheson and Handel,[27] and Hamburg was looking forward to a performance of the newly written setting of Brockes's Passion. Mattheson avers that this was written in London "and was sent by the post in a score written very minutely." Later writers cast doubts on this statement and preferred to have the Passion written in Germany during this tour. In default of positive evidence it is uncharitable to question Mattheson's veracity on this point. In any case Handel was clearly travelling a good deal during this vacation.

He was, among other places, at Ansbach, on some mission contrived by the Princess Caroline. Here he met an old associate in Johann Christoph Schmidt. Schmidt was impecunious, and Handel recommended London as a city in which broken fortunes might be mended. Schmidt accordingly went to London, shortly afterwards sending for his family to join him. Thus Handel combined self-interest (he needed a secretary) and charity.

Handel's Passion was performed at Hamburg after he left Germany. Its later history is not without interest. Bach came across it and, with the help of Anna Magdalena, made a copy for use at Leipzig.[28]

[27] Mattheson, *Ehren-Pforte.*

[28] Schweitzer, *J. S. Bach.* i. 94. Twenty-three pages were copied by Bach and thirty-seven by Anna Magdalena. Telemann also thought highly of this work, for once withholding his own music in its honour in a performance given at the Collegium Musicum at Hamburg in 1722. (Rolland, op. cit., p. 116.)

In January 1717 King George, refreshed by beer and oysters, solaced by Mesdames Schulenburg and Kielmansegge, and rested from the unconscionable English, who disapproved paraded paramours who were fat and foreign, returned to London. Back went Handel.

Chapter 4

"An Act for Naturalisating . . ."

THE PRINCIPAL PROFITEER out of the War of Spanish
Succession was James Brydges, who had paid the accounts, as Paymaster-General to the Forces, of Marlborough's overseas armies and kept a good deal of the
change. In 1711 the disappearance of £35,000,000
caused a parliamentary stir, and Brydges, though defend-
ed with warmth by Mr. Secretary,[1] was named as partly
responsible. Nevertheless, the fuss died down, and like
many military heroes whose duties keep them at a safe
distance from the firing-line, Brydges won the customary
rewards of successful peculation. In 1714 he became Vis-
count Wilton and Earl of Carnarvon, and five years later
Marquis of Carnarvon and Duke of Chandos. In the middle of this prosperity (retribution later overtook him in
ill-judged speculation in the South Sea Bubble and lost
him £300,000) he built a palace at Canons, by Edgware,
and as a necessary adjunct a chapel.

> The Chapel is a singularity not only in its building
> and the beauty of its workmanship, but in this also,
> that the Duke maintains there a full Choir and has the
> Worship performed there with the best musick, after
> the manner of the Chapel Royal, . . . Nor is this
> chapel only furnished with such excellent musick, but
> the Duke has a set of them to entertain him every day
> at dinner.[2]

[1] Swift, op. cit., Letter XXI.
[2] Defoe, *Tour in England*, 1725.

The duke's first director of music was Pepusch. The maxim

He wins this Patron, who can tickle best,[3]

however, worked to his disadvantage, and Handel soon after his return from Germany superseded him. His royal associations—he still continued in his capacity as music-master to the king's grandchildren—and his virtuosity in performance and composition fitted Handel better for the baroque atmosphere of Canons than did learning Pepusch. From Handel's point of view this appointment was a welcome addition to his emoluments, there being a lull in operatic interest in town. He celebrated the grand duke worthily in the Chandos anthems as well as in the *Te Deum*. In the early days at Canons he collected a number of harpsichord pieces, those which perplexed royal fingers, and other pieces with which he had been accustomed to impress his select audiences; these he published in 1720 with Cluer under the title of *Suites de Pièces pour le Clavecin*. "I have," wrote Handel in an introductory note which reflects the amoral habits of piratical publishers,

> been obliged to publish some of the following lessons, because surrepticious and incorrect copies of them had got abroad. I have added several new ones to make the work more useful, which if it meets with a favourable reception, I will still proceed to publish more, reckoning it my duty, with my small talent [tongue well in cheek here!], to serve a nation from which I have received so generous a protection.

Two significant works of larger stature were produced under the ducal aegis; *Acis and Galatea* and *Haman and Mordecai*, or *Esther*. The libretto of the first was done by Gay, though assisted by Hughes and Pope,[4] and was prompted by Handel's previous affection for this Sicilian

[3] Pope, *Dunciad*, ii. 196.
[4] Passages from Pope's *Autumn* (ll. 43–6) and *Iliad* (xiii. ll. 17–33) appear almost unaltered in *Acis and Galatea*.

fable. *Esther,* reputed to have been performed in August
1720 and to have brought from the duke a gift of
£1,000, was prepared by Pope (in 1732 it was added
to by Humphreys) from Racine. These two works, privately rehearsed, indicated new direction: towards landscape and towards oratorio. But in 1720 their significance
was not apparent to their author. He was by now newly
involved in an ill-fated operatic adventure.

The Hanoverian dynasty securely fixed, Jacobitism
gone underground or to Saint-Germain since the miscar-
riage of 1715, the Tories suffering political exclusion and
no greater excitement than could be provided by the
Mohocks to hand, aristocracy turned its head towards
culture. Therefore was launched the Royal Academy of
Music. This, in 1719–20, appeared a no less profitable
speculation than anything else. In fact, more than in the
case of most newly formed companies of that time, there
was a definite chance of the thing working. There were
composers, librettists and managers available and there
was a probable market. A capital of £50,000 was raised
in £100 shares, and the king was induced to contribute
£1,000 to the scheme.

Under the governorship of the Duke of Newcastle, and
with Lord Bingley as his second-in-command, twenty directors were elected. These included the Dukes of Port-
land and Queensberry, the Earls of Burlington (who apparently didn't mind Handel's desertion to Canons), Stair
and Waldegrave, Lords Chetwynd and Stanhope, a collection of military gentlemen, including the celebrated
roadmaker General Wade and Scarlatti's pupil Colonel
Blathwayt, Sir John Vanbrugh and William Pulteney. Burlington, whose voice was raised authoritatively on artistic
matters, had the bright idea of inviting Buononcini to come
from Rome; somebody else suggested Attilio Ariosti. By
1720 they were banded with Handel in brief amiability.
The next development was the engagement of singers. To
effect this Handel was dispatched abroad.

A new lease of life to opera was a congenial prospect
to Handel. He undertook his responsibilities in connection therewith with high seriousness. He complains in

letters to Mattheson, whose request for a biographical
entry for the *Ehren-Pforte* he disappointingly refused and
whose questions on Greek modes receive a pragmatic
answer,[5] and to his brother-in-law, of pressure of work.

> Do not [he writes to Michaelsen,[6]] judge of my desire
> to see you by the delay connected with my departure;
> for, to my great regret, I find myself detained here by
> indispensible business, on which it is not too much to
> say that my whole fortune depends, and which lasts
> much longer than I expected.

Handel's sister Dorothea had lately died of consumption,
so that personal grief overshadowed the excitement of
the inception of the Royal Academy. However, shortly
after writing Handel was *en route* for the Continent.

Business took him to Düsseldorf and Dresden, and
painful pleasure to Halle. Here he stayed for too short a
period to allow of a meeting with Bach who, hearing of
his presence there, undertook a fruitless walk from Anhalt-
Cöthen. At Düsseldorf Handel impressed Baldassari, at
Dresden Durastanti. In the middle of his Dresden negotiations Handel wrote to the Earl of Burlington. Because the
letter has not previously been published it is given in full:

My Lord

> C'est toujours autant par une vive reconnoissance,
> que par devoir, que je me donne l'honneur de Vous
> dire le zele et l'attachement que j'ay pour Vôtre per-
> sonne. Je Vous dois de plus un conte exact de ce que
> j'ay entrepris, et de la reussite du sujet de mon long
> voyage.

> Je suis icy à attendre que les engagements de Sine-
> sino, Berselli, et Guizzardi, soyent finis, et que ces

[5] Letter from Handel to Mattheson, 24th February 1719: "As
to the Greek Modes, Sir, I find that you have said all that can
be said upon the subject. It is no doubt necessary that those who
wish to practise and execute Music composed in those Modes
should study them: but, since we have escaped from the narrow
bounds of antient Music, I cannot see in what way the Greek
Modes can be useful in connection with the Music of modern
times. This, Sir, is my opinion: . . ."

[6] 20th February 1719.

Messieurs d'ailleurs bien disposés, s'engagent avec moy pour la Grande Bretagne. Tout sera decidé en quelques jours; j'ay des bonnes esperances, et dès que j'auray conclû quelque chose de réel, je Vous l'ecrirai My Lord comme a mon bienfaiteur, à mon Protecteur. Conservez moy, My Lord, Vos graces, elles me seront pretieuses, et ce sera toujours avec ardeur et fidelité que je suivray Vôtre service, et Vos nobles volontés. C'est avec une soumission egalement sincere et profonde que je serai à jamais

à Dresde
ce 26/15 de Juillet
1719

> My Lord
> Vôtre
> tres humble tres obeissant, et tres devoue
> Serviteur
> GEORGE FRIDERIC HANDEL[7]

The negotiations with Senesino and Berselli went satisfactorily, but not with Guizzardi, who never came to England. However, Salvai and Boschi made up for that deficiency. In addition to contriving these arrangements Handel was playing the harpsichord at the Dresden court. For this the elector, with generosity under the circumstances, made him a present of 100 ducats. As for German noblemen, Handel found them inferior to the English variety, and the Count von Fleming, annoyed at shallow excuses for inability to be social, wrote to Melusine von Schulenburg[8] in London, that Handel was a little mad. That was on 6th October, so Handel had been a long time at Dresden. His newly engaged singers relieved themselves quickly of electoral responsibility by displaying such bouts of temperament that the elector was glad to terminate their contract.

Back in London Handel began *Radamisto,* his first contribution to the repertory of the Royal Academy. His

---

[7] Devonshire MSS., 1st Series, 150, 0.

[8] She was a daughter of the Duchess of Kendal, formerly Madame von Schulenburg, a pupil of Handel's, and in 1733 married the Earl of Chesterfield.

librettist was Haym and the story from Tacitus. Handel's optimism for the new scheme led him to take the house in Lower Brook Street, No. 57,[9] which was his home for the rest of his life.

The opera season opened on 2nd April 1720 with Porta's *Numitor,* which gave way after half a dozen performances to *Radamisto.* This attracted a tremendous first-night audience: the royal family was there, and so great was the crush that free fights ensued in the admission queues with damage to persons and property: women fainted, and of those who didn't many had their dresses torn off their backs. In view of impending developments and disappointment it should be mentioned that this opera season came, with more than a fair share of publicity, after a fallow period in the entertainment world. *Radamisto* is notable among Handelian operas, but fine craftsmanship was beside the point to the majority of those whose lives were governed by a sequence of events whose primary purpose was to relieve boredom. Handel took himself seriously: only a few other people of discernment did. When Dr. William Stukeley told Sir Isaac Newton that he had attended a rehearsal of *Radamisto,* Newton expressed a distaste for the subject.[10] As for Handel's playing Newton was reported to have found "nothing worthy to remark but the elasticity of his fingers."[11] But that Newton got so far as to comment on Handel is symptomatic of the pressure of the Handel cult. Nothing, however, is more delusive than to be the temporary hero of fashion.

Radamisto came and went and was followed by Domenico Scarlatti's *Narciso,* conducted by that unhappy genius Thomas Roseingrave. The chief singers during the season were Baldassari, Durastanti, Anastasia Robinson, Mrs. Turner Robinson—wife of the organist of Westminster Abbey—and the athletic Gordon.

In March the singers from Dresden arrived. Of these the most eagerly awaited was Senesino, who came to fill

[9] As renumbered, No. 25 Brook Street.
[10] William Stukeley, *Family Memoirs,* i. 59.
[11] Hawkins, *Life of Johnson,* iii. 176 n.

the void left by Nicolini. The cult of the *castrato* helped to ruin opera in England, where men were preferred as men. From Handel's point of view, however, considerations of masculinity were secondary to those of vocal ability and the box-office. The great *castrati* could sing magnificently, and their Mediterranean manners engaged the attention of the ladies. This encouraged such vainglorious idiosyncrasies as Handel found unbearable. *Radamisto* in the meantime was published with Meares and Christopher Smith (formerly Schmidt) and *Esther* was got ready for Canons.

The next opera to be performed at the Haymarket was Buononcini's *Astarto,* one of the Earl of Burlington's favourite works. The combination of Buononcini and Senesino was irresistible. In the patchwork operas of Queen Anne's day Buononcini's arias had been highly popular. He was a good composer, an elegant melodist, a competent judge of the requirements of public opinion and an astute courtier. His style, says Hawkins, "was tender, elegant, and pathetic. Handel's had all these qualities, and numberless others, and his invention was inexhaustible."[12] Unfortunately Handel had a superfluity of excellence, so that vociferous and ignorant critics were always able to find something to displease them in the differences which separated Handel from Buononcini. That his orchestration was heavy and his counterpoint severe was therefore relatively true. All this tended towards the division of the musical into two factions. *Radamisto* was again revived after *Astarto,* but Buononcini's opera, which had run for ten nights before and ten after Christmas, put him in the ascendant. The season closed with him well pleased, and he disappeared to Twickenham in an aura of self-satisfaction to idle the summer away with Senesino and Mrs. Robinson. He cultivated the quality and supped occasionally with Lady Mary Wortley Montagu.[13]

The Buononcini faction was largely Whig, his chief

[12] Hawkins, v. 276.
[13] Letter from Lady Mary Wortley Montagu to the Countess of Mar, 6th September 1721.

support coming from his disgruntled Marlboroughs with the Duke of Newcastle furnishing a good second string. Handel's associates were of the discredited Tory school and, while his political ideas were necessarily not particularly bound, the fact that he had been among the Arbuthnot, Swift (although there is no direct evidence of a meeting between Handel and Swift it is inconceivable that they were not acquainted),[14] Pope, Gay and Parnell circle would not have gone unnoticed. Moreover, he was a king's man, and that was not conducive to popularity; nor was a character unpliable to condescension. The letter to Burlington may appear Heep-like, but in private conversation Handel spoke to all and sundry as man to man.

In the spring of 1721 *Muzio Scevola,* of which the acts were composed in turn by Filippo Mattei, Buononcini and Handel, afforded an opportunity to view the protagonists in close juxtaposition. Handel's *Floridante,* later in the season, was a failure, and Buononcini was able to establish a commanding lead by the popularity of his *Crispo* and *Griselda.*

At this juncture Handel fell back on the expedient of introducing a new singer. This was Francesca Cuzzoni, an ugly little Venetian virago with a dominating personality, a flair for self-advertisement, a pathetic husband (Sandoni her accompanist, whom she married on landing in England) and "a nest of nightingales in her belly." This pregnant remark was bawled from the gallery by a groom privileged to hear Handel's *Ottone,* which at the beginning of 1723 introduced Cuzzoni to an enraptured public. *Ottone* undermined Buononcini's operatic future, which had already suffered from his arrogant demands on the directorate of the Royal Academy. He retreated to enjoy a handsome pension from the Duchess of Marlborough. Cuzzoni drove from the stage Anastasia Robinson, whose voice had been reduced by illness and her interest in the theatre by the importunities of the Earl of Peterborough. Handel thus survived his first depression

[14] Swift was a particular friend of Mrs. Pendarves's uncle, Sir John Stanley, to whom frequent reference is made in the *Journal to Stella.*

and celebrated it by a fit of choler at the expense of his new prima donna.

Having refused to sing the first air in *Ottone* in rehearsal, Cuzzoni suffered: "Madame, je sais que vous êtes une véritable diablesse, mais je vous ferai savoir, moi, que je suis Béelzebub, le chef des diables." This was followed up by an intention to throw her through a conveniently open window. But at that point she capitulated.

After *Ottone* came *Flavio,* in which Gordon's threat to jump on the harpsichord provoked Handel to comment that that would be more attractive an entertainment than his singing. And after *Flavio* came *Giulio Cesare.* Cuzzoni and Senesino were carrying all before them; but the latter suffered some diminution in fame by his abjection at the disturbance caused by a falling piece of scenery in *Giulio Cesare* and by his recent horse-whipping at the hands of Peterborough. On 25th May 1724 Ambrose Philips let Cuzzoni know that her tenure of popularity was not eternal:

> *Little* Siren *of the stage*
> *Charmer of an idle age,*
> *Empty warbler, breathing lyre,*
> *Wanton gale of fond desire,*
> *Bane of every heavenly art,*
> *Sweet enfeebler of the breast,*
> *O, too pleasing is thy strain,*
> *Hence to southern climes again;*
> *Tuneful mischief, vocal spell,*
> *To this island bid farewell;*
> *Leave us as we ought to be,*
> *Leave the* Britons *rough and free.*[15]

A year earlier Philips had put a straw in the wind by his publication of *A Collection of Old Ballads,* including *Robin Hood* and *The Children in the Wood.* There were others. Hogarth, at the outset of his career, was, in "Masquerades and Operas," displaying a righteous indignation

[15] "To Signora Cuzzoni May 25, 1724," *Pastorals, Epistles, Odes, and other Original Poems,* 1765.

at the sympathies of high society. His butts were Burlington, whom he regarded as an effete play-boy, and Heidegger, who was promoting *ridotti* and masquerades of lewd distinction. Easeful life and the Walpolian policy of a peaceful England were reducing morality to shreds. Heidegger was doing his best to complete the process. "The rules that are observed by this new society," says Addison acidly, "are wonderfully contrived for the advancement of cuckoldom."[16] Handel looked on at the attacks on the opera and considered *Esther* an insurance against the religious revival which Heidegger would undoubtedly stimulate. Already the Bishop of London was inveighing against him and Fielding was coming in to the attack.

Tamerlano, Rodelinda and *Scipione* kept the Academy precariously afloat until 1726. *Rodelinda* was sensational for no other reason than that in it Cuzzoni scored a sartorial triumph by appearing in a brown and silver dress which set the pace for ladies' fashions for a long time. Handel found refuge from such irrelevancies in a nostalgic letter,[17] the first for some time as he ruefully admits, to his brother-in-law. Michaelsen was acting *in loco filii,* but Handel was anxious to revisit Halle. In England, however, he saw trouble ahead if he did not take adequate measures to safeguard the future: therefore he filed a petition to the House of Lords which ran as follows:

> To the Right Honourable The Lords Spiritual and Temporal in Parliament assembled. The Humble Petition of George Frideric Handel sheweth That your Petitioner was born at Halle, in Saxony, out of His Majesty's Allegiance, but hath constantly professed the Protestant Religion, and hath given Testimony of his Loyalty and Fidelity to His Majesty and the Good of this Kingdom.
>
> Therefore the Petitioner humbly prays That he may be added to the Bill now pending entitled "An Act for Naturalisating Louis Sechehaye." And the petitioner will ever pray, etc.
>
> GEORGE FRIDERIC HANDEL.

[16] *Spectator,* No. 8.
[17] 11th/22nd June 1725.

On 20th February 1726 the king signed the Bill. Having made his *civis britannicus sum* gesture, Handel was now eligible for employment as "Composer of Musick for the Chapel Royal," from which aliens were debarred, and "Composer to the Court."

The affairs of the Academy languishing, the directors committed themselves to the further extravagance of engaging a new singer, at £2,000 a year, in the person of Faustina Bordoni. Considering the eminence in military circles of so many of the directors, it can only be regarded as providential that their inane tactical behaviour was confined to the realm of artistic operations. "The umbrage given to Cuzzoni by her [Faustina's] coming hither, proves that as Turkish monarchs can bear no brother near the throne, an aspiring sister is as obnoxious to a theatrical Queen."[18] The degree of enmity engendered between these two was worse "than even the theological and political parties of high church and low, or Whig and Tory, which then raged in this country."[19] The main supporters of Cuzzoni were the Countess of Pembroke, Sir Wilfred Lawson, Sir William Gage and Mr. Simon Smith; of Faustina, more impressively, Sir Robert Walpole, the Countess of Burlington, Lady Delawar and Lady Cowper.

They were jointly featured by Handel in *Alessandro,* which ran from 5th May until the end of the season on 7th June. Not unnaturally there were good houses. Handel's preoccupation on this score was to effect such division of virtuosity that neither of his ladies felt affronted. The only casualty was Senesino, who, forgotten in this welter of new adulation, advertised his chagrin in the conventional way by falling ill and retiring to Italy for a rest cure.

During the season Quantz was in London. He observed the battle of the singers, but was on the whole more interested in the orchestra which, led by Castrucci and directed by Handel, impressed him. Handel played the harpsichord and the organ; other players were

---

[18] Burney, *History,* iv. 306.
[19] Ibid, iv. 309.

Geminiani, a great master on the violin; Dubourg, his scholar, an Englishman, who was a pleasing performer on that instrument; the two Castrucci's, who were brothers, and tolerable solo players; Weidemann, a German, and Festing, an Englishman, on the German flute, with Mauro d'Alaia, who came to England with Faustina; he was an excellent performer on the violin, and an excellent leader; his manner of playing was clear and distinct, but he never ventured at great difficulties.[20]

Quantz had an idea of staying in London and received encouragement from Handel, but—and we may hope that Handel appreciated this—"as he was still a servant of the King of Poland, he did not chuse to perform in public, thinking it a duty to his prince to offer him the first fruits of his travels."[21]

Senesino returned from Italy in time for Ariosti's *Lucio Vero* on 7th January 1727. In succession to it came Handel's *Admeto,* which kept the flames of Cuzzoni-Faustina animosity well ablaze until Buononcini's *Astyanax* provided the grand conflagration. Polly Peachum and Lucy Lockit behaved as ladies in comparison with the rival singers, who delighted a vast audience with a hair-tearing display which not only stimulated Gay but also Arbuthnot, who celebrated it in *The Devil to pay at St. James's,* and Cibber, who produced honorifically *The Rival Queens.*

On 11th June George I died in his electorate, of apoplexy, at Osnabrück. On the 15th, the news having tardily reached England, George II was proclaimed. For his coronation in October Handel wrote what must be the paragon of all ceremonial music, not less than four anthems. This was a busy period. Music for the court balls was also requisitioned, and *Admeto* was put on at the Haymarket on 3rd October. On 11th November a *pièce d'occasion* was presented in the shape of *Riccardo primo, re d'Inghilterra.*

[20] Burney, *Travels,* ii. 191 et seq.
[21] Ibid.

I was yesterday at the rehearsal of Mr. Handel's new opera called Richard I—'tis delightful. There I saw Captain Elliot. I was in Lady Sutherland's box . . . and he came and sate behind me. . . . Masquerades are not to be forbid, but there is to be another entertainment *barefaced,* which are balls. . . . There is to be a handsome collation, and they will have Heidegger's rooms to perform in. Some prudes already have attacked the reputation of those ladies that will accept of the tickets, but as all the subscribers are men, I don't see what scandal can ensue, only spiteful people make harm of everything.[22]

Not even Mrs. Pendarves (*née* Mary Granville and later to be Mrs. Delany) could resist the counter-attractions. Small wonder, then, that *Richard I* played for only eleven nights. And round the corner was another surprise.

[22] Mrs. Pendarves to Anne Granville, 11th November 1727.

Chapter 5

English or Italian?

There's Madam Faustina, Catso
And eek Madam Cuzzoni;
Likewise Signor Senesino
Are tutti Abbandonni:
Ha, Ha, Ha, Ha, Do, Re, Mi, Fa,
Are now but farce and folly;
We're ravish'd all with Toll, Loll, Loll,
And pretty, pretty Polly.[1]

THUS CHEERFULLY HARRY CAREY epitomized the state of affairs at the beginning of 1728. *The Beggar's Opera* had its *première* on 29th January. To his title-page Gay added, over-modestly, from Martial: "Nos haec novimus esse nihil." The influence of this work, undertaken at the suggestion of Swift, was tremendous. Italian opera, the philandering Walpole, corrupt politicians and lascivious courtiers all came under the lash, and English drama was enriched. In the rumbustiousness of the text Ben Jonson was recalled, in the sharp-edged satire Dryden, in the songs the open-air artlessness of the natural pastoralist. Of all poetry English is, according to Voltaire, the most moral: *The Beggar's Opera* is the prime example. The music was not of less consequence than the libretto. Herein lies Gay's genius. Only a musician could have contrived it. Pepusch scored the work, but the tunes were those to which Gay had been brought up. Handel must often have heard the same tunes, which ravished the general ear when Gay fluted privately at Burlington House.

---

[1] "Polly Peachum," Carey, op. cit.

64

Moreover, Gay knew the ways of opera. Prison scenes were commonplace. Handel provided them in *Tamerlano, Radamisto, Floridante* and, most movingly, *Rodelinda,* while in *Floridante* an excellent farewell scene between Elmira and Floridante suggested that between Polly and Macheath.

But of malice towards Handel Gay must be acquitted, nor was Handel the sort of person to have suggested it. At Burlington House they had got on excellently well together and later Handel had subscribed for a copy of *Poems on Several Occasions.*[2] Further, they were linked by a mutual friendship for Aaron Hill, a fellow Devonian with Gay. That *The Beggar's Opera* ran for sixty-three nights was a surprise to everybody: in advance Rich, who produced it at Lincoln's Inn Fields, had been very dubious, so had Bolingbroke when acquainted with the project, so had Gay's patron the Duke of Queensberry, and so had Jimmy Quin, who refused Macheath. However, in the curious fashion of literary-dramatic affairs it defied the previous dismalling and exceeded its author's most sanguine expectations.

Handel's *Siroe,* produced in February, containing nothing more extraordinary than Signora Mignotti trousered, lasted nineteen performances, and its successor *Tolomeo* only seven. And that was the end of £ 50,000, the Royal Academy and apparently of Faustina, Cuzzoni, Senesino and Handel. Faustina, fortified by the energy of London life, went off to Venice. There she disappeared into respectability and matrimony. She married Hasse in 1730. Senesino also went to Venice, where for a time he sang with Faustina. At another Venetian theatre at the same time could have been found Cuzzoni, Boschi, Nicolini and Farinelli.

Carey solemnized the departure of Senesino in *A Sorrowful Lamentation for the Loss of a Man and No Man.*[3] Handel settled down with customary determination to revive the faded glories by proposing partnership with

[2] Phoebe Fenwick Gaye, *John Gay,* p. 201.
[3] Carey, op. cit.

Heidegger and by taking the King's Theatre for a five-year period. The first step was to replace the vanished singers, and this necessitated another Italian visit. In Italy he signed on—the whole business seems to foreshadow latter-day commercial sport technique—Bernacchi, a *castrato;* Fabri, a tenor (tenor singers had not yet arrived at idolization); Signora Fabri; Merighi and Bertolli, *contralti;* and Strada, to whom the English with their usual flair for graceless observation promptly attached the loveless sobriquet of "The Pig."

In Italy Handel renewed acquaintance with Joseph Smith[4] and exhibited a nice tact in declining an invitation from Colonna[5] at Rome on account of the Pretender's holding court in the city. From Italy to Germany. At Hamburg Gottfried Riemschneider was persuaded to come to England to take the place of Boschi. At Halle Handel saw his mother for the last time, blind and paralysed. Again he received overtures from Bach, who wished Handel to visit him at Leipzig; but there was no opportunity for a *rencontre*. To be truthful, it looks as though Handel was lacking in enthusiasm. He was a busy man, he probably reasoned, and provincial cantors had a habit of tedious severity in conversation unpalatable to the travelled and worldly-wise.

Handel went before and the singers followed after, arriving in London in time for *Lotario,* which was to open the 1729–30 season on 16th November. "Being thus embarqued on his own bottom,"[6] as Mainwaring picturesquely puts it, Handel proceeded to forget the misdemeanours of the former Academy directorate in the enthusiasm of his new scheme. Not that affairs were, at the outset, particularly propitious. *Lotario* and *Partenope* were indifferently received despite the splendid songs written for Fabri. The moderate capacity for stimulation

[4] Letter from Handel to Michaelsen, 11th March 1729. "You have only to address your letters to Mr. Joseph Smith, Banker, at Venice (as I have already explained), and he will forward them to me, in whatever part of Italy I may be staying."

[5] Mainwaring, p. 113.

[6] Ibid.

possessed by the singers is instructively indicated by Mrs. Pendarves:

> Bernacchi has a vast compass, his voice mellow and clear, but not so sweet as Senesino, his manner better; his person not so good, for he is as big as a Spanish friar. Fabri has a tenor voice, sweet, clear, and firm, but not strong enough, I doubt, for the stage: he sings like a gentleman, without making faces, and his manner is particularly agreeable; he is the greatest master of musick that ever sung upon the stage. The third is the bass, a very good distinct voice, without any harshness. La Strada is the first woman; her voice is without exception fine, her manner near perfection, but her person is *very bad,* and she makes *frightful mouths.* La Merighi is the next to her; her voice is not so extraordinarily good or bad, she is tall and has a very graceful person, with a tolerable face: she seems to be a woman about forty, she sings easily and agreeably. The last is Bertoli, she has neither voice, ear nor manner to recommend her; but she is a perfect beauty, quite a Cleopatra, that sort of complexion with regular features, fine teeth, and when she sings has a smile about her mouth which is extreme pretty, and I believe has practised to sing before a glass, for she has never any distortion of her face.[7]

Bernacchi was dismissed and Senesino re-engaged, through the intermediary offices of His Majesty's Envoy Extraordinary at Florence, Francis Colman,[8] at a fee of 1,400 guineas for the season. The amount is large in view of the fact that Handel had no directors behind him: but his financial transactions were conducted on a large scale,[9] and what he earned by music was increased by judicious investment. The re-engagement of Senesino worked, de-

---

[7] Mrs. Pendarves to Anne Granville, 1728.

[8] Letters from Handel to Colman, 19th/30th June 1730 and 7th/16th October 1730.

[9] A summary of Handel's financial transactions is given in Appendix E.

spite the rumblings of abuse which came from those who subscribed to Carey's

> *Curse on this damn'd Italian pathic mode,*
> *To Sodom and to Hell the ready road,*[10]

and trundled off to take pugilistic advice from Figg, to enjoy manly sports at Hockley-in-the-Hole, and to demonstrate Macheath-like the benefits to be conferred on a virile nation by the pursuit of strumpets. Senesino brought large audiences to the Haymarket during the 1730–1 season who were regaled with revivals of *Scipione,* the evergreen *Rinaldo,* whose name *The Beggar's Opera* had done much to make familiar, *Rodelinda* and the new *Poro.* The second act of this opera was composed in a week, and if any reason is required to explain the speed of Handel's execution none other is necessary than his busyness. When he wasn't discussing his finances with his City friends, or struggling with the vagaries of singers (in general "he resolved to subdue these Italian humours, not by lenitives, but sharp corrosives"[11]), or teaching, or performing at private concerts, he was engaged in the normal pleasures of a normal person.

From here and there fragments may be pieced together to form a composite picture of the man. He had no great library,[12] one small book-case mentioned in the inventory of his effects after his death appears to have sufficed; but his views on literature were put to shrewd use in his later dealings with oratorio librettists. Pictures were a source of considerable pleasure, and two Rembrandts eventually

---

[10] "A Satire on the Luxury and Effeminacy of the Age," Carey, op. cit. Carey, like Addison, writes his prejudices with magnificent anger. The reason therefor is contained in a couplet of universal application:

> *But such is the good-nature of the town,*
> *'Tis now the mode to cry the English down.*

[11] Mainwaring, p. 108.

[12] Hawkins, v. 410. "His attainments in literature cannot be supposed to have been very great . . . but . . . Of the English also he had such a degree of knowledge, as to be susceptible of the beauties of our best poets. . . ."

found their way into the hands of Bernard Granville (who
had given them to Handel in the first place), while Jennens received his Denners. Among the fleshly pleasures
eating and drinking were conspicuous. Many anecdotes
abounded concerning his intemperance in these respects,
and Goupy perpetuated it by a malicious cartoon. It may
be that Goupy had a private score to settle, for he had
had dealings with Handel years before 1730, when his
cartoon appeared, when he was employed as a scene-
painter for the Royal Academy.[13] Mainwaring parsoni-
cally proclaims that "he paid more attention to it [food]
than is becoming in any man."[14] Which, if true, suggests
that the capacity of the eighteenth-century stomach was
less than the general evidence leads us to suppose.[15] In
most respects Handel was a typical Georgian, and such
exaggeration as finds its way into fable is that which inevitably follows the name of a conspicuous member of
society. And by this period of his life Handel was conspicuous. The roughness of his manners was limited to
professional points of exasperation; otherwise his relationship with friends and acquaintances is marked by amiability. So he frequented country houses (Handel's rural
painting, such as shown in *L'Allegro,* was based on ample
experience of the English countryside): he used to stay
at Salisbury with the Harris family,[16] at Ashford, in Kent,
with Sir Wyndham Knatchbull,[17] with Jennens in Leices-

[13] Goupy must have been forgiven (what a capacity for this
virtue Handel must have possessed!), as Hawkins (v. 412) men-
tions him as one of Handel's intimates.

[14] Mainwaring, p. 140.

[15] Ned Ward and his friends (*London Spy,* Chapter III) could
manage two calves' heads and a couple of geese as a *first course,*
and then, without notifiable discomfort, follow it up with a
"stately Cheshire cheese, of a groaning size."

[16] Streatfeild, pp. 185–6 n.

[17] At the end of August 1734 Handel had to decline a week-
end at Merstham-le-Hatch, near Ashford; but the friendship was
a durable one in that we find Handel sending his respectful compliments to Sir William (Wyndham?) Knatchbull via Jennens in
1741. Lady Knatchbull was a daughter of James Harris, of Salisbury, and was married in 1730.

tershire[18] and as far afield as Calwich,[19] in Staffordshire, with Bernard Granville or at Teddesley Hall in the same county with Fisher Littleton.[20] His favourite house, however, was that of Mrs. Pendarves. Mrs. Pendarves, whose first marriage was turbulently miserable and whose second was quietly uneventful, had a wealth of sympathy, wit, literary and artistic sensibility and musical knowledge. She could also achieve the conquests of flippant flirtation. All these things attracted Handel and, while we have no reason to doubt that the friendship was of other than the platonic order, he would call frequently to play over new works, to interrupt Mrs. Pendarves in her correspondence or to *desipere in loco*. The parties which Mrs. Pendarves gave had that blend of entertaining refreshment and refreshing entertainment to which we may glance nostalgically:

I must tell you of a little entertainment I had last week; I never wished more heartily for you and my mother than on that occasion. I had Lady Rich and her daughter; Lady Cath. Hammer and her husband, Mr. and Mrs. Percival, Sir John Stanley and my brother, Mrs. Donellan, Strada and Mr. Coot. Lord Shaftesbury begged of Mr. Percival to bring him, and being a *profess'd friend* of Mr. Handel (who was here also) was admitted: I never was *so well* entertained at *an opera!* Mr. Handel was in the best humour in the world, and played lessons and accompanied Strada and all the ladies that sung from seven o' the clock till eleven. I gave them tea and coffee, and about half an hour after nine had a salver brought in of chocolate, mulled

[18] Newman Flower, *passim*.

[19] *History of Ashbourne*, 1839, and Lady Mary Fortescue, *History of Calwich Abbey*.

[20] The father of the late Lord Hatherton, of Teddesley Hall, who lived to the age of ninety, used to relate that Handel was accustomed to play with Fisher Littleton's amateur band at concerts at Teddesley. An interesting and detailed account of a visit by Handel to Lord Gainsborough's country seat at Exton, Rutland, is given in a letter from James Noel (23rd January 1745) quoted in "Unpublished Letters concerning Handel," Betty Matthews, *Music and Letters*, July 1959, pp. 264–5.

white wine and biscuits. Everybody was easy and seemed pleased, Bunny [Bernard Granville] staid with me after the company was gone, eat a cold chick with me, and we chatted till one o' the clock.[21]

The curious conclusion has frequently been drawn that Handel's sole mistress was Art (always with a capital A). Handel was a bachelor, but that condition did not preclude the eighteenth-century gentleman from becoming acquainted with the delectable possibilities of female companionship. Pope, Gay, Congreve, Prior, Atterbury and Savage were all bachelors: it was not unfashionable to avoid the rigours of matrimony. Regarding Handel an anonymous commentator, said to have been George III, observed that he "scorned the advice of any but the Woman he loved, but his Amours were rather of short duration, always within the pale of his own profession . . . ."[22] Rolli, in a scurrilous outburst, made rude insinuations concerning Handel and Strada.[23] It may be remarked, as a matter of fact, that the only creditor who pressed hardly on Handel in a period of financial instability was Strada's husband.

But this is to anticipate. Returning to the opera, we find the 1731-2 season less successful than its predecessor despite the début of yet another remarkable bass in the person of Antonio Montagnana, who graced the first performances of *Ezio* and *Sosarme*.

In 1732 a fortuitous set of circumstances diverted Handel from a too rueful contemplation of his operatic disappointments. On 23rd February, Bernard Gates, Master of the Chapel Royal, a member of the Academy of Ancient Music and a zealous Handelian, performed at his house in Westminister *Esther* as a birthday offering. Gates had been one of the original singers in the Canons per-

---

[21] Letter from Mrs. Pendarves to Anne Granville, 1734.

[22] *Vide* Newman Flower, p. 188 n. Is Mrs. Pendarves indicated?

[23] Letter to *The Craftsman*, 7th April 1733. ". . . *Strada del Pò*, who is much in his favour. . . ." In *Anecdotes of Handel* (p. 28) two anonymous ladies are mentioned who would have married Handel had he been willing to eschew his undignified profession of musician. They were of rank and fortune.

formance. In 1732 he used the services of his choir-boys. The debt owed by English drama and music to generations of singing-boys is incalculable. A further private performance was given in the rooms of the Academy of Ancient Music at the "Crown and Anchor." Emboldened by appreciation Handel took a further step. The *Daily Journal* advertised at the beginning of April as follows:

> Never performed in public, at the great room in Villar's Street, Yorkbuildings, by the best vocal and instrumental Musick, Esther an Oratorio, or sacred drama, will be performed, on Thursday, April 20th., as it was composed for the most noble James Duke of Chandos, by George Frederick Handel. Each ticket five shillings.

The evening before this event a further advertisement appeared to the effect that

> By his Majesty's command, at the King's Theatre in the Haymarket, on Tuesday the 2nd. day of May, will be performed the sacred story of Esther; an oratorio in English, formerly composed by Mr. Handel, and now revised by him with several additions, and to be performed by a great number of voices and instruments. N.B. There will be no acting on the stage, but the house will be fitted up in a decent manner, for the audience. The Musick to be disposed after the manner of the coronation service. Tickets to be delivered at the usual prices.

That the oratorio was performed in static undress was due to the Bishop of London, who, fearful lest true religion should founder on the rocks of histrionic excess, forbade a production after the operatic manner. It is unjust to cavil at the bishop's veto. He, not unaware of the reputation of the Haymarket, must have been much exercised in mind at the projected liaison between the Word of God and the music of the theatre. The wonder is that the performance ever took place. However, it did and was approved by king and court.

On 17th May a pirated version of *Acis and Galatea*

was done at the Little Theatre in Lincoln's Inn Fields, under the management of Rich, at the instigation of the eccentric Arne—father of Thomas and Susanna and, according to Addison, an arm-chair politician[24] who made his own arm-chairs—who saw money in the new-style Handel and an opportunity of starting his daughter on her career. Handel retaliated against this exploitation of his labour and promptly put on at his own theatre a refurbished *Acis*

> . . . by a great number of the best voices and instruments. There will be *no action* on the stage [did Handel mistake his hero and heroine for *St. Acis* and *St. Galatea*?], but the scene will represent, in a picturesque manner, a rural prospect, with rocks, groves, fountains, and grottos, among which will be dispersed a chorus of nymphs and shepherds, the habits and every other decoration suited to the subject.

The singers were Strada, Senesino, Montagnana, a choir-boy for the part of Damon, Mrs. Davis, Miss Robinson (? Anastasia's sister). An enlarged cast was necessary, for Handel, forced to expand his original score by Arne's thunder-stealing, had incorporated part of his Italian *Aci, Galatea e Polifemo*. Thus the audiences who patronized the King's Theatre enjoyed macaronically the best of both works. Susanna Arne's appearance had given a fillip to the growing school of English protagonists, and Handel might have done well at this juncture to jettison Italian libretti altogether. Aaron Hill thought so, and later in the year proposed

> that you would be resolute enough to deliver us from an Italian bondage, and demonstrate that English is soft enough for opera, when composed by poets who know how to distinguish the sweetness of our tongue from the strength of it, when the last is less necessary.[25]

Hill had in mind, no doubt, the skill of the lately de-

[24] Addison, *Tatler*, Nos. 155 and 160.
[25] Letter from Aaron Hill, 5th December 1732.

ceased Gay, whose opera *Achilles* was still awaiting performance and whose heroic theme was ill suited to the pleasant jingle of ballad tunes suggested by the author. But English opera had taken a side turning in 1728 and Handel was reluctant to bring it back to the main road. Italian opera had its vicissitudes, but at best it was extremely remunerative, and at worst no more disastrous than unsuccessful English opera. Besides which oratorio was the new delight. Its record in 1732 was propitious: on 2nd August Handel paid £2,300 into his account at the Bank of England.

Orlando was completed on 20th November and produced on 27th January 1733; it was followed by a revival of *Floridante*. In Lent *Deborah*, the text being by Samuel Humphreys, who had had a hand in the 1732 version of *Esther*, came next in the oratorio succession. The royal family was in attendance, which at this juncture was unfortunate. Handel, as has previously been noticed, was often the victim of circumstances over which he could have had no direct control. That Walpole was proposing the introduction of an Excise Bill, and that the Prince of Wales, in the best tradition of his family, was in opposition to his father and therefore to his father's prime minister, were factors for which Handel could hardly be held responsible. But Handel's loyalty to the Crown, combined with the increased price of admission to the oratorios, necessary, so Handel and Heidegger protested, to meet the increased expenses in production, were sufficient to call forth Rolli's letter in the *Craftsman* of 7th April, concluding:

Quoth W—e to H—l, shall We Two agree,
And excise *the whole Nation?*
                                          H. Si, Caro, Si.
Of what use are Sheep *if the Shepherd can't shear them*
At the Hay-market *I, you at* Westminster.
                                          W. Hear him!
Call'd to order, their Seconds *appear in their place;*
One fam'd for his Morals, *and one for his* Face.
In half they succeeded, in half they were crost:
The EXCISE *was obtained, but poor* DEBORAH *lost.*

This crude attack, supervening on a house of no more than 260 persons, and a growing deterioration in health worried Handel.

In June the nobility under the direction of Frederick, Prince of Wales, and Marlborough[26] set up a rival opera to Handel's, substituting Porpora for their former champion Buononcini, now thoroughly in disgrace for palming off a madrigal of Lotti's as his own. Singers were seduced from Handel's service, first Senesino, then Cuzzoni and then Montagnana: only Strada remained faithful. In this wretched year two gestures relieved the gloom. The first was a vigorous polemic by Arbuthnot in defence of Handel and entitled *Harmony in an Uproar;* the second an invitation from the University of Oxford which, in honouring Handel, was paying lip-service to the house of Hanover and thereby giving the lie to its alleged Jacobitism. If Handel was offered a degree he refused it, possibly because tact forbade receiving the honour from a politically suspect institution or possibly because so many people of whom he disapproved, including Maurice Greene, were doctors. Handel preferred the less honorific Mr. to being associated with Greene.[27]

On the whole Oxford greeted Handel with warmth, and what he made out of a series of concerts there amply compensated for the lean period in the earlier part of the year. On 5th July *Esther* was given, on the 7th it was repeated, on the 8th the *Utrecht Te Deum* at St. Mary's, on the 10th "a spick and span new oratorio, called *Athaliah*," on the 11th *Athaliah* again, and on the 12th, to conclude the festival, *Deborah*. Earless dons, purse-empty undergraduates and recalcitrant Jacobites might carp at the attention paid to "Handell and (his lousy crew) a

[26] Charles Spencer, succeeded to the title on the death, in 1753, of his maternal aunt Henrietta, who had been duchess in her own right since the death of her father, the first duke, in 1722.

[27] *Vide Harmony in an Uproar:* "Why Dr. Pushpin [Pepusch] and Dr. Blue [Greene] laugh at you, and scorn to keep you company; and they have vowed to me, that it is scarcely possible to imagine how much better they composed after the commencement gown was thrown over their shoulders than before; it was as if a musical—had laid hands upon them, and inspired them with the enthusiasm of harmony."

great number of foreign fiddlers,"[28] but the *Gentleman's Magazine* reported that *Athaliah* was greeted "with vast applause, before an audience [this must have been the sum of the two audiences] of 3,700 persons."

But after this interlude the ugly business of fighting the operatic opposition had to be faced. The nobility put in Porpora to bat first. *Ariadne* filled Lincoln's Inn Fields from 29th December. Handel responded with a similarly titled opera (*Arianna*) of his own on 26th January. In this he featured a new *castrato*—Carestini, who had been engaged during a continental tour undertaken after Oxford with this end in view. Lady Bristol described Carestini as "an extream good singer. The rest are all scrubbs, except old Durastanti, that sings as well as ever she did." Nor was Lady Bristol far wrong. Handel faced the nobility with an inferior team, and he had played into their hands by preferring Carestini to the much more famous Farinelli.

Meanwhile opera in English was improving in popularity if not always in quality. In the tradition of ballad opera came Charles Johnson's *Village Opera* and Bickerstaff's *Love in a Village*. In direct competition with Handel Carey produced, in 1732, *Amelia* and *Teraminta*, the first music by Lampe and the second by John Christopher Smith. *Amelia* gave Susanna Arne her first opportunity, and not only encouraged her father in Handelian depredation, but also put ideas into her brilliant brother's head. He proceeded to take the threadbare script of Addison's *Rosamund* and to give it another trial. With no more famous singers than old Leveridge, a relic of the Purcellian era, one of Rich's pantomimers, a reliable drinker and a massive *basso* who lived ripely on to the age of eighty-eight; Mrs. Barbier, more celebrated as the heroine of an elopement escapade than as a singer; Mr. Corfe; Miss Chambers; Mrs. Jones; Miss Arne; and a younger brother, Master Arne, *Rosamund* achieved ten performances and a benefit night for the composer. Carey with his genius for lampoon was at the same time handling grandiose exoticism in general extremely roughly in *Chrononhotontho-*

[28] Hearne, *Reliquiae Hearnianae.*

logos which, with its nomenclature (Aldiborontiphoscop-hornio, Rigdum-Funnidos, the Queen of Queerum-mania), its rude allusions to

A sudden diarrhoea's rapid force

which stimulated disastrously the peristaltic motion of the queen, and with its "Rough Music of Salt-boxes and Roll-ing-pins, Gridirons and Tongs, Sow-gelders Horns, Mar-row-bones and Cleavers" (an orchestration later adopted by Burney) sent gusts of ribald laughter round London at the expense of more serious entertainment.

Nor was oratorio left as a Handelian monopoly. De-fesch, a Fleming and leader of the band at Marylebone, composed a work in this *genre* to a text by Huggins. The work is known to posterity through Hogarth's castigation in caricature. Maurice Greene, to whom, as has been noted, Handel was particularly allergic, tried his hand at part of *The Song of Deborah*. And Porpora was in the same occupation as a relief from opera.

> Yesterday [wrote Mrs. Pendarves] in the afternoon Phil and I went to the oratorio at Lincoln's Inn, com-posed by Porpora, an Italian, famous for church music, who is now in England: it is a fine solemn piece of music, but I confess I think the subject too solemn for a theatre. To have words of piety made use of *only* to introduce good music, is *reversing* what it ought to be, and most of the people that hear the oratorio make no reflection on the meaning of the words, though God is addressed in the most solemn manner; some of the choruses and recitatives are extremely fine and touch-ing, but they say it is not equal to Mr. Handel's ora-torio of *Esther* or *Deborah*.[29]

Mrs. Pendarves was a fair critic and Handel would not have had it otherwise.

In the spring of 1734 Handel fulfilled an occasional engagement by compiling out of *Athaliah* a *Parnasso in festa* and by writing an anthem to celebrate the marriage

[29] Letter to Anne Granville, 28th March 1734.

of the Princess Royal with the Prince of Orange. At the end of the season Handel's agreement with Heidegger was terminated, and before he had had time to readjust his affairs the nobility rushed into the Haymarket. There was in their party sound business direction. They took the best theatre and then produced a sensational addition to their company—Farinelli. With Farinelli, Montagnana, Cuzzoni and Senesino the directorate could confront Handel with the ace, king, queen and knave of hearts.

Chapter 6

The Transition

ON HIS [FARINELLI'S] arrival here, at the first private
rehearsal at Cuzzoni's apartments, Lord Cowper, then
principal manager of the opera under Porpora, observing that the band did not follow him, but were all gaping with wonder, as if thunder-struck, desired them to
be attentive; when they all confessed, that they were
unable to keep pace with him: having not only been
disabled by astonishment, but overpowered by his talents. This band was small, consisting only of Carbonelli, Mich. Christ. Festing, Valentine Snow, afterwards
sergeant-trumpeter, and Mr. Vezan, a dancing-master,
who was likewise a steady and excellent player on the
violin, and constantly employed whenever Carbonelli
or Festing was the leader: it was from this worthy that
I had this anecdote.[1]

The prince of *castrati* stayed in London for three years,
sufficiently long to be in at the kill of Italian opera, to see
Handel reduced to financial disorder and society to a state
of emotional exhaustion. The incredible furore his presence created is without parallel in the long history of stage
idolatry. He happened to be the best singer of his kind in
Europe, but this was not entirely relevant. His acclamation came because he was the Farinelli. Towards the end
of his sojourn he had the mortification of playing to near-
empty houses, but his fortune was made and he could retire to Spain to endorse the truth of Mattheson's remark
that "he who in the present time wants to make a profit

[1] Burney, *History*, iv. 380.

out of music betakes himself to England." Handsome fees
were dispensed by private purses when the presence of
Farinelli was indicative of social standing. Among his patrons were the Spanish ambassador, the Portuguese chap-
lain for whom Farinelli sang "on the occasion of the Princess of Brazil's being brought to bed of a daughter," the
Duke of Leeds and the Prince of Wales.

> His Royal Highness the Prince of Wales was pleased
> to make a present of a fine wrought snuff-box, richly
> set with diamonds and rubies, in which was inclosed a
> pair of brilliant diamond knee-buckles, as also a purse
> of one hundred guineas, to the famous Signor Farinelli,
> who had constantly attended all his Royal Highness's
> concerts since he came from Italy.[2]

"One God, one Farinelli!" shouted Lady Bingley with ac-
curate impiety at the opera, thus achieving immortality in
Hogarth's denunciation of the whole disgusting orgy of
castrato worship in the fourth scene of "Marriage à la
Mode." In "The Rake's Progress" (Scene ii) the gifts
enumerated above are listed, with T. Rakewell both perti-
nently and impertinently named as donor, as the elee-
mosynary outcome of *Artaserse,* Farinelli's first opera at
the Haymarket. This scene of Hogarth's illuminates dis-
tressingly the degeneracy of fashionable artistic proclivities. There are Figg, the instructor in quarter-staff, Dubois
the fencing-master, Essex the professor of dancing, hat-
ters, tailors and other miscellaneous clients, a horn-player
blowing indiscriminate noises and Handel (the wig is of
the ripe variety favoured by him, although the figure is
less massive than we have been accustomed to imagine).
The latter rehearses with blissful unconcern the score of
The Rape of the Sabines at the harpsichord. The repul-
siveness of Farinelli exercised a particular fascination on
Hogarth, who lashed the idol again in his "Farinelli, Cuzzoni and Senesino" of 1734.

Handel, excluded from the King's Theatre, took the
smaller house, under Rich's management, in Lincoln's Inn

Fields. It is suggested by Streatfeild that this theatre was temporarily taken[3] for the benefit of the Princess of Orange, who was anxious to hear some music before leaving for Holland. He stayed at Lincoln's Inn Fields until 18th December with *Arianna* and *Il pastor fido,* the latter being rearranged to include dances for the Parisian ballerina, if the term is not too euphemistic, Sallé, who had been used for her talents of dubious propriety in earlier pantomime. After 18th December Handel moved to Covent Garden.

For the new year his singers were Carestini, Beard, Waltz, Stoppelaer, Strada, Negri and Cecilia Young. John Beard was a former chorister of the Chapel Royal under Gates. He was a singer of charm and intelligence, but of limited technique. Cecilia Young was one of three sisters, all of whom sang themselves into marriage: Cecilia with Arne, Isabella with Lampe and Esther, less notably, with one Jones. Waltz, the other singer who calls for comment, was reputed to have served Handel as cook,[4] and had certainly sung in the Oxford celebrations in place of the miscreant Montagnana. Previously Waltz had put himself in temporary disgrace by taking part in Arne's *Acis and Galatea* production.

Against *Artaserse* and *Polifemo* at the Haymarket Handel set *Ariodante* at Covent Garden. The king generously, and with a deprecatory sigh at those of the nobility who made such sacrifice necessary by attempting "the ruin of one poor fellow," contributed £1,000 towards the running expenses. For Lent, Handel, "as his capital singers were inferior in number and renown to those of his rival . . . very wisely discontinued the performance of operas for a considerable time, and rested his fame and fortune on his choral strength in the composition of oratorios."[5] Burney felt strongly here: after all as a young man he had had the honour of playing for Handel, and as a schoolboy he had experienced the greater thrill of witnessing the

[3] Streatfeild, p. 134.

[4] See "Gustavus Waltz: was he Handel's cook?" in *Concerning Handel,* W. C. Smith, 1948.

[5] Burney, *History,* iv. 383.

great man so ordinarily engaged as in drinking a cup of coffee and smoking a pipe. He continued his communiqué with gallant satisfaction at Porpora's discomfiture after sending a *David* into the oratorio sector of the battle. "In this attack he seems to have sunk under his antagonist's superior force and fire. For this oratorio was executed but three times. . . ." *Esther* was given six times, *Athaliah* five and *Deborah* three. Between the acts of *Esther* Handel "performs a part in two concertos, that are the finest things I ever heard in my life."

In introducing organ concertos Handel was wise. Many would come to hear him play who found less to interest them in the singing of indifferent singers. Handel was a great organ-lover with modern tendencies and was apparently instrumental in inducing the Germans to adopt the English-invented swell-box. As far back as 1722 his playing stimulated the Rev. Daniel Prat, M.A., to Browning-esque enthusiasm:

> *Yet as thy volant touch pursues*
> *Through all proportions low and high*
> *The wondrous fugue, it peace renews*
> *Serene as the unsullied sky.*[6]

The concertos indicate that the touch was still volant[7] in 1734.

On 16th April *Alcina,* with a preliminary puff in the *London Daily Post* stating that "the new opera will exceed any composition of Mr. Handel's hitherto performed," completed the season. In the other house, during the performance of *Polifemo,* unnecessary notoriety was gained by a show of anarchy on the part of the footmen who terrified the ladies "by crowding into the lobby with lighted flambeaux, and refusing to retire when ordered by the gentlemen." The assistance of the guards was called for and "the Marquis of Tweedale's servant received a wound of which he died a few days after."[8] An episode such as

[6] "Ode to Mr. Handel, on his Playing on the Organ, 1722" in Nichols's *Select Collection of Poems, 1781,* vii. 150–6.

[7] *Vide* Hawkins, v. 413.

[8] Burney, *History,* iv. 384.

this often enlivened the theatre of the heroic age. With Handel's triumph in *Alcina,* a lightweight among his operas designed more than was usual with Handel to suit popular taste, and including more dances for the disreputable Sallé, was mingled the by now familiar touch of disillusionment. Carestini, affronted by his director's corrosive treatment (the old story of the singer refusing to sing an aria and being subjected to a salutary course of browbeating repeats itself), affirmed his intention of leaving the cast. Handel thereupon took £300 from the bank and left town for the summer. Some time during the recess he had another of Mattheson's periodic requests for autobiographical matter. To this Handel returned his customary polite refusal: "It would be impossible for me to recall the events of my past life, since continued application to the service of this Court and Nobility prevents me from giving my attention to any other matters.[9] Which wasn't quite true, as a letter written to Jennens at the same time shows:

> I received your very agreeable letter with the inclosed oratorio. I am just going to Tunbridge; yet what I could read of it in haste, gave me a great deal of satisfaction. I shall have more leisure time there to read it with all the attention it deserves. There is no certainty of any scheme for next season, but it is probable that something or other may be done, of which I shall take the liberty to give you notice, being extremely obliged to you for the generous concern you show upon this account. . . .[10]

In 1736, after diplomatic disappointment over the miscarried "double marriage project," designed to detach Prussia from Austria, the Prince of Wales was married to the Princess of Saxe-Gotha on 27th April. Handel carried out his proper duties and added a wedding anthem to his list of royal offerings. *Sing unto God* was about the only token of piety in a sordid affair. The prince, indifferent to

[9] 29th July 1735.
[10] 28th July 1735.

considerations other than those of unpleasant consequence
to his father and to women who were honest, seized the
opportunity to make the occasion a parliamentary issue
in which his financial position gave the Opposition a stick
with which to beat the Government. The debate was notable for the appearance on the floor of the House of Cor-
net Pitt, who was, for his championship of the prince,
deprived of his rank. Occasional music was in these conditions a minor issue. Nevertheless Porpora put on *The
Feast of Hymen* to keep the scores even, anticipating that
Handel would cap his wedding anthem with a piece of
secular *réjouissance*.

At the beginning of this year Handel, embarrassed by
the late secession of Carestini, had turned Purcellian in a
setting of one of Dryden's odes for St. Cecilia. *Alexander's
Feast,* in a version prepared by Newburgh Hamilton, was
highly successful, probably for no other reason than that
it was in English. John Walsh the younger, having paid
Handel £105, published the work—with chorus, which
was unusual—more or less entire. In May *Atalanta*
brought back the opera under princely protection, as it
was by way of being the expected *Festgesang*. The description of this work in the *Daily Post* recalls the glories
of the Jonsonian masque. There

> was a new set of scenes painted in honour of the union,
> which took up the full length of the stage; the fore part
> of the scene represented an avenue to the temple of
> Hymen, adorned with statues of heathen deities. Next
> was a triumphal arch, on the summit of which were the
> arms of their Royal Highnesses. Under the arch was
> the figure of Fame on a cloud [under it would have been
> more fitting], sounding the praises of the happy pair.
> The names Fredericus and Augusta appeared above, in
> transparent characters. The opera concluded with a
> grand chorus, during which several beautiful illumina-
> tions were displayed.

The prince and princess from now on were staunch Handelians, to the temporary annoyance of the king, who felt,

as a matter of principle, obliged to withdraw his support.

In the summer and autumn Handel took comfort from the obviously declining fortunes of the opera of the nobility. Senesino had already gone and Farinelli was on the point of departure. Handel himself had lately engaged new singers—Gioacchino Conti (alias Gizziello), a soprano who had appeared in *Atalanta* and possessed, according to Burney, delicacy and tenderness; and Domenico Annibali, a contralto from Dresden. The scores of the operas for the coming season were prepared and as completed were taken round for Mrs. Pendarves's approval.[11]

By November the scene was set for the final show-down between the rival schools: Handel in good heart, although his health was a source of anxiety; the nobility banking on their new arrivals—Merighi, Chimenti and Francesina. The new singers on both sides were paraded before the queen and the princesses at Kensington and impartially approved. Strada, back from a vacation in Holland, acclimatized herself by singing at the Swan Tavern.

Handel got off this season to a flying start with revivals of *Atalanta* (with "several fine devices in fireworks" in honour of the Princess of Wales's birthday) and *Poro,* whose production was somewhat delayed by Strada's sore throat, under royal patronage. In the new year came *Arminio* (12th January), *Giustino* (16th February) and *Berenice* (18th May). But little success attended these works, and Handel's health was no longer proof against rapid deterioration. He survived the oratorio performances during Lent—the days were Wednesdays, Fridays and the first four days of Holy Week—but on 30th April the *London Daily Post* referred to Mr. Handel's indisposition with rheumatism and his hopes of being sufficiently recovered to accompany *Giustino* on 4th May. During his illness his cast staged an untraceable *Dido. Berenice,* which had been composed between 18th December and 18th January, was the season's last opera. Handel closed his theatre on 1st June.

At the Haymarket affairs were in no better state. Op-

11 Streatfeild, p. 140.

eras failed with monotonous regularity, operas with inter-mezzi (*Il Giocatore,* introduced between the acts of Hasse's *Siroe,* was the first ever seen on the stage in England) failed, Hasse, Porpora, Pescetti failed, and Fari-nelli, perturbed by houses worth no more than £35, de-veloped a cold, thus preventing further performances of the concluding *Sabrina,* and cleared out of the country having completely knocked the bottom out of the aspira-tions of the nobility.

Giustino had featured a sea monster. Harry Carey grinned broadly, picked up his ready pen, scribbled a farce, dragged in the agreeable Lampe and threw into London the pleasant ribaldries of *The Dragon of Wantley.* To visualize Handel enjoying this burlesque[12] is to recog-nize the greatness of his heart and the instinct for chivalry which prompted him to approve Carey's opportunism. The Dragon was killed by a kick on the backside. This (sixty-three performances during the season) was also the death-blow of Italian opera. Carey refreshed his audiences by action and words which were intelligible, by a York-shire accent and by slapstick comedy. His final chorus mocked at the noise of Italian vowels, and winked wicked-ly at the new Lenten occupation of oratorio. Thus was morale restored:

> *Sing, sing, and rorio*
> *An Oratorio*
> *To gallant Morio,*
>   *Of More-Hall.*
> *To Margereenia*
> *Of Roth'ram Greenia,*
> *Beauty's bright Queenia*
>   *Bellow and bawl.*

Upon which supervened a concluding salvo of loud huzzas.

Handel's illness has previously been referred to as rheu-matism. In the summer it culminated in a paralytic disor-der which affected his right side (according to the *London*

12 *Wentworth Papers,* p. 539.

Evening Post of May 14) and, more disastrously, the balance of his mind. For cure he was recommended to the waters of Aix-la-Chapelle. Having been soused with (sulphurous) holy water by attendant nuns, he returned to England much restored, miraculously so they said, in health early in November. It is worth remarking that those who refer to Handel as bankrupt at this period do him an injustice. He had lost pretty heavily by operatic misadventure, but in 1737 his banking account was in credit, nor did his name appear in the published lists of bankrupts.[13]

He returned to London in time to celebrate the obsequies of Queen Caroline in *The Ways of Zion do mourn.* "This fine anthem of Mr. Handel's," says the *Daily Post* in reference to the melancholy events of 17th December,

> was performed about nine; the vocal parts were performed by the several choirs of the Chapel Royal, Westminster Abbey, St. Paul, and Windsor, and the boys of the Chapel Royal and Westminster Abbey; and several musical gentlemen of distinction attended in surplices, and sung in the burial service. There were near 80 *vocal* performers and 100 *instrumental,* from His Majesty's band and from the Opera, etc.

The queen's death sent the town into mourning, and Handel's *Faramondo,* which had been begun early in November, was set aside until the new year. Neither this nor the patchwork *Alessandro Severo* nor *Serse* (*Xerxes*) materially improved Handel's fortunes; but a benefit concert, given in March, did. More than this (and more than the fact that its receipts enabled Strada to be paid and her husband quieted), the concert, consisting of oratorio excerpts and organ concertos, renewed Handel's confidence in his friends. A furthur demonstration in his favour occurred when, a little later in the year, Tyers, the prosperous proprietor of Vauxhall Gardens, spent £300 on

---

[13] "Bankruptcy is the status of a debtor who has been declared by judicial process to be unable to pay his debts."—*Ency. Brit.,* iii. 56.

the erection of that Roubiliac statue which now greets the customers of Messrs. Novello. John Lockman was inspired to this quatrain:

> *That* Orpheus *drew a grove, a rock, a stream*
> *By musick's powers, will not a fiction seem;*
> *For here as great a miracle is shown—*
> *Fam'd Handel breathing, tho' transformed to stone.*[14]

Tyers's gesture was prompted by the use he had made of Handel's music in enhancing the pleasures of his playground. According to the Russian Nkarintsev[15] Handel was a "people's composer." If so, no better evidence can be afforded than by the amount of his music presented to the citizens and citizenesses who nightly flocked to Vauxhall for a variety of diversions, some innocent, others not. There, said a gentleman of Oxford,

> . . . *plac'd marmoric in the vocal grove*
> *He guides the measures listening throngs approve.*[16]

In view of the major events of biography which are chronicled in headlines it may tend to be assumed that in between opera and oratorio production Handel was lacking in occupation. The present period is a case in point. Nothing of great significance appears, but all the time Handel is engaged fully: preparing material for publication (Handel was the most frequently published of all eighteenth-century composers), interviewing Heidegger as to the prospects of renewed partnership, exercising his charitable instincts, as in the foundation, in 1738, of the Society of Musicians, or essaying collaboration with Jennens.

To refer to the century under review as the Age of

[14] *London Magazine*, May, 1738: On the artistic quality of Roubiliac's statue Margaret Whinney writes that it is "a brilliant example of that interest in a transitory mood that desires to catch a fleeting moment rather than to record the permanent ideal, which is characteristic of Rococo art." (*Handel and Roubiliac,* in *Musical Times,* February 1961, pp. 82–3.)

[15] *Pictures from the Life of Handel* (Moscow, 1937).

[16] *Gentleman's Magazine,* October 1740.

Reason, or as the Classical Era, is to obscure its principal attributes. It was the age of high romance, of glorious irrationality, of the novel. Above all, it was the age of the individual. The life of London (population in 1750 was 676,250[17]) was still sufficiently compact for people to be known, and the precision of classical education, which impinged even on the relatively illiterate, combined with a native genius for idiosyncratic observation enlarged names into characters. And conversation, not then a lost art, took leisurely opportunity at coffee-house, tavern or pleasure garden to embellish familiar characters with picturesque anecdote. When the royal linen, that perennial source of indignant amusement, had been disposed of, conversation turned to this and that. Handel stories were frequent. Sometimes his appetite set the inventive going. One day Handel ordered dinner for three and, on being asked whether he would wait for the company, replied pontifically: "Bring up the dinner *prestissimo*. I am the company." Stories like this were improved by being put into the pidgin-English which Handel was reputed to have spoken. (So far as can be judged from quoted examples of Handel's speech it would seem that he changed his consonants as in the Halle dialect of boyhood German.) In 1738 the clubbable were diverted to hear that Handel and Jennens were on agreeable terms.

Charles Jennens, of Gopsall in Leicestershire, was a notable conversation piece. Rich and a bachelor, he could afford to live in undisturbed and luxurious eccentricity. In town Jennens graced Great Ormond Street and impressed the impressionable by the ostentation of his wealth on the one hand (he used to drive the distance of a penny bus ride with four footmen in attendance, one deputed on descent to clear the footpath of garbage) and his patronage of the polite arts on the other. He understood, although Steevens and Johnson held a different opinion, literature, music and painting. And in time they called him "Solyman the Magnificent."

Jennens met Handel and projected ideas for oratorios.

[17] M. Dorothy George, *London Life in the XVIIIth Century*, p. 329.

He sent a libretto, which may well have been that of *Saul,*
to Handel in 1735. (*Saul* was in other people's minds as
a possible subject, and one act of a dramatic work thereon, by Aaron Hill, appeared in the *Gentleman's Magazine*
for February 1736.) A good deal of the autumn of 1738
was spent in fruitful collaboration, the outcome being *Saul*
and *Israel in Egypt.* The important partner, according to
Jennens, was Jennens. While we may sympathize with
Handel for having to work with an opinionated poetaster
we should not overlook the fact that in matters of art he
was not slow in expressing himself with rough dogmatism.
And the aftermath of his illness was often disturbing in
social repercussions. However, Jennens had the grace to
keep his opinions private and to circulate them only in
family correspondence. A letter to the Earl of Guernsey,
written by Jennens on 19th September 1738, hints at domestic disorder:

Mr. Handel's head is more full of maggots than ever.
I found yesterday in his room a very queer instrument
which he calls carillon (Anglice, a bell) and says some
call it a Tubalcain, I suppose because it is both in the
make and tone like a set of Hammers striking upon anvils. 'Tis played upon with keys like a Harpischord and
with this Cyclopean instrument he designs to make poor
Saul mad. His second maggot is an organ of £500
price which (because he is overstocked with money) he
has bespoke of one Moss of Barnet. This organ, he says,
is so constructed that as he sits at it he has a better command of his performers than he used to have, and he is
highly delighted to think with what exactness his Oratorio will be performed by the help of this organ; so that
for the future instead of beating time at his oratorios, he
is to sit at the organ all the time with his back to the Audience. His third maggot is a Hallelujah which he has
trump'd up at the end of his oratorio since I went into the
Country, because he thought the conclusion of the oratorio not Grand enough; tho' if that were the case 'twas
his own fault, for the words would have bore as Grand
Musick as he could have set 'em to: but this Hallelujah,

Grand as it is, comes in very nonsensically, having no manner of relation to what goes before. And this is the more extraordinary, because he refused to set a Hallelujah at the end of the first Chorus in the Oratorio, where I had placed one and where it was to be introduced with the utmost propriety, upon a pretence that it would make the entertainment too long. I could tell you more of his maggots: but it grows late and I must defer the rest till I write next, by which time, I doubt not, more new ones will breed in his Brain.

The maggots came from mental derangement on the one hand and flooding inspiration on the other. So that any host was likely to have had his patience stretched. The Tubalcain (the name was surely a joke at Jennens's expense) is indicative of Handel's Straussian outlook on orchestral colour and is a warning to extreme purism. Through mention of the organ a glimpse can be obtained of the anarchic conditions which obtained in choral singing, and which justified Carey's "roratorios." Moreover Mr. Moss's new organ explains the prominence given to the instrument in the score of *Saul,* which, all in all, includes two more or less complete organ concertos.[18] Both *Saul,* finished on 27th September, and *Israel in Egypt,* finished on 1st November, are impressive in their intensity. Handel, like Swift and Kit Smart, fought the nightmare of mental disturbance with deep concentration.

The completion of these works was therefore the triumph which their author desired. That neither succeeded worried him little. Some of his critics complained of the noise, a perennial annoyance to the witless who regarded any instruments which overpowered conversation as supernumerary. The kettledrums borrowed from the Tower would have effectively put an end to gossip. Then some of the singers were castigated. But the truth was that the psychological insight of *Saul* and the *Lear*-like vasture of *Israel in Egypt* were out of time and out of place. Nor did the latter succeed when Handel interspersed it with operatic arias for Beard and prefaced it with the *Funeral*

[18] *Vide* HHA Edition of *Saul* (1962), Percy M. Young.

Anthem. Beard, incidentally, had stimulated drawing-room tittle-tattle by marrying, above his station, Lady Harriet Herbert in the previous year. Lady Mary Wortley Montagu[19] was much distressed. The failure of his two oratorios drove Handel to his side line of pasticcio: *Jupiter in Argos,* based on the libretto of Lotti's opera of that name, which Handel had seen twenty years before at Dresden, was advertised for performance on 1st May. It was never performed.

The year 1739 was a bad one altogether. No one was in the mood for music. As Jenkins was bringing his ear out of pickle, and opinion was hardening against foreigners in general and Spaniards in particular, opera and oratorio became insignificant against the necessity for moving the stubbornly pacific Walpole to declare war.

In October the king moved to St. James's from Kensington and on the night of the 27th went to the Playhouse with the duke and the princesses, "where the Tune of Britons Strike Home, etc. being played for a Dance the House seconded it with a loud and long Huzza."[20] That was the feeling of the times. In Lincoln's Inn Fields on 22nd November "it being St. Cecilia's day [Handel] first performed *Dryden's Second Ode,*[21] with two concertos for several instruments, preceded by *Alexander's Feast,* and a concerto on the organ, at opera prices." A month later *Acis and Galatea* was again revived and two more *Concerti grossi* (all twelve were written this year) appeared.

In the winter the roasting of oxen on the frozen Thames was a familiar sight, but the elements responsible for so elevating and so olfactory a spectacle put the draught-riddled seats of Lincoln's Inn Fields out of bounds. Handel was a notable curser: his vocabulary was fully exercised at this time. Nevertheless he picked up Jennens's "improvements" to Milton and turned out the enchanting music of *L'Allegro.* And still dallying with his old love he

---

[19] Letter to the Countess of Pomfret, 1738.

[20] *Gentleman's Magazine,* October 1739.

[21] i.e. The *Ode* (Dryden's *Song) for St. Cecilia's Day; cf.* pp. 61 and 71.

prepared two more operas. *Imeneo* (*Hymen*) had two performances in November. *Deidamia*, the last of his operas, three in January and February 1741.

An advertisement during March 1741 in the *London Daily Post* read:

> For the benefit and increase of a fund established for the support of decayed musicians and their families, at the King's Theatre, on Saturday next (14) will be performed, with the original scenes and habits, *Parnasso in festa*, composed by Mr. Handel for Her Royal Highness the Princess of Orange's wedding.

So Handel eased his discontent by helping to alleviate the misfortunes of others.

On 8th April *L'Allegro* and the *Ode for St. Cecilia's Day* furnished the programme for a farewell concert.

Chapter 7

"Sacred Grand Oratorio"

DUBLIN IN 1741 had not yet reached its peak in architectural achievement: Gandon's crowning glories were still to come. But among European capitals Dublin held high place, despite the Liberties, for elegance in town-planning and for beauty in situation. Trinity College focused attention in the city centre; medieval Dublin spoke proudly through the curiously Irish crenellations of her parish churches; Christ Church sat in grave ruination on its own eminence overlooking the changing colours of the Liffey; not far away St. Patrick's nursed a sick dean and entertained the lords of state. The bay of Dublin, flanked by its headlands, welcomed the English visitor and the quiet serenity of the Wicklow mountains hinted at not-too-distant rural enchantment. Society in Dublin was feverishly gay. For many years appointment to the Irish service had been a pleasant insult to those who had failed, or proved disagreeable in other ways, in English government or diplomacy. The rusticated, therefore, concentrated on the pleasantest way of killing time. Posterity should be grateful that this took the form of building houses, making libraries, beautifying a city, engaging in that brilliance of conversation which was the foundation of the great Anglo-Irish literary tradition, patronizing the fine arts in general with taste and understanding and in reading nostalgically the news from England.

The great name in English music was that of Handel. Handel's fortunes were declining. What better opportunity could there be, then, argued Castle circles, for Dublin to restore his fame by fêting him in Ireland? Dr. Delany, who, when he wasn't in London dancing attendance on Mrs. Pendarves, was in Dublin, knew all about Handel. He approved him as a friend of Mrs. Pendarves and reflected that a course in oratorio would help to spread godliness among a society not conspicuous for its cult. The lord lieutenant, William Cavendish, fourth Duke of Devonshire, was impressed by what he heard and issued an invitation which Handel gratefully accepted.

Between 22nd August and 14th September Handel, again with the collaboration of Jennens, had written a new oratorio: *Messiah*. By 11th October he had done the most of *Samson,* the text ably extracted from Milton by Newburgh Hamilton. After this furious burst of energy Handel went north. For some days he waited at Chester for the contrary winds to subside before hazarding the notorious waters of St. George's Channel. Young Burney saw Handel at the "Golden Falcon" in Bridge Street and got all the details of the *Messiah* rehearsal, at which mediocrity and self-satisfaction were pricked by Handelian sarcasm, from Baker, the cathedral organist and Burney's music-master. And so to Ireland.

Among old friends there were Dubourg, leader of the viceroy's band, and Mrs. Cibber (*née* Susanna Arne), whose exquisite Polly Peachum excused those moral lapses which had driven her to Ireland out of the range of the anger of Theophilus and the scandals of litigation. Other performers went with Handel. A new concert hall had lately been built not far from Christ Church: Neal's Music Hall in Fishamble Street. The architect was a German immigrant—Richard Cassels—who had already designed Leinster House, the Rotunda, the dining hall of Trinity and a series of mansions for the wealthy. He was, as the examples quoted still show, a good architect, and in his concert hall he triumphed, where most architects fail, in producing good acoustics. This pleased Handel. Indeed, everything pleased Handel (except when they miscalled him doctor), and he wrote with old-time enthusiasm to Jennens on 29th December:

The Nobility did me the honour to make among

themselves a Subscription for 6 Nights, which did fill a Room of 600 Persons, so that I needed not to sell one single ticket at the Door, and without Vanity the Performance was received with a general Approbation. Sig.ra Avolio, which I brought with me from London, pleases extraordinary. I have found another Tenor Voice which gives great Satisfaction, the Basses and Counter Tenors are very good, and the rest of the Chorus Singers (by my Direction) do exceedingly well. As for the Instruments they are really excellent, Mr. Dubourgh being at the Head of them, and the Musick sounds delightfully in this charming room, which puts me in good Spirits (and my Health being so good) that I exert myself on my Organ with more than usual success.

I open'd with the *Allegro, Penseroso, and Moderato,* and I assure you that the words of the *Moderato* are vastly admired. The Audience being composed (besides the Flower of Ladies of Distinction and other People of the greatest Quality) of so many Bishops, Deans, heads of the Colledge, the most eminent People in the Law, as the Chancellor, Auditor General, etc. etc., all of which are very much taken with the Poetry, so that I am desired to perform it again the next time. I cannot sufficiently express the kind treatment I receive here, but the Politeness of this generous Nation cannot be unknown to you, so I let you judge of the satisfaction I enjoy, passing my time with honour, profit, and pleasure.

These six subscription concerts were followed by six more. And Dublin, which had previously welcomed[1] such of Handel's music as had come its way, rallied round a god's-plenty of *Alexander's Feast,* the *St. Cecilia Ode, Esther,* a revision of *Imeneo,* renamed *Hymen,* and unspecified orchestral works. In one of these latter occurred Dubourg's celebrated cadenza which, having returned from labyrinthine modulation to the safe haven of the

[1] *Vide Pue's Occurrences,* 1st April 1736, and *Dublin News-Letter,* 12th-16th January 1741.

tonic, provoked Handel's "You are welcome home, Mr. Dubourg." That was the sort of comment which went (and still goes) down well in Dublin. Handel's rooms in Abbey Street, near a later centre of laudable artistic achievement, were a hive of activity in February and March. *Messiah* was coming. On 8th March a crowded rehearsal greeted it with acclamation. The first performance was given, and to increase the accommodation ladies were requested to attend hoopless,[2] on 13th April.

> On Tuesday last Mr. Handel's Sacred Grand Oratorio, *The Messiah* [*sic*] was performed in the New Musick Hall in Fishamble Street; the best judges allowed it to be the most finished piece of Musick. Words are wanting to express the exquisite Delight it afforded to the admiring crowded Audience. The Sublime, the Grand, and the Tender, adapted to the most elevated, majestick and moving Words, conspired to transport and charm the ravished Heart and Ear. It is but Justice to Mr. Handel that the World should know he generously gave the Money arising from this Grand Performance, to be equally shared by the Society for relieving Prisoners, the Charitable Infirmary, and Mercer's Hospital, for which they will ever gratefully remember his Name; and that the Gentlemen of the Two Choirs [Christ Church and St. Patrick's], Mr. Dubourg, Mrs. Avolio, and Mrs. Cibber, who all performed their Parts to Admiration acted also on the same disinterested Principle, satisfied with the deserved Applause of the Publick, and the conscious Pleasure of promoting such useful and extensive Charity. There were above 700 People in the Room, and the Sum collected amounted to about £400, out of which £127 goes to each of the three great and pious Charities.

What the self-conscious correspondent of *Faulkner's*

---

[2] The wording of the "hoopless" advertisement in *Faulkner's Journal* (6th-10th April 1742) suggests that *Messiah* was a commissioned work: "Many Ladies and Gentlemen who are well-wishers to this Noble and Grand Charity *for which this Oratorio was composed* . . ." (my italics—P. M. Y.).

Journal fails to note is the Christian charity which Dr. Delany was impelled to display at Mrs. Cibber's "He was despised." His comment was: "Woman, for this thy sins be forgiven thee."

Messiah was performed again on 3rd June, and other summer activities were *Saul* (25th May), Avolio's benefit on 16th July and Mrs. Arne's benefit on 21st July. In between whiles Handel told funny stories to Dr. Quin and Mrs. Vernon and exercised their understanding in Italian, French, German and English, all of which languages he used indiscriminately. What else he did we should know had his letters from Ireland to Bernard Granville not been lost. He went away with the full intention, unfulfilled, of returning to Ireland the next year.

Back in London early in September Handel was at something of a loose end. A report that he was to take over the opera again was without foundation in fact. He had left opera for good and had arrived at the stage when he could laugh at its absurdities. The ageing Handel—he was by now fifty-seven—looked at life more gravely. Added piety came resultant on recovery from illness, and a new evangelical spirit infused his outlook on his work. "My Lord," he said to Lord Kinnoul after the London production of *Messiah,* "I should be sorry if I only entertained them; I wished to make them better."

Samson was quickly finished on returning home and with *Messiah* formed the mainstay of the 1743 season. *Samson* went down well, *Messiah* badly. *Samson* was sufficiently pagan to avoid damaging the susceptibilities of piety, induced by William Law and John Wesley, whereas *Messiah* had a blasphemous look in the title which was accordingly disallowed on the play-bills. None the less, *Messiah* impressed the eclectic and at its first performance—it had three this season as against eight of *Samson*—George II set the fashion (which might quite well now be discontinued) of standing during the "Hallelujah" chorus.

---

[3] Letter to Jennens, 29th December 1741: "The first Opera [*Alessandro in Persia*] I heard myself before I left London, and it made me very merry all along my journey. . . ."

In 1743 the king was a man of war and distinguished himself by being the last reigning monarch in England to appear at the head of his troops in the field. In the war, which had been greeted so ecstatically four years before, things were going badly, but at Dettingen, de Noaille's pincers movement going wrong, a surprising and unwarranted victory was snatched from defeat. Hence the *Dettingen Te Deum,* which enraptured all who heard it and which was pronounced by Mrs. Pendarves "heavenly." During the year Handel had another bout of illness. "Handel has had a palsy and can't compose," noted Horace Walpole.

At this period Mrs. Delany (on 9th June 1743 the *Gentleman's Magazine* advised the world of the marriage of the Rev. Dr. Delany "to the Relict of Alex. Pendarvis Esq.") was very busy. Marrying a clergyman, seconding his efforts to gain preferment, cutting down unbecoming flirtation and writing for and about Handel took the best part of her time. In May 1744 she was pleased for her husband's sake that he was elected to the vacant deanery of Downpatrick, but her pleasure was permanently tempered with anxiety for Handel. She records a row, of short duration, between Handel and the Prince of Wales—it was at Carlton House, where rehearsals frequently used to take place—and praises *Semele*. "But it being a profane story D.D. [Dr. Delany] does not think it proper for him to go." *Semele,* a reversion to the masque form of *Acis and Galatea,* suffered, like all Handel's music, opposition—from "the fine ladies, petit [*sic*] maitres, and *ignoramus's*. All the opera people are enraged at Handel, but Lady Cobham, Lady Westmoreland, and Lady Chesterfield never fail it."[4] On 10th March Mrs. Delany wrote to her sister a letter which has greater interest:

The oratorios fill very well, notwithstanding the spite of the opera party; nine of the twelve are over. Joseph is to be performed (I hope) once more, then Saul, and the Messiah finishes; as they have taken very well, I

4 Letter to Mrs. Dewes (*née* Anne Granville), 21st February 1744.

fancy Handel will have a second subscription; and how do you think *I have lately been employed?* Why, I have made a drama for an oratorio, out of Milton's *Paradise Lost,* to give Mr. Handel to compose to; it has cost me a great deal of thought and contrivance; D.D. approves of my performance, and that gives me some reason to think it is not bad, though all I have had to do has been collecting and making the connection between the fine parts. I begin with Satan's threatenings to seduce the woman, her being seduced follows, and it ends with the man's yielding to the temptation; I would not have a word or a thought of Milton's altered [a rare act of eighteenth-century self-denial]: and I hope to prevail with Handel to set it *without* having *any of the lines put into verse,* for that will take from its dignity."[5]

Handel, however, avoided the task set for him. The story was hardly in his line: not sufficiently strong in that clash of heroic personality which was his especial province. What happened to Mrs. Delany's text is not known. Professor Dent suggests the possibility that it furnished the original of Haydn's *Creation,* and that Lidley was the nearest that German scholarship could approximate to Delany.

From Covent Garden Handel returned to the Haymarket in November 1744. The theatre had again become available through the inability of Lord Middlesex, whose efforts at opera management had amused Handel previously, to succeed where better than he had failed. Subscription concerts, *Hercules* and *Belshazzar* were ill received, to Handel's "great loss, and the nation's disgrace," and once again he was taken ill.

Lady Shaftesbury went to *Alexander's Feast,*

but it was such a melancholy pleasure as drew tears of sorrow to see the great though unhappy Handel, dejected man and dark, sitting by, not playing on the harpsichord, and to think how his light had been spent by being overplied in music's cause. I was sorry, too, to

[5] Letter to Mrs. Dewes, 10th March 1744.

find the audience so insipid and tasteless (I may add unkind) not to give the poor man the benefit of applause; but affectation and conceit cannot discern or attend to merit.[6]

Society wanted amusement and novelty. Handel to the generality was too familiar, too severe and too incomprehensible. In his youth he had provided gay fantasy; in his old age, so it seemed, his line was moral philosophy. Lord —— saw in the oratorio an opportunity to attack the outworks of Amelia's virtue.[7] The bucks at the masquerade gave their opinion of oratorio when they discovered Dr. Harrison's philippic against adultery:

"Tom," says one of them, "let us set the ditty to music; let us subscribe to have it set by Handel; it will make an excellent oratorio."

"D——n me, Jack," says another, "we'll have it set to a psalm-tune, and we'll sing it next Sunday at St. James's Church, and I'll bear a bob, d——n me."[8]

In the summer of 1745 Charles Edward Stuart landed at Moidart. For six months he kept England in agitated suspense. He "liberated" Scotland, passed through Carlisle and Manchester, and reached as far south as Derby. At Ashbourne he was proclaimed king in the market-place. For Handel this was an uncomfortable thought. He knew Ashbourne, for Calwich Abbey near by, in what is now known as the George Eliot country, was the seat of Bernard Granville. Handel was a frequent visitor. The local tradition that *Messiah* was written at Calwich is improbable in view of the fact that Granville's new house was not yet ready in 1741. However, it may be reasonably assumed that Handel's fullest inspiration did not always come in London. Between Prince Charlie and London, as he had by-passed Wade's forces, lay only the indomitable volunteers. In them only insobriety would have reposed confidence. They had changed little since the early

[6] *Malmesbury Papers*, i. 2.
[7] Henry Fielding, *Amelia*, iv, Chapter IX.
[8] Ibid., x, Chapter II.

days of the century when they were affectionately designated "The Cuckolds-all-in-a-row" and thus pleasantly delineated by the effervescent Ned Ward:

I could not forbear laughing to see so many greasy cooks, tun-bellied lick-spiggots, and fat wheezing butchers, sweating in their buff doublets, under the command of some pig-faced brewer, whose belly was hooped in with a golden sash, which the clod-skulled hero became as well as one of his dray-horses would an embroidered saddle.[9]

But the train-bands, despite Handel's exhortation in a "Song made for the Gentlemen Volunteers of the City of London," were not called on. Charles Edward misjudged his strategy, retreated from Derby to have his forces finally routed by the bloody Duke of Cumberland at Culloden, on 16th April 1746. In 1745 Handel had been unable to complete his series of subscription concerts. The disappointment of his patrons he mitigated by giving them the *Occasional Oratorio*. This successfully celebrated the duke, who

allur'd by glory's charms
Flew with a lover's haste to arms[10]

and gave disappointed ticket-holders their money's worth. Thus honourably did Handel always keep to the spirit of his commitments.

The year 1745 is significant in Handel's life. It divides the old unhappiness and disappointment from an autumnal season of mellowed brilliance and general esteem. The *Occasional Oratorio* preluded a period of *ad hoc* composition. Its successor was *Judas Maccabaeus*. The librettist was Thomas Morell, D.D. Like other librettists Morell had no high standing in letters. Writing to Walpole of some odes, Mason remarked: "They are so lopped and mangled, that they are worse now than the productions of Handel's poet, Dr. Morell."[11] But, as Garrick said, he

[9] Ned Ward, *London Spy*.
[10] *Gentleman's Magazine*, May 1746.

was a scholar,[12] and what was more he could see Handel's point of view.

Fortunately his observations on the inception of an oratorio are extant. They make illuminating reading:

> . . . As to myself, great lover as I am of music, I should never have thought of such an undertaking (in which, for the reasons above, little or no credit is to be gained) had not Mr. Handel applied to me when at Kew in 1746, and added to his request the honour of a recommendation from Prince Frederick. Upon this I thought I could do as well as some who had gone before me, and within two or three days carried him the first act of *Judas Maccabaeus,* which he approved of. "Well," says he, "and how are you to go on?" "Why, we are to suppose an engagement, and that the Israelites have conquered, and so begin with a chorus as 'Fallen is the foe,' or something like it." "No, I will have this," and began working it, as it is, upon the harpsichord. "Well, go on." "I will bring you more to-morrow." "No, something now." "So fall thy foes, O Lord———." "That will do," and immediately carried on the composition as we have it in that most admirable chorus. That incomparable air, "Wise men, flattering, may deceive us" (which was his last chorus) was de-signed for *Belshazzar,* but that not being performed, he happily flung it into *Judas Maccabaeus.* N.B.—The plan of *Judas Maccabaeus* was designed as a compli-ment to the Duke of Cumberland, upon his returning victorious from Scotland. I had introduced several inci-dents more apropos, but it was thought they would make it too long, and they were therefore omitted. The Duke, however, made me a handsome present by the hands of Mr. Poyntz. The success of the oratorio was very great, and I have often wished that at first I had asked in jest for the benefit of the 30th night instead of a 3rd. I am sure he would have given it to me; on

---

[11] Walpole, *Letters,* v. 420.
[12] Hill, *Boswell,* v. 350.

which night there was above £400 in the house. He left me a legacy, however, of £200.[13]

Judas was produced on 1st April 1747 at Covent Garden. Rosenberg, with his "This *Judas Maccabaeus* (composed on the occasion of the great battle won by the English over the Scots) was simply a song of praise on victory,"[14] would have been disturbed at the enthusiasm with which Handel was on this occasion greeted by the Jews. There were in England at that time probably 5,000 Jews: their chief synagogue had been established in Duke's Place, Aldgate, in 1722.[15] Persecution had brought them or their forbears to England, and Handel's flamboyant glorification of the Maccabees filled them with pride and gratitude. It would appear that George Amyand, Handel's friend and executor, had Jewish blood,[16] so that an interest in Jewry was of personal origin. Morell, therefore, was instructed to choose another Jewish subject. The result was *Alexander Balus*.

Burney saw a good deal of Handel domestically at this time. He had lately come to London and was preparing his own literary career by noting the characteristics of the great whom it was his privilege to meet.

Handel's general look was somewhat heavy and sour; but when he did smile, it was his sire the sun, bursting out of a black cloud. There was a sudden flash of intel-

[13] Historical MSS. Commission, Report XV, Appendix, Pt. 2.
[14] Alfred Rosenberg, *Georg Friedrich Händel* (Berlin, 1937). "Dieser Judas Maccabaeus—komponiert aus dem Anlass der gewonnenen grossen Schlacht der Engländer gegen die Schotten —war ein einziger Lobgesang des Sieges."
[15] M. Dorothy George, op. cit., p. 126.
[16] George Amyand, after Handel's death M.P. for Barnstaple and created baronet in 1764, was the second son of Claudius Amyand and his wife Mary Rabache, and grandson of Isaac Amyand and Anne Hottot, refugees from Mornac, Saintonge. He was a "Hamburg merchant" and married in April 1746 the daughter of the "late John Abraham Korten." Handel met Amyand at court, where Claudius was principal surgeon to George II from 1729–40.—*Gentleman's Magazine* and Daphne Drake, *Members of Parliament for Barnstaple.*

ligence, wit, and good humour, beaming in his coun-
tenance, which I hardly ever saw in any other.[17]

Thus we can picture Handel. At Carlton House in rehearsal, severe and concentrated; tempestuous at the
prince's late arrival; swearing at undertones of maid-of-
honour conversation ("Hush! hush! Handel's in a passion," urged the Princess of Wales); wig vibrating in
moments of satisfaction, discarded as a sign of dissatis-
faction. In the afternoons walking in the park, talking
to himself. "The devil! the father was deceived; the mother
was deceived—but I was not deceived; he is a damned
scoundrel—and good for nothing," he was once heard
to mutter after a charity boy entrusted to his care had
betrayed his testimonials and absconded. In the evenings,
and particularly on Sundays, occupied in amiable conversation at Mrs. Cibber's or Frasi's. If he was a little in
love with Mrs. Cibber his taste was commendable. She
was a lovely woman, honest—hence she cast off the odi-
ous Theophilus, intelligent, full enough of conviction to
defy convention in more ways than one. She was a
Catholic. She was also a great actress with an unrivalled
career as Juliet to her credit and a singer of attractive
accomplishment.

No person of sensibility, who has had the good fortune to hear Mrs. Cibber sing in the oratorio of *The
Messiah,* will find it very difficult to give credit to
accounts of the most wonderful effects of music produced from so powerful a union. And yet it was not
to any extraordinary powers of voice (whereof she has
but a moderate share), nor to a greater degree of skill
in music (wherein many of the Italians must be allowed
to exceed her) that she owed her excellence, but to
expression only, her acknowledged superiority in which
could proceed from nothing but skill in her profession.[18]

With Mrs. Cibber should be mentioned Jimmy Quin,
a staunch friend of Handel's since the day on which he

[17] Burney, *Commem.,* p. 53.
[18] Sheridan, *British Education,* p. 369.

walked out of *The Beggar's Opera* to devote his Hibernian affection to the destruction of the anti-Handelians. He too was a great actor: a notable Othello, Falstaff and Lear. Handel went to the theatre sometimes, and in addition to his two particular friends would have seen David Garrick.

Occasionally Handel still went for recreation to the opera, more often to St. Martin's-in-the-Fields to hear Kelway play the organ. Kelway was a great player, possessed of "a masterly wildness" and a highly individual style, "bold, rapid, and fanciful."[19] He was also a devotee of Domenico Scarlatti. But Handel went to church not only for the purpose of listening to the organ. His piety was not inconsiderable. It was reported that he prayed twice a day. He certainly exhibited his faith beneficially through works. He was rarely absent from the charity concerts for the benefit of decayed musicians and their families and was a great supporter, as the next chapter will show, of Captain Coram's new foundation.

Handel still worked in terrific bursts, spasmodically. A libretto was ready. He put everything on one side and wrote his music in a fortnight or three weeks. He was no believer in cold iron. *Alexander Balus* took from 1st June to 4th July 1747; *Joshua* from the end of July to 19th August; *Solomon* from 5th May to 13th June 1748; *Susanna* from 11th July to 24th August. The precision with which Handel's works can thus be dated is due to his methodical habits of annotation. *Susanna* bears the following inscriptions:

Ouverture Sussana Oratorio angefangen 11 July.)
17. . . .
Fine della parte prima geendiget July 21 ♃ 1748
Fine della parte 2da | völlig Agost 21 —
Fine dell Atto 3^{zo} | S.D.G. G.F. Handel Agost 9 ♂
1748
aetatis 63 völlig geendiget | Agost 24 ☿ 1748[20]

[19] Burney, *History,* iv. 665.
[20] The astrological signs for the days of the week were consistently used by Handel after 1737.

The five languages here employed give some hint of Handel's linguistic capacity which, in conversation (plus a wealth of broad oaths), must have been impressive.

In October 1748 the Peace of Aix-la-Chapelle was signed. So ended another war. No doubt on the conclusion of this egregious campaign Handel reflected on Jonathan's air:

> *From cities storm'd, and battles won,*
> *What glory can accrue;*
> *By this the hero best is known,*
> *He can himself subdue.*

But dutifully he turned his attention to a royal command for fitting music.

Chapter 8

Tellus Superata

Country Tradesman
When will Profusion leave a Bankrupt realm?
When Folly cease? and Prudence guide the helm?

Court Politician
O! When will dull mechanics cease to prate,
With blind presumption, on affairs of state!
To break a glorious peace lest France *should dare,*
'Tis right to shew, We've powder still to spare.[1]

To CELEBRATE THE return of peace with a royal salute of 101 brass ordnance (viz. 71 six-pounders, 20 twelve-pounders and 10 twenty-pounders), with a near-lethal display of fireworks, and with music arranged for warlike instruments obviously was not everybody's idea of propriety. But it was that of George II and his masters of ceremonies. Handel, who wrote music with godlike detachment for any occasion attractive to puny mortality, flung all the wind and percussion he could lay hands on into the April celebrations of 1749. Twenty-four hautboys, twelve bassoons, nine trumpets, nine horns, three pairs of kettledrums, a serpent (although this is crossed out) and a double bass are all listed in the score of the *Fireworks Music*.

The wonder is that this virtuous age, which fulfils Handel's putative intentions by regaling itself with gargantuan stews of reorchestrations, can resist a proper-scale, near-original performance of the *Fireworks Music* in Hyde Park (the Albert Hall if wet). Judging by what happened

[1] *Gentleman's Magazine*, January 1749.

on 21st April 1749 the result would be highly diverting. On that day a rehearsal at Vauxhall drew 12,000 people, stopped the traffic over London Bridge for three hours, and led to disorderly queues in which heads were duly broken. This rehearsal was one sensation in a bout of glorious licentiousness. Another was the masquerade at Ranelagh. There George II, disguised in an old English habit, viewed with lewd satisfaction the classical nudity (emphasized by a modest covering of flimsy gauze) of Elizabeth Chudleigh arrayed as "Iphigenia for the sacrifice but so naked, the high priest might easily inspect the entrails of the victim. The Maids-of-Honour (not of maids the strictest) were so offended they would not speak to her." The Princess of Wales threw a shawl over the lady and a veil over the proceedings.[2]

On 27th April Peace came into her own with impressive salvos from the aforementioned guns (a bombardier lost his life in preparing them[3]), with Handel's music, with fireworks which would not at first function and which, when they did, set ablaze the great temple erected *ad hoc* by the Chevalier Servandoni, and with lesser orgies of Georgian amusement.

A few days later Handel turned his thoughts to the Foundling Hospital. He attended a committee on 5th May and offered for performance in aid of the foundation the *Fireworks Music;* the anthem on the peace; selected pieces from *Solomon* relating to the dedication of the temple; and several pieces composed for the occasion. With this began (publicly speaking) an association which still happily persists: the genius of Handel still honours the hospital and the hospital with charming fidelity still remembers its greatest governor. The foundation was due to two widely contrasted facets of eighteenth-century life: on the one hand gin,[4] which reduced women to depravity and

[2] Mrs. Elizabeth Montagu.

[3] *Gentleman's Magazine*, April 1749.

[4] Because of the prevalence of gin-drinking children were "starved and naked at home" and "either become a burthen to their parishes or . . . are forced to beg whilst they are children, and as they grow up learn to pilfer and steal."—*Order Book*, Middlesex Sessions, January 1735–6.

their unwanted offspring to the dubious hospitality of the pavement; on the other to the crescent power of middle-class initiative. Captain Coram urged that something must be done (the wheels of government eventually turned, but not before amateur organization had achieved a monument of empirical piety), and something was done. This independence of action was after Handel's own heart. He did not place much trust in governments, as his anger at the hospital's intention to have its interest in *Messiah* safe-guarded by Act of Parliament shows. "Mine musick shall not go to the Parliament." But added to an appreciation of Coram's gesture was lonely bachelordom and growing age, both of which helped to turn the full magnificence of a broad sympathy to the fatherless and destitute. In 1750 he presented an organ to the hospital and opened it himself with *Messiah*. Thereafter he presided annually at a Foundling Hospital *Messiah* and was instrumental thereby in enriching the hospital to the extent of nearly £7,000.[5] A fair copy and parts of the oratorio were bequeathed to the foundation in his will. The suggestion frequently made that Handel was segregated from intellectual activities outside of music is not borne out by his connection with the Foundling Hospital. On 9th May 1750 he was elected a governor. In this capacity he was called into consultation, not only on musical matters, but "also in affairs connected with the interior ornamentation of the Chapel."[6] And an interest in heraldry, attached to a nostalgia which naturalization and long residence never entirely removed, is romantically signified in the coat of arms granted to the hospital in 1749. This contains a "Crescent Argent between two Mullets of six points Or": a part also of the arms of the town of Halle.[7]

In 1749 Handel mourned the death of his old friend Sir Wyndham Knatchbull, who died on 23rd July. But being given to sublimating his private griefs in assistance for the living he busied himself with the composition of

[5] Burney, *Commem.*, p. 43.
[6] Nichols and Wray, *The History of the Foundling Hospital*, p. 204.
[7] Ibid., p. 250.

Theodora, in the consideration of music for Smollett's *Alceste* (which was never performed but which was re-hashed in *The Choice of Hercules*) and in advising Jennens on the subject of organ specification. The clergy, who are frequently anxious for information on this head, are recommended to Handel's good sense and austerity. He wrote to Jennens on 30th September:

> Yesterday I received Your letter to which I here-under specify my Opinion of an Organ which I think will answer the Ends you propose, being everything that is necessary for a good and grand Organ, without reed Stops, which I have omitted, because they are continually wanting to be tuned, which in the Country is very inconvenient, and should it remain useless on that account, it would still be very expensive althou' that may not be your consideration [herein out-peers German frugality]. I very well approve of Mr. Bridge who without any objection is a very good Organ builder, and I shall willingly (when he has finished it) give you my Opinion of it. I have referr'd you to the Flute Shop in Mr. Freeman's Organ being excellent in this kind, but as I do not referr you in that Organ.
>
> The System of the Organ I advise is. Vizt.
>
> The Compass to be up to D and down to Gamut, full Octave, Church Work,
> One Row of Keys, whole Stops and none in halves.
>
> STOPS
>
> | | |
> |---|---|
> | An Open Diapason | — of Metal throughout to be in Front |
> | A Stopt Diapason | — the Treble Metal and the Bass Wood |
> | A Principal | — of Metal throughout |
> | A Twelfth | — of Metal throughout |
> | A Fifteenth | — of Metal throughout |
> | A Great Tierce | — of Metal throughout |
> | A Flute Stop | — such a one is in Freeman's[8] Organ. |

Theodora came off with indifferent success in March 1750. Handel was annoyed. Among his oratorios the work

---

[8] Probably William Freeman of "Hemels" in Hertfordshire, to whom the libretto of *Alexander Balus* is inscribed.

was his favourite. But he chose the wrong year for its production. It was the year of the great earthquake, and superstition having been so little eradicated by the rationalism of the age people began to set their affairs in order against the apparent imminence of the last trumpet. Handel was angry or amusing. It depended on his gout. "Oh, your servant, mine Herren!" he said to two gentlemen who applied for "orders of admission" to the May performance of *Messiah,* "you are damnable dainty! You would not go to *Theodora*—there was room enough to dance there, when that was perform." To another who remarked on the exiguity of audience: "Never mind; the music will sound the better."

In this year's *Messiah* Cuzzoni, old and voiceless, was charitably given an engagement. But she was a shadow from another world. She sang for Handel and for the newly arrived Giardini at the Little Theatre in the Haymarket and "returned to the continent, more miserable than she came," to die in a short time in the pauper's ward of a Bolognese hospital.[9] Other ancient history was revived by the defalcations of Dr. Croza, the latest in the tribe of opera managers. On 15th May Handel would have smiled sardonically at a newspaper advertisement, signed by Henry Gibbs, a tea-merchant of Covent Garden, offering £30 for the production of the person of the said Croza.[10]

During the summer Handel left England for a holiday in Germany. A coach accident between The Hague and Haarlem nearly achieved a second remarkable coincidence of history. Bach, born within a month of Handel, died in that year. But on 21st August the *General Advertiser* announced that Handel was out of danger.

At the beginning of 1751 *Jephtha* was written. As he wrote Handel had some idea that this might be his last major work. On 13th February he had to stop work because of his failing sight. Ten days later he felt better and resumed his score with a determination that this should be a fitting close to a career which he knew to be

[9] Burney, *History,* iv. 460.
[10] Ibid.

not without distinction. *Jephtha* is (in one opinion at all events) the most magnificent of all the oratorios. On 18th April and 16th May there were *Messiah* performances at the Foundling Hospital, and afterwards an unavailing effort to recapture elusive health by a visit to Cheltenham. By the end of the year sight was so far gone as to admit of none but drastic treatment. Handel resigned himself to the hands of Samuel Sharp.

Sharp, lest all medicine and surgery of the eighteenth century should be regarded as a compound of old wives' tale and elemental butchery, was an influential figure in medical history. He was the first great surgeon of Guy's, to which he was elected in 1733, a lecturer to naval surgeons and the author of learned works which proved him to be an innovator in surgical technique. As a traveller, a *littérateur* and the husband of a wealthy wife he anticipated later consultative practice.[11] But he was unable to cure Handel. The best he could do after operating unsuccessfully was to suggest that Handel should go into partnership with John Stanley. "If the blind lead the blind, shall they not both fall into the ditch?" was the observation of Handel's grim humour.

By 1753, despite the further attentions of William Bramfield and the Chevalier Taylor, blindness was all but complete. Indeed reports got about that Handel was preparing for death by composing his own funeral anthem to be sung in the chapel of the Foundling Hospital. This rumour distressed the governors of the hospital so that they issued a statement saying:

> the said Paragraph has given this Committee great concern they being highly sensible that all well-wishers to this Charity must be desirous for the continuance of his life, who has been and is so great and generous a benefactor thereto.

> *Total eclipse! No sun, no moon!*
> *All dark amid the blaze of noon.*

[11] Wilks and Bettany, *Biographical History of Guy's Hospital*, p. 120, et seq., and *Gentleman's Magazine*.

When Beard sang those words a great wave of sympathy swept over his audience and many were seen in tears. But Handel was courageous as ever. If Gay had ever told him stories of the old sea-dogs of Devon Handel would have recognized in them men after his own heart. He carried on, calling in Christopher Smith to manage his affairs, to act as amanuensis and to control the rough edge of his tongue,[12] playing at the oratorio, corresponding with his friends and composing.

Habit rather than inspiration kept the latter faculty in operation, and nothing of greater moment than a duet and chorus for *Judas Maccabaeus* ("Zion now her head shall raise") and a revision of the *Trionfo del Tempo* (*The Triumph of Time and Truth*) appeared.

In 1754 we are reintroduced to Telemann.[13] He had been reported as dead, so that, on confirmation of the falseness of this report, Handel wrote to him with relief and promising to send some flowers which Telemann had requested. So a friendship of fifty years draws to its close, fragrantly and in the garden.

The last years of Handel's life were uneventful. He rested in the satisfaction that his music was the most durable of all that was written in England during his lifetime. He heard with pleasure of the popularity of his oratorios in the west country where the Three Choirs Festival was emerging to occupy its particular niche in the history of English music. In 1757 *Messiah* was first performed at this festival. With the faithful Beard new singers appeared, and among them a high preponderance of English: there were Mence and Wass, Baildon and Denham, Miss Turner and Frasi; among the players Adcock, Millar, Vincent, Malchair, Richards and Storace.[14] Mention of the last-named, father of Ann and Stephen, indicates the passing of the years. A new era was opening, that of

---

[12] Particularly when Handel had a sudden quarrel with old Smith, which led to the (temporary) withdrawal of Smith's name from his will.

[13] Letter from Handel, 20th September.

[14] Lysons, *Origin and Progress of the Meeting of the Three Choirs* (1895 edition), p. 36. Portions of *Messiah* had been performed in Salisbury Cathedral in 1752.

Haydn and Mozart. In the world too events were inexorably pressing forward. The Great Commoner was in power at the close of Handel's life, the Seven Years War was in progress, imperial conquests were at hand, and Josiah Wedgwood was prefacing the Industrial Revolution with rural spoliation and exquisite craft. Of all these things Handel was only dimly aware. His life was in his music and among his friends.[15]

On 30th March and 6th April 1759 *Messiah* was, as usual, performed for the Foundling Hospital. Handel was present on the first occasion, and this was his last appearance in public. He was taken home unwell. On 11th April he added a third codicil to his will. On 14th April, being the Saturday before Easter Day, he died.

According to your request to me when you left London [wrote James Smyth to Bernard Granville], that I would let you know when our good friend departed this life—on Saturday last, at eight o'clock in the morn, died the great and good Mr. Handel. He was sensible to the last moment; made a codicil to his will on Tuesday; ordered to be buried privately in Westminster Abbey, and a monument not to exceed £600 for him. I had the pleasure to reconcile him to his old friends[16]: he saw them and forgave them, and let all their legacies stand! In the codicil he left many legacies to his friends; and among the rest he left me £600, and has left to you the two pictures you formerly gave him. He took leave of all his friends on Friday morning, and desired to see nobody but the doctor, and apothecary, and myself. At seven o'clock in the evening he took leave of me, and told me we "should meet again." As soon as I was gone, he told his servant not to let me come to him any more, for that he had now done with the world. He died as he lived, a good Christian, with true sense of his duty to GOD and man, and in perfect char-

---

[15] To those already mentioned should be added "one Hunter, a scarlet-dyer at Old Ford" and Gael Morris, "a broker of the first eminence."—Hawkins, v. 410–11.

[16] Including old Smith, presumably.

ity with all the world. If there is anything that I can be of farther service to you, please let me know. I was to have set out for Bath to-morrow, but must attend the funeral, and shall then go next week.

London made amends for earlier lapses in its behaviour by sending 3,000 of its citizens to the obsequies. These took place with due solemnity in Westminster Abbey on the evening of 20th April. The music, including Dr. Croft's *Funeral Anthem,* was sung by the Gentlemen of His Majesty's Chapels Royal, the choirs of St. Paul's and the Abbey. The sermon was preached by Dr. Zachary Pearce, Dean of the Abbey and Bishop of Rochester. The grave was placed in the Poets' Corner and now has as near neighbour that of Charles Dickens. The proximity of their ashes may, perhaps, be symbolic of the similar massive influence which each has exercised on the hearts and minds of generations they never knew. The fitting epitaph for Handel (Roubiliac added none to his monument) was written over a thousand years before his time by another musician—Boethius:

Tellus superata
Sidera donat.

Chapter 9

Style

THERE EXISTS A popular fallacy that all music of the first half of the eighteenth century not written by Bach was written by Handel. Thus a song cast in this mould:

being obviously non-Bachian, would provoke the averagely well-read to father it on Handel. In fact, the responsible composer was James Oswald,[1] a relatively obscure figure in musical history whose misfortune it is, alongside Greene, Arne, Boyce, Carey and any other English musician of the period, to be counted out as insignificant because an imitator of Handel. *The Moderate Wish*[2] is chosen, more or less at random, to illustrate particular

[1] A Scotsman, an assiduous editor, a music-seller and publisher in St. Martin's Lane. Founder of the Society of the Temple of Apollo and a putative composer of "God save the King." The above quotation comes from *Ten Favourite Songs sung by Miss Formantel at Ranelagh* (1747).

[2] Oswald's title. The poem is, of course, Pope's juvenile *Ode on Solitude*.

qualities characteristic of the eighteenth century. Balance, proportion, mellifluence, lyrical aptness and harmonic insouciance are combined so as to satisfy the hedonistic ear. And, peeping through, comes the amiable modesty of urban pastoralization. Now to dismiss so charming a by-product as merely *Ersatz* Handel is to misunderstand the basis of eighteenth-century style and to allow the romantic picture of the great Cham of music to obscure that clarity of intellectual vision which the age consciously invites.

That a family likeness is apparent between the works of Handel and any contemporary of his is due not to the fact that Handel was the prime source of formal inspiration, but that homogeneity of thought prevailed with regard to the purpose of music in the community and the style in which it should generally be cast. That music should convey more or less specific ideas was the key-stone of musical philosophy and that lucidity of expression should prevail was regarded as a necessary symbol of good breeding. In emphasizing the necessity for clear communication the eighteenth century was doing service to art if disservice to itself. It rendered music generally intelligible, but invited the later charge of uninspired uniformity. At this point Dryden's apophthegm that "a great thought comes dressed in words so commonly received, that it is understood by the meanest apprehensions, as the best meat is the most easily digested" may be introduced to indicate the deeper significance of the classical outlook. Style may remain constant, but the underlying ethos can still preserve independence and individuality. Thus it is that in Handel we meet the paradox of an individualist without obvious individuality.

A common mode of speech is the ideal towards which art perpetually aspires, and at certain stages in history the ideal has not been far from realization. Dante's master, Brunetto Latini, writing in the days when the romance-poem carried itself to universal comprehension through the medium of French, commented that "la parleuse en est plus délitable et plus commune à toutes gens." A similar community of expression led the medieval pilgrim to find in the ubiquity of Gothic architecture a genius making every foreign city a home from home. After the Renaissance a particular set of circumstances developed a mode of musical address more than at any other period in the history of music *plus commune à toutes gens*. Under those conditions which obtain when a style is generally accepted and approved a major artist tends to be accepted as representative of his age. Chaucer, Leonardo, Goethe are cases in point. Each is more than himself, confluential. All the tributaries of the eighteenth century flow into Handel and so he stands apotheosized.

A robust and generative period concerns itself more with the summarization of anterior effort than with the novelty of experiment. Therefore most of what appears characteristically eighteenth-century is in fact discoverable in the seventeenth. The simple mechanics of both centuries involved melody, counterpoint, the harmonic basis of triadic repose interspersed with regulated discord and utilitarian rhythm controlled by dance and poetry. In the later period emphasis was laid on certain points so that retrospectively we recognize inevitable mannerisms. It may, however, be considered that superior observation on the presence of such mannerisms is the result of mental restlessness rather than of objective criticism. The perfect cadence and the easeful modulation, to take two obvious and easily recognized habits, were to the style of Handel as the pointed arch to Gothic architecture, essential to large-scale and monumental planning.

The tripartite aria, regularized by Alessandro Scarlatti, the forms of recitative peculiar to seventeenth-century dramatic music, the conventions of suite, sonata, fugue, overture, ground-bass were all ready for Handel's employment, but on whatever form he used he impressed a sense of fluency only comparable to that of Mozart. Fluency, however, is not *per se* a complete virtue: Handel achieved fluency, but he did more. Matthew Arnold added to Chaucer's other qualities a "large, free, simple, clear yet kindly view of human life—so unlike the total want, in the romance-poets, of all intelligent command of it." The observation fits Handel and should be borne in mind throughout any attempt to estimate his significance.

The language of Handel was that of his contemporaries, but often they were lacking in the capacity for deep penetration. In so familiar an example as the "Dead March" from *Saul* Handel's profundity of sympathy extends itself through nothing more complex than a four-bar sequence of tonic and dominant harmony. Placing this movement by the side of a not dissimilar passage from the overture to Clayton's ill-fated *Rosamund* music, we shall see that

what Clayton achieved is negative: This is merely not unpleasant and has no particular dramatic sense.

Handel was pre-eminently a dramatic writer, and in the simplest passages he demonstrates the two essentials of dramatic intention: timing and placing. Among the moving passages in Handel one of the most intense occurs in *Hercules* where Iole laments her dead father in the strangely Schubertian "Peaceful Rest." With grave memory Iole reflects:

The extension of thought engendered by the orchestral repetition of the operative phrase is miraculous. Nothing could be simpler nor more obvious, yet placed in its setting of poignant pulsation the spacious crotchet movement is entirely fitting. Inspired simplicity of this order recalls the emotional finality of Lear's "I am a very foolish fond old man." Within this aria Handel reserves one more telling blow until the end:

This aptitude for realizing unerringly the point of climax was partly the gift of the gods and partly—industry is rarely neglected by the great—the result of extensive experience, wide reading and absorbent memory. It has already been stated that the eighteenth century was a recapitulatory epoch, and the scholar will not be slow to point out that Handel was so typical in this respect that he reiterated often the spirit and sometimes the substance of other men's music. And yet the unassailable fact remains that what he wrote was so dramatically synthesized that it never leaves the impression of being the music of any one but Handel. At this point we may tread lightly round the plagiaristic slough which has led so many "sapient trouble-tombs" from the contemplation of music to the anatomy of morals and merely comment that the two common and alternative theses, (1) that it was a great blemish to copy out Muffat, Erba, Kerl, Stradella, Urio or Habermann, (2) that since Handel turned mediocrity into perfection it was satisfactory behaviour (although not too prominently so), ignore the major issues of musical philosophy.[3]

In the eighteenth as in the thirteenth and the sixteenth century there was, despite such contrary appearances as are indicated by political rivalries, a reciprocity which viewed artistic achievement with massive impartiality. The achievement was the thing, and whether Pope employed agents to translate his Homer or Handel represented an incorporated society mattered as little to their audiences as did the fact that Shakespeare looked over Marlowe's shoulder and quarried in Holinshed to his. Epochal literature came because it outcropped from the seams of lively conversation. Music of comparable quality also grew from the fecundity of commonplace phraseology. The desiccation of both music and literature by the academies leads sometimes to the suppression of this vital point, but without its absorption the rapidity of Handel's creation and the normality of his clichés become of inflated significance. The speed in execution was inevitable when mastery of language was so complete, and the continual appearance of particular idioms equally inevitable when each was universally regarded as a useful vehicle of competent expression. Triteness develops not when clichés are used, but when they are used in the wrong place. There is a resemblance in method and achievement between Handel and Virgil. Virgil was dependent on what earlier poets had

[3] This matter is treated more fully in Appendix F.

said: words, stories, technical devices came from every-
where; complete lines from Homer and Ennius.

> The impulse to say the verse or tell the story over
> and over again [came], partly because there was a mys-
> terious, self-sufficient delight in the poetry, and partly
> because it fitted Virgil's own feelings, expressed them,
> clarified them, and made them acceptable and friendly
> to himself. . . . Everything went into the dream world
> . . . the "hooked atoms" parted and recombined.[4]

So in Handel's case the "esemplastic" imagination worked
in fertility to produce new combinations of integrative
miracle.

The places of Handel's residence explain his technical
antecedents in the main. The influence of Italy, however,
is proportionately more significant than his brief sojourn
there would suggest, the reason being that from the beginning of the seventeenth century all music was tending
towards the Italianate. Italy was the first home of madrigal, opera, oratorio and the major instrumental forms of
sonata, concerto and suite: these and their virtuosic ex-
ponents were nurtured under the shadow of Renaissance
humanism and at the expense of princely patrons whose
interest came not entirely from ostentation. Under enlight-
ened patronage circumstances were helpful and music was
subjected to a degree of refinement unknown since the
monastic organization of polyphony. The tendency of the
age was away from the austerity of the ancient *a cappella*
style (which was as outmoded then as Stainer is now)
towards virtuosic display, an obvious adjunct of specializa-
tion, and towards that expressiveness perceived through
the medium of musico-dramatic performance. Reacting
against the inherent moralization of old counterpoint,
Galuppi, Vivaldi, Corelli and the Scarlattis evolved a new
melodic sensibility in long, sensuous melismatic lines,
pointed with wit, grace, fire or whatever dramatic quality
was considered proper, and supported by slender pillars
of conventional chording. The revolution was noteworthy
in the same way as that which produced walls of painted

---

[4] *The Times Literary Supplement*, 1st April 1944.

glass in late Perpendicular. The insistence on melodic integrity which culminated in the Scarlatti-Handel aria was an unconscious reversion to the self-sufficiency of Gregorian chant, to the popular approach of troubadour art and to the simpler urge of folksong. Once again the nature of the melody in Handel depends on environment, and on further examination the range suggested will not seem extravagant. The outlook of the age was summed up by Telemann thus: "Singen is das Fundament zur Music in allen Dingen."[5]

Although aristocratic in setting, seventeenth- and eighteenth-century music aimed at popular understanding in that its basic concern was with that interplay of tonal nuance such as can hardly leave unaffected even the confessedly unmusical. Handel learned more than formality from Italy: he learned the theory that what is to be quickly influential must be effective in immediate application. Thus his melodies are ever warmed with the rich voluptuousness of the south and are readily apprehensible. The danger in Italian teaching lay in the facility it promoted, and on occasion Handel fell victim to that "Deluge of unbounded *Extravaganzi*, which the unskillful call Invention, and which are merely calculated to shew an Execution, without either Propriety or Grace."[6] Hence the fluent emptiness of the following in *Hercules,* where for a moment the customary irradiation of personality is lacking:

---

[5] "Singing is the foundation of music in all things."—Romain Rolland, op. cit., p. 73.

[6] Avison, *An Essay on Musical Expression*, 1753.

That Handel so seldom pursued fluency for its own sake was due to influences other than that of Italy. He had early been nourished on the strong meat of Teutonic severity. Rugged Lutheranism turned the attention of art to the power of personal experience and to the continual wrestling of contrary mental forces: thus *Sturm und Drang* imbue religious music from Schütz to Bach. Handel betrays his German origin when he leads us into agony with Iole:

or when he sacrifices dramatic logic to massive counterpoint as in the stupendous "Wretched lovers" of *Acis and Galatea*. Elsewhere, chorale influence[7] serves to make di-

[7] Passion music and Funeral Anthem. Whether the second subject of the "Hallelujah" chorus in *Messiah* is derived from "Wachet auf" must be decided by the reader. Some authorities are fervent in support of this thesis, but direct quotation from a German chorale would seem to have been a pointless procedure.

rect reference to Germany, and dramatic recitatives recall the forgotten talent of Keiser.

Between the extremes of German intensity and Italian virtuosity English style characteristically steers a middle course. And it is the influence of England (though the slighter influence of France should not be forgotten)[8] which acts catalytically for Handel. The particular may be taken first. Purcell was not forgotten when Handel first arrived in London. His music could be still heard in the cathedrals, at Britton's, where also scores were available for reference,[9] and elsewhere domestically. From Purcell Handel learned the possibilities of rhythmic extension along the lines of resilient syncopation. The lesson was well learned for it was Handel who wrote:

in *Theodora,* and casual listening will reveal that Handel uses this turn of rhythm with continual enthusiasm.[10]

In 1745 Gluck visited England and Handel, but was discouraged by the latter in a moment of disillusionment from extending his visit. He did, however, discover that England had some contribution to make to the development of musical thought.

> He then studied the English taste; remarked particularly what the audience seemed most to feel; and finding that plainness and simplicity had the greatest effect upon them he has endeavoured to write for the voice,

[8] Cf., for example, the connection between Handel's *Water Music* and Lalande's *Concert de Trompettes pour les Festes sur le Canal de Versailles,* written for Louis XIV.

[9] Britton's well-stocked library included the music for *Dioclesian, Ode for St. Cecilia's Day, Te Deum and Jubilate,* two volumes of *Harmonia Sacra,* airs from the operas, catches and miscellaneous music, all by Purcell. There were also scores by Lupo and Ferrabosco, to whose period reference is made in Chapter XV.

[10] This mannerism is usually laid at Purcell's door although it appears in Locke's *Macbeth* music. That is if Locke was the composer.

more in the natural tones of the human affections and passions, than to flatter the lovers of deep science or difficult execution; and it may be remarked, that most of his arias in *Orfeo* are as plain and simple as English ballads; and the additions made to it when first performed in England, by Messrs. Bach [J. C.] and Guglielmi, were of so different a texture, though excellent in another way, that they destroyed the *unity* of style and characteristic simplicity, for which, when performed at Vienna, this production was so much admired."[11]

It was simplicity and directness of approach which Handel too detected and admired in the English response: hence the primeval strokes of triadic majesty in the Jews' chorus "Recall, O King" in *Belshazzar,* in "Make them to be numbered with Thy saints" in the *Dettingen Te Deum,* in "Moses and the Children of Israel" in *Israel in Egypt* and in the superlative "But their name liveth evermore" in the *Funeral Anthem* for Queen Caroline.[12] This last chorus, with its cross-rhythms (throughout Handel conductors may be urged to treat bar-lines without exaggerated respect), consciously renews the glories of Renais-

(voice parts only)

sance polyphony. Here it may be interjected that with rare exceptions, one of which is the clumsy handling of

[11] Burney, *Travels,* 1. 268–9.

[12] "In this, and the preceding movement, HANDEL has made a happy use of a modulation which was very frequent in the sixteenth century: the giving a common chord to the flat seventh of a major key, just before a close." Burney, *Commem.,* p. 37 n. This chorus is, in fact, a transcription of the motet *Ecce quomodo moritur justus,* by Jacob Handl, a work which was sung at Passiontide at the Thomaskirche in Leipzig when Handel lived in neighbouring Halle.

The dou-ble, dou-ble, dou-ble beat of the thun-d'ring drum

in the *Ode for St. Cecilia,* Handel's treatment of the English language is, from an accentual point of view, so meticulous as to suggest that he not only understood it as well as most Englishmen but that he loved it. Could otherwise

Andantino con moto

Come and trip it as you go, On the light fan - tas-tic toe,
trip it, trip it, Come and trip it as you go . . . .
On the light fan-tas-tic toe

which with its succeeding chorus recalls the first scene of *The Fairy Queen,* have been penned? This leads to the observation that the English outlook on music is largely literary, with the result that songs from Dowland to Warlock have a studied lyricism based on the dictation of melodic and rhythmic contour by the shape and situation of individual words. Handel's extension of the Purcellian technique in this respect softens the Italian-inspired roulades and divisions so beloved by contemporary singers, so indifferently mastered by those of later generations, and gives point to virtuosic embellishment. Frequently Handel allowed the delicacy of verbal rhythm to catch his imagination and proceeded to eliminate bar-line tyranny. One instance, from *Jephtha,* will serve representatively in this respect:

Allegro

Laud her, all ye virgin train, In glad songs of choicest strain:

Charles Lamb and Handel are odd bedfellows, but in one respect they are well matched—in a philosophic realization that the surface of life runs at every turn over the main springs of human emotion. Eclecticism belonged to Italy, large-eyed wonder to Germany; to England an eccentricity that saw silk purses in every sow's ear. "I have sat through an Italian Opera," says the unrepentant and unmusical Elia,

> till, for sheer pain, and inexplicable anguish, I have rushed out into the noisiest places of the crowded streets, to solace myself with sounds which I was not obliged to follow, and get rid of the distracting torment of endless, fruitless, barren attention! I take refuge in the unpretending assemblage of honest common-life sounds; and the purgatory of the Enraged Musician becomes my paradise.[13]

Handel took inspiration from, rather than refuge in, honest common-life sounds. Therefore he rushes to meet Hercules with the noise of bucolic bagpipery:

David, in *Saul,* with the cheering glitter of Flemish carillon; the infant Jesus with the recollected naïveté of the *pifa.* A Roman holiday in *Theodora* is celebrated with a ripe tavern song—hiccups in the rhythm and top Cs indicate that English tenors should hesitate to essay "Venus laughing from the skies" when sober—whose fitting place is in those collections of catches and glees, catholicly embracing almost every composer from Morley to Harrington, which when pleasure was taken gladly used to keep the tap-room alive with harmonious gurgitation. That Handel recognized degrees in intoxication may be gathered from a comparison of this plebeian revelry with the dignified Commemoration Dinner merriment of Belshazzar's court: his nobles invoke their tutelar gods with well-trained octave passages and the king sings the praise of wine in the sort of rum-tum-tum measure one might have expect-

[13] *A Chapter on Ears.*

ed from an eighteenth-century don. It may be suspected that the picture was truer of London than of Babylon.

Handel himself confessed that street cries fascinated and inspired him:[14] the direct evidence is in *Serse,* and the flower-seller's song, honoured frequently enough by reference but never by quotation, may be found below on page 170. The quality of rusticity achieved in *L'Allegro* and *Susanna* suggests that Handel was susceptible to the influence of folksong.[15] The sunny charm of

and the Helston Furry excitement of

summarize this aspect of Handelian universality. The merry bells of *Saul* have already been heard: in later contrast come the thunderous peals of ominous profundity which darken the canvas in "Envy, eldest born of Hell" and threaten the wicked with a horrific *Dies irae* prospect. *L'Allegro* places all sorts of bells in happy neighbourhood: there are the pleasant Sunday morning chimes of "Or let the merry bells," the rich urban ring of "Populous cities," the distant enchantment of the faintly heard curfew and the domestic jangle of the bellman's instrument of office. Clearly one might say *nullum tetigit quod non ornavit.*

The synoptic outlook of Handel, which is his most distinctive quality, recalls Waller's epitaph on Ben Jonson:

[14] Lady Luxborough to Shenstone: "The great Handel has told me that the hints of his very best songs have several of them been owing to the sounds in his ears of cries in the streets" (*Luxborough Correspondence,* 1775, p. 58).

[15] An Irish folksong, "The poor Irish Boy," appears in Handel's Fitzwilliam MSS.

"Mirror of poets! mirror of our age!" Therein we may leave the comprehensiveness of Handel temporarily suspended.

In a period so prolific as the eighteenth century supply and demand were particularly interdependent. The consideration of what Handel, or anybody else for that matter, wrote cannot be fully undertaken without some conception of the obligations laid upon them by society. When art functions actively in a community which regards some degree of artistic endeavour as normal rather than abnormal it is not unhealthy that those who pay the piper should take some responsibility for calling the tune. Frequently Handel outdistanced his patrons in imaginative exploration, but from time to time he called himself back to the standards required. What these standards were is defined by Burney at the outset of his *History*. His definitions may help us to discover to what extent Handel was representative of his age and to what extent he outgrew its limitations.

MUSIC is an innocent luxury, unnecessary, indeed, to our existence, but a great improvement and gratification of the sense of hearing. It consists, at present, of MELODY, TIME, CONSONANCE, and DISSONANCE.

By MELODY is implied a series of sounds more fixed, and generally more lengthened, than those of common speech; arranged with grace, and, with respect to TIME, of proportional lengths, such as the mind can easily measure, and the voice express. These sounds are regulated by a scale, consisting of tones and semitones; but admit a variety of arrangements as unbounded as imagination.

CONSONANCE is derived from a coincidence of two or more sounds, which being heard together, by their agreement and union, afford to ears capable of judging and feeling, a delight of a most grateful kind. The combination and succession of CONCORDS or SOUNDS in Consonance, constitute HARMONY; as the selection and texture of Single Sounds produce MELODY.

DISSONANCE is the want of that agreeable union be-

tween two or more sounds, which constitutes Consonance: in musical composition it is occasioned by the
suspension or anticipation of some sound before, or
after, it becomes a Concord. It is the DOLCE PICCANTE
of Music, and operates on the ear as a poignant sauce
on the palate: it is a zest, without which the auditory
sense would be as much cloyed as the appetite, if it had
nothing to feed on but sweets.

Of MUSICAL TONES the most grateful to the ear are
such as are produced by the vocal organ. And, next to
singing, the most pleasing kinds are those which approach the nearest to vocal; such as can be sustained,
swelled, and diminished, at pleasure. Of these, the first
in rank are such as the most excellent performers produce from the Violin, Flute, and Hautbois. If it were
to be asked what instrument is capable of affording the
GREATEST EFFECTS? I should answer, the Organ; which
can not only imitate a number of other instruments,
but is so comprehensive as to possess the power of a
numerous orchestra. It is, however, very remote from
perfection, as it wants expression, and a more perfect
intonation.

With respect to EXCELLENCE OF STYLE AND COM-
POSITION, it may perhaps be said that to practised ears
the most pleasing Music is such as has the merit of
novelty, added to refinement, and ingenious contrivance;
and to the ignorant, such as is most familiar and common.

There, in a fair-sized nutshell, is a monument to the
rational hedonism which Handel sought to serve.

It may be complained that morality, such as should
surely fit a composer of oratorio, is ignored. Avison does
something to fill this gap when he speaks of "the peculiar
Quality of Music to raise the *sociable* and *happy Passions,*
and to *subdue* the *contrary ones.*" But a musician's first
duty was to please: after that he could take a risk and,
like Dr. Johnson and the B.B.C., try his hand at instruction through pleasure. The glory of Handel is that he
worked through all these stages until he arrived by intel-

ligible steps at the *ne plus ultra* of musical expression. This was because he worked in a style which had, so far as music ever can have, utilitarian significance. A utilitarian style, approved and generally understood by an intelligent and not insensitive community, is indivisible. Therefore opera and oratorio use the same language. A comparison may not be inapt with the architectural style of the Tudors wherein both God and man were served in the same homely, well-bred idiom.

Chapter 10

The Orchestra

AT THE BEGINNING of the eighteenth century there was, as we understand it, no orchestra: there were instrumentalists who on occasion played together. Their function, both individually and collectively, was a subordinate one; to assist prandial conversation, to enliven the pageantry of city streets, to serve the gaiety of the dance, to enwrap the amorous excursions of royalty, to furnish pompous atmosphere for military display, to support ecclesiastical ceremony, to add zest to holiday and to sauce the conceit of operatic heroes and heroines. For each of these purposes music was necessary, and what in the way of players happened to be available was united in relative concord. This relativity varied from place to place, but a general deduction is that those were congenial days for players to whom faulty tonality came naturally. Cacophonous memories are contained in Avison's remark about "the irremediable Disagreement of their [wind instruments] rising in their Pitch, while the others are probably falling."[1] That strings had their limitations too is indicated by Corelli's protest against Handel's impatience. This episode immediately suggests that Handel had orchestral vision beyond what was then considered normal. But whatever his aspirations, he was constrained always to make the best use of the material to hand.

It is always the privilege of one generation to regard previous generations as barbaric. It happened in the eighteenth century, it happens to-day, and in no respect more markedly than when eyes accustomed to the systematized

[1] Avison, op. cit.

scoring of the contemporary orchestra review a Handel score. To see such a score in proper perspective it is necessary to see it from an eighteenth-century angle.

The first factor for realization is that then music possessed a unique sense of homogeneity. Sophistication had not so far progressed as to remove music from the focal position it should occupy in life in general. There was still apparent an Elizabethan or Jacobean influence which contained music, despite the forward-looking aspirations of the virtuosic, within almost universal limits of comprehension. Airs from opera and oratorio with movements from concertos kept in agreeable spirits the patrons of Vauxhall, Ranelagh or Marylebone: the same works, together with divers suites, sonatas and lessons, found their way into the editions of Walsh, Arnold or Cluer, or else less expensively through supplements to the *Lady's* or the *Gentleman's Magazine,* to the hands of the Sophia Westerns of the countryside. Amateur music-making flourished so extensively that it was possible for teachers of instrumental music to make fortunes from their teaching, the flautist John Festing, for instance, leaving the sum of £8,000 as a monument to his industry. It was also not regarded as improper by professional players that the quality should associate with them on equal terms. In country houses music was indulged in with such frequency that, were we to fall victim to jingoism, we should protest that English music in a practical way had a spirited reply to make to the Continent. James Harris at Salisbury and Fisher Littleton at Teddesley each had bands in which it is recorded that Handel used to play. Court Dewes, who married Mrs. Delany's sister and lived at Wellesbourne in Warwickshire, had a concert daily at which the vicar, presumably as a necessary part of his pastoral function, played the bass viol. Hogarth's "Music Party" mixes tea-drinking, conversation, the cat's milk and music in the proportions which might have been expected at Mrs. Delany's. A later picture by Zoffany shows the Sharp family making water music. In the eighteenth century it was difficult to escape the sound of music, and so much energy being apparent in its culture compels the opinion that it was then more likely to be understood than when, as in the succeeding century, musicians were regarded as "ingenious puppets, sir, who live in a box and look out on the world only when it is gaping for amusement."[2]

The variety of instruments used by Handel in combination related to the improvisatory character of performances of the time. Whether in private house or theatre, there were always differences in the number and quality of instruments available; but this factor of uncertainty partly led to the mastery achieved by Handel over the orchestral forces at his disposal. The variety met with in his scores may be gathered from a survey of selected works. In the autograph copy of *Messiah* strings, trumpets and drums are employed (a harpsichord should be taken as constant in every score, whether expressly indicated or not); in 1759 the Foundling Hospital noted with uncommon precision the number of players involved in a *Messiah* performance—and a new scoring is apparent: twelve violins, three "tenners," three cellos, two double basses, four hautboys, four bassoons, two horns, two trumpets, kettledrums and organ. In *Esther* provision was made for flutes, hautboys, bassoons, theorbo, harp and organ. In *Orlando* are used *violette marine, per gli Signori Castrucci. Alexander's Feast* has three bassoon parts, *Alexander Balus* a mandoline, the *Fireworks* music a double bassoon, *Semele* a side-drum and *Saul* three trombones. Clearly the period was one of experiment: thus archaic and startlingly modern effects stand side by side. Handel, as will be seen shortly, was a founder of orchestral music, and if we ignore his manipulation of different *ensembles* in performance we lose a great part of his music. With him each player or singer has a potentiality not to be disregarded in the working-out of his plot, and where his genius for transmuting the conventional into the extraordinary appears most prominently is in his orchestration.

The prestige of an instrumentalist was lower than that of a successful singer; consequently the names of the majority of Handel's orchestral performers are lost in anonymity. Nevertheless some remain. Of violinists the most

[2] George Eliot, *Daniel Deronda*, book iii, Chapter XXII.

celebrated were William Corbett, Banister, Carbonelli, Castrucci, Veracini, Pasquali, Michael Festing, John Clegg, Richard Charke, Defesch and Richard Collet. Caporale, Pasqualino, Filippo ("Pippo") Mattei—one of the *Muzio Scevola* collaborators—Abaco and the long-nosed and long-lived Cervetto[3] established the cello. Caporale was a notably expressive player, Cervetto and Pasqualino technically finished but tonally raw. The great flautists were Lœillet, Jack Festing and Weidemann. Among oboists we hear of Kytsch, San Martini, Galliard and Richard Vincent, among bassoonists Karba, Lampe, Hebden and Miller, while the surpassing trumpeter was Valentine Snow, sergeant trumpeter in the king's service. Most of these players performed on more than one instrument, so that, in the case of a special instrument being required for an exceptional effect, changes were made in performance in similar manner to that familiarized by the contemporary dance-band musician. Some of them were also composers. There could have been few complaints concerning lack of employment. The king's band, the theatres, the pleasure gardens, Hickford's Music Rooms, the taverns and private clients gave as much work as most had time for.

Music which may be supposed to have been "popular" is recorded in this programme of Carbonelli's benefit concert in 1722[4] (the division into acts signifies the omnipotence of operatic design):

Act I. A new concerto for two trumpets, composed and performed by *Grano* and others; a new concerto by *Albinoni,* just brought over; song by *Mrs. Barbier;* concerto composed by Signor *Carbonelli.*

Act II. A concerto with two hautbois and two flutes, composed by *Dieupart;* a concerto on the base-violin by *Pippo;* song, *Mrs. Barbier;* by desire, the eighth concerto of *Arcangello Corelli.*

Act III. Concerto by *Carbonelli;* solo on the arch-

---

[3] Of whom there is an excellent portrait by Zoffany.

[4] Programme from the *Daily Courant,* quoted by Burney, *History,* iv. 648.

lute by Signor *Vebar;* song, *Mrs. Barbier;* a new concerto on the little flute, composed by *Woodcock,* and
performed by *Baston;* solo, Signor *Carbonelli;* and for
finale, a concerto on two trumpets by *Grano,* etc.

It is not specified how long this concert lasted, but it is
evident that the virtuosic and the bizarre were principal
attractions. In 1729 the hearts of those who revelled in
these qualities must have been gladdened by the appearance of one Joachim Frederic Creta, who at several
concerts "blew the first and second treble on two French-
horns, in the same manner as is usually done by two persons." It is to be regretted that this singular art died with
its creator.

Handel dealt tactfully, from an artistic point of view,
with singers, leaving them their exhibitionism but sublimating it to higher ends. In the same way he made use
of the mechanical inventiveness of his instrumentalists
while keeping in check their aptitude for music-hall display. And so their acrobatic feats fitted naturally into a
more idealistic setting. Conspicuous examples are the
trumpet parts, of which those to "And the trumpet shall
sound" and "Let the bright Seraphim" will be immediately
familiar. Then there are the magnificent canonic entry at
the beginning of the *Dettingen Te Deum* and the brief
flourish which follows "Thou shalt come to be our
Judge":

This latter is indicative of so many aspects of Handel
that it merits closer attention. Obviously the trumpeters
enjoyed it and so did the audience. On the other hand
there is more to it than this simple equation of enjoyment.
The passage is dramatically impressive. It halts the flow
of *Te Deum* at the sombre and leaves the judicial vision
of the hereafter poised in mid thought while by the asso-

ciation of ideas the crimson dignity of the assize court is evoked.

It will be remembered that Handel was a collector of pictures, that he had an eye as well as an ear. The conclusion drawn from his music at many points is that

> whether life or nature be his subject . . . he has seen with his own eyes: he gives the image which he receives, not weakened or distorted by the intervention of any other mind: the ignorant feel his representations to be just, and the learned see that they are compleat.[5]

In music as in literature the classical theory of *mimesis* had particular validity in the eighteenth century. "Every man's performance," says Johnson, "must be compared with the state of the age in which he lived, and with his own particular opportunities." Therefore the response of Handel to the theory that music in general and orchestral music in particular held up the mirror to nature must now be considered.

There is, from our point of view, a naïveté in

in the bucolic

in the harp *obbligato* in "Praise the Lord with cheerful noise" from *Esther,* in the murmurous insect life of *Israel in Egypt,* in the lute and flute dialogue of St. Cecilia's "Soft complaining flute" and in countless similar descriptive passages. But such behaviour was part of the eighteenth-century stylistic convention. Avison, in summarizing contemporary thought, writes:

[5] Johnson, *Preface to Shakespeare.*

Thus Music, either by imitating these various Sounds (of Nature) in due Subordination to the Laws of *Air* and *Harmony,* or by any other Method of Association, bringing the Objects of our Passions before us (especially where those Objects are determined, and made as it were visibly, and intimately present to the Imagination by the Help of Words) does naturally raise a Variety of Passions in the human Breast, similar to the Sounds which are expressed. . . .[6]

By the side of this may be placed Mattheson's statement from *Der Musikalische Patriot:* "All that produces an effect upon men is theatrical. . . . The whole world is a gigantic theatre." The working out of this general theory brings us to the inevitable fact that "there are various instruments suited to the different Kinds of musical Compositions." Trumpets, horns, kettledrums are meet for "the rough handling proper for Battles, Sieges, and whatever is great or terrible," while love, tenderness and beauty are the province of the lute or harp. Of descriptive sounds Avison[7] comments first that

their Tendency is rather to fix the Hearer's Attention on the Similitude between the Sounds and the Things which they describe, and thereby to excite a reflex Act of the Understanding, than to affect the Heart and raise the Passions of the Soul.

Yet such sounds are legitimate so long as the "expression" is contained in the vocal line and the bird and allied noises are placed at a discreet distance in the accompanying parts. This was at Handel's expense. Handel could never refrain from giving his singers some share in the picturesque.

It is difficult to see how the orchestra would have developed but for programmatic considerations, and Handel's large palette was in large measure, like those of Berlioz and Wagner, the result of the search for verisimilitudinous colour. Thus the little flute breaks into bird-song

[6] Avison, op. cit.
[7] op. cit.

in *Riccardo I;* clarinets make tentative pastoral entry in
Tamerlano (thirty years before, or thereabouts, Denner
had produced the clarinet, although it was not until about
1770 that it became finally accepted as a member of the
woodwind fraternity); the double bassoon, first made by
Stanesby in 1739 and probably at Handel's suggestion,
is introduced in *L'Allegro;* four horns exotically enhance
the scoring of *Giulio Cesare;* three . trumpets imperially
add their ardour to the coronation music and to the *Dettingen Te Deum* (one marked "Principal" indicates, according to Heinrich Christoph Koch,[8] a particular "crash-
ing (or martial) Style of performance, for which only the
middle tones of this instrument are used"); three trombones are uniquely employed in *Saul,* a work which holds
incredible fascination in its opulent instrumentation and
the ready answer to those who ignorantly rail at the indif-
ference of Handel's orchestral technique. Realism led
Handel, who had a notable habit of following every idea
to its logical conclusion, to anticipate Tchaikovsky in producing gun-fire as a musical climax. "Handel," wrote Mrs.
Elizabeth Carter, "has literally introduced firearms . . .
and they have a good effect." The reference was to *Judas
Maccabaeus,* and the innovation was so startling as to
provoke Sheridan at a later date to explain off-stage gun-
shots thus: "See, I borrowed this from Handel."[9] It was
not every one who approved these experiments: it was in
fact a customary complaint that Handel made too much
noise with his orchestra. Pope glances sidelong at the
vogue for noisy theatrical effects in that passage in the
Dunciad which begins:

> *'Tis yours to shake the soul*
> *With Thunder rumbling from the mustard bowl,*
> *With horns and trumpets now to madness swell,*
> *Now sink in sorrows with a tolling bell.*

This may or may not have some connection with Han-

[8] Heinrich Christoph Koch, *Musikalisches Lexicon,* 1802. While
on the subject of trumpets, it may be noted that in the *Rinaldo*
march Handel uses four.

[9] Sheridan, *Jupiter.*

del's zest for massive and unprecedented orchestral climaxes, but it does indicate how effects in drama and in music were of inspiring variety. The tendency towards extravagance was not confined to Handel, nor to England. "One no longer hears the voice; the orchestra is deafening," complained the conservatives in Germany.[10]

Before dismissing such criticism as unreasonable, it may be noted objectively that in general string tone was inadequate to cope with large additions of brass and woodwind: as a rule, about a dozen strings with harpsichord were expected to hold their own. Moreover, obscuration of the melodic line was regarded as an unpardonable offence against the canons of good taste, and without considerable augmentation of the string department such obscuration was at times inevitable.

The fact remains, however, that Handel was indicating progress in the employment of new combinations of colour. After directing attention to the mimetic a second factor supervenes. Avison laid down in brief that certain instruments were apt for certain forms of direct imitation; he also hinted at the attachment of other instruments to more indefinite and more philosophic ideas. Not that this represented anything new. In the Shakespearian theatre flutes made funereal impact on the mind; from the earliest times hautboys or their ancestors had stood for pastoral atmosphere; God, in the mystery plays, had been haloed by string tone. These ancient associations held point in the eighteenth century, as indeed they obviously do today; but Handel, with the keenest dramatic insight of his age, subtilized these general impressions. In so doing he urged romanticism from the wings.

"He was the first," said Volbach, "to assert the expressive personality of the violoncello." Thus rich melancholy steals into *L'Allegro,* clad sombrely in cello and bassoon tone:

10 Romain Rolland, op. cit, p. 76.

and sadness and virginity at a later point in the same work
find sympathetic delineation in the voluptuous folds of a
solo passage which any cellist would relish as an exercise
in soulful dissertation. The viola was accepted in the
eighteenth-century orchestra only on sufferance and it
was the custom to insist on "placing one of the worst
hands to the Tenor," much to Avison's annoyance. If
Handel failed to raise this instrument to its true dignity,
he did indicate the importance he attached to its particular timbre by withholding violins at the beginning of the
second act of *Alexander's Feast* and by painting the ghost-
ly with a dark combination of two violas, three bassoons,
cello, basses and organ. In *Giulio Cesare* Caesar's "Dall'
ondoso periglio" is introduced with this dialogue in the
strings:

Therein the viola receives more attention than was then
common.

The gently suggestive use of woodwind colour is
ubiquitous, and in such music as "As steals the morn"
in *L'Allegro,* where the oboe sings its own aubade, or
"Ferma l'ali" from *La Resurrezione,* where two flutes and
muted violins undulate over a pedal, or in Oriane's "Dolce
vita" from *Amadigi,* where the picture of distressed beauty
is thus delicately flavoured:

or in the colloquy between voice and oboe in Melissa's
"Ah! spietato!" from the same opera:

the delicacy of aquarelle invites an intimacy between performer and listener which is not apparent unless the fact that in Handel's day the orchestra had not left the domestic atmosphere of chamber music is realized.

At the opposite pole comes Handel's sense of tonal climax: instrument piled on instrument to achieve the golden enchantment of Parnassus in *Giulio Cesare.* Two orchestras are used with strings, oboes, harp, gamba, theorbo and bassoons. The music runs:

and then the second orchestra enters with answering phrase. The dramatic perfection of this movement lies less in the actual music than in the seductive colouring. Another point to be noted is that Handel was sensible that the numerical strength of the instruments employed was not necessarily in relation to the dynamic power intended. Mozart struck at the truth, even though by his supererogation he endeavoured to undermine it, when he observed "Handel understands effect better than any of us—when he chooses, he strikes like a thunderbolt." The last part of this has been remembered, the first part too often inconveniently forgotten. The mastery of effect was all-embracing.

As for the thunderbolts, we look for them chorally. But the massive trumpet climaxes which crown the full choral fury are overlooked, largely because they can never be heard. When they can they possess an Elgarian inevitability, as when they surprise the imagination in the Gloria of *Messiah* or when they anoint the regality of "Thou hast set a crown of pure gold upon his head" in the first *Coronation Anthem,* or when, undarkened either by horns or trombones, they help the acclamation of "God save the King." With regard to his brass Handel had clear-cut ideas: trumpets were noble, horns—four of them at any rate—exotic, trombones priestly. The secret of their effectiveness lay in their rarity of appearance. When they did appear they were felt.

Chapter 11

Chamber Music

THE ESSENCE OF chamber music is domesticity. Handel wrote at a time when most music still retained something of its *camera* origins and for that reason, and because Handel was of amiable disposition in congenial company, his suites, sonatas and concertos are pleasantly evocative of fireside warmth. This is a great though often neglected quality, for when music loses its fraternal power to "fetch out in smiles the mutual soul," as Leigh Hunt wrote of it to Thomas Alsager, the graciousness of courteous hospitality is denuded of one of its chief agents. The proper setting for Handel's music, other than that obviously designed for public performance, was between Mrs. Delany's conversation and her mulled white wine: the two extremes of extemporaneous sagacity, wit and philosophy and discriminating hedonism. Music in the eighteenth century was disposed to stimulate pleasure, but an unwritten law decreed that pleasure should have such blend of intellectual and sensual appeal as became a set of comfortable eclectics. With the eclectics Handel was at home, and his music is monumental to his clubbableness; it is not esoteric like so much of Bach, nor shot with the febrile brilliance of Domenico Scarlatti, nor overrun with the tintinnabulations of the vulgar who, like the Rev. William Felton, had no more than "a neat finger for common divisions and the rapid multiplication of notes," but plainly pleasing.

It is symptomatic that the most eligible party piece for the not too precociously musical schoolgirl is the set of variations from the E major (No. 5) Suite (Set I, 1720), commonly miscalled *The Harmonious Blacksmith*. The long story of why this title and the attendant fable are mythical will do no good by repetition (a generation bred on Hollywood will be loth to believe that pretty inaptness in nomenclature is no great aid to musical appreciation), so let it simply be stated that there is no recorded instance of Handel's having had dealings with blacksmiths, harmonious or otherwise, at Edgware or anywhere else. The music of these variations has that artless, narrative pleasantry equally attractive to the child and to the naïve adult who enjoys the simplicity of innocent pleasures. Handel was not above taking children seriously, nor did he underestimate their capacity for understanding. His educational interests showed their effectiveness in the loyalties of the Princesses Anne and Amelia and of Frederick, Prince of Wales, while a nice piece of prescience prompted this anecdote of the future George III in Southey's *Commonplace Book:*

> Handel asked the King, then a young child, and listening very earnestly while he played, if he liked the music, and the Prince warmly expressed his pleasure. "A good boy, a good boy," he cried, "you shall protect my fame when I am dead."

It was for those *in statu pupillari* that many of the harpsichord pieces were written: some clearly betray their *étude* origin and need no long critical examination. But elsewhere Handel speaks for himself more particularly. In the Prelude to the first Suite, in A major, the characteristic flourish of extemporization is represented in little more than a shorthand abstract. In the succeeding Allemande that gentle quality which, for want of a term of nearer precision, had best be defined as pastoral, demonstrates how much more musical thought meant to Handel than the implications of a set form. The suave counterpoint of the opening:

and the sinuosity of the last cadence:

have a cool French quality of rationalized whimsicality. The Courante has similar poise and recollects in its closing bars the particular note-disposition of the Allemande cadence. If inspiration fails, it is in the gigues of the harpsichord suites, which with their slickly tailored efficiency please once. An exception is the rumbustiously percussive finale to the Suite in G minor (No. 6, Set II, 1733). This, unbuttoned and Beethovenian, is of more than normally generous proportion and elbows its rough way thus impulsively:

If this defeats the capacity of the harpsichord the same may be said of the Ouverture, also in G minor, to Suite VII (Set I). This intense prelude is too tragic for its context and suggests a sketch for some epic tale of high passion. Fuguing was a constant delight to Handel, but not as an exercise in academic rectitude. The purpose of a Handelian fugue was to demonstrate the personality of his subject. If students would learn how not to satisfy examiners they should model their counterpoint on that of Handel; if, however, they would realize the incentive to musical thought given by epigram they should study the suggestiveness of such themes as:

or the darkly anachronistic romanticism of the second movement of the Suite in F minor (No. 8, Set I). The third fugue in the set of six published in 1735, which also furnishes most of the Sinfonia to the Passion of 1716, gives further publicity to the St. Anne motiv and, underlining the common sources of eighteenth-century musical diction, emphasizes the dangers of recognizing personal influence by fortuitous thematic coincidence.

Those who have looked at the suites will realize that often as between movement and movement there is some philosophic connection which imposes a sense of unity on what would otherwise be a collection of heterogeneous fragments. This is not simply a matter of key consistency, but an offshoot of Handel's fertile dramatic ability to present problems and situations with comprehension. An interest in the dramatic capacity of melody led inevitably to experiment with *Leitmotive*. The possibilities of this artificial aid to consistency were foreseen tentatively long before Handel's day, in fact the folksong-dependent mass-writers of the sixteenth century were first in this field; But Handel had a habit of anticipating Berlioz and Wagner in so many other respects that this practice, not fundamentally of the eighteenth century, cannot pass without notice. In Handel's case, however, it may often be attributed to accident rather than design. Thematic identity at the outset of successive movements, such as occurs in Suite 4 (Set I):

suggests the improviser calculating the future plan of development while automatically delivering what remains fresh in the mind. Sometimes, on the other hand, thematic reiteration comes as the result of deliberation: the most effective instance being in the "Se mai turbo" duet in *Poro*, "in which the lovers, Porus and Cleosilda, are ironically repeating the former promises which they had made to each other of fidelity and confidence."[1]

[1] Burney, *History*, iv. 351.

In contrast to this subtlety lies the conservatism which generally pervades Handel's use of variations. Here too often the volant finger has little to proclaim except its own dexterity. Here and there, however, a masculine perversity recalls the acidulous flavour of the Elizabethan virginalists. The Chaconne in F is thus antiquely reminiscent, while elsewhere, and particularly in the organ concertos, monotony is relieved by Chippendale delicacy. Variations were to Handel a recreation. High seriousness he reserved for opera and oratorio, though accidents sometimes happened and let into the drawing-room an occasional glimpse of tragedy; and the ground basses which symbolize intensity of feeling in *Poro, Orlando, Hercules* and *Saul* demonstrate Handel's outlook on the relative functions of opera and oratorio on the one hand and domestic music on the other.

This sense of fitness for purpose is one of the keys to Handel's omnipotence. It was not that opera and oratorio had a higher sanction than chamber music, but that when they were performed there was more likelihood of listening being more attentive than in the case of that homely music which entered the one ear not engaged in the absorption of whispered scandal. From all accounts Quin was a mighty Lear, but conversely he was a delicious raconteur. Handel had the same zest for rich expression, and the necessary complement to profundity may be discovered in the violin sonatas, written for Dubourg or possibly for Dubourg's pupil, the Prince of Wales, in the oboe sonatas, characteristically available for German flute or violin, and in the various works for trio. Of these it may be said that they implicitly express approval of Telemann's "Wer auf Instrumenten spielt muss des Singens kundig seyn."[2] Otherwise they impress by high technical competence and by mellifluence which jointly predominate over imaginative adventure.

In the smaller chamber works there are many instances of recollection or anticipation of ideas familiarized in other settings. The 1735 collection of fugues presents

[2] Whoever plays an instrument must be conversant with singing.

those which fit horrifically into *Israel in Egypt* ("He smote all the first-born in Egypt" and "They loathed to drink of the river"); the *Allegro* of the violin Sonata in D major appears symphonically in *Jephtha;* "Why so full of grief" from the sixth Chandos anthem is reflected in the first of the 1733 trio sonatas and the fourth of the 1738 set remodels the overture to *Athaliah.*

If the organ concertos are considered among the chamber works organists may feel encouraged to regard them without pomposity, and to refrain from enveloping their clarity in orgiastic outbursts from the swell reeds. The largest organs of the eighteenth century, in England at any rate, where choral singing was well able to dispense with massive accompanimental support, were slight of build, clear-voiced, bright-eyed with mutation work, effective in contrast with the string ensemble and accordingly acceptable in theatre or house as well as in church. Pedal boards were rare in England; that they were not altogether unknown is shown by Handel's note that pedals should be used in Concerto I of the second (1740) set. In general, the style of writing for the organ was that proper for the harpsichord. In relation to modern interpretation this suggests a reduction of tone-colour to near conformity with eighteenth-century standards. This makes evident the integrity of the melodic line, the delicacy of contrast and ornamentation, the gentle persuasiveness of the orchestral scoring (how eloquently flutes and oboes can maintain silence!) and the intimate dialogue. And sufficient is left unsaid—this is important in all Handelian interpretation and particularly in *ff* which should never be pushed to the vulgar extremity of *fff* with the solo tuba—for the listener to be able to follow the direction of the thought in his own imagination. It may be that the best way of presenting the organ concertos to a modern audience is via pianoforte or harpsichord and chamber orchestra. That is so long as the alternative combines the violence of the out-voluntary with the clamour of "full" orchestra.

"Our Composers," said Avison,[3] "have run all their

---

[3] op. cit.

concertos into little else than tedious Divisions." The unsympathetic may hold this generalization to Handel and suspect that it applies. But once again it is necessary to view the matter from an eighteenth-century angle: then purpose will begin to appear. Concertos were an exhibition of skill (presumably they still are) into which the orchestra entered as a foil to pyrotechnic display. This display often stood out in a strong light because the concertos were, as Avison remarks, generally under-rehearsed. Concertos in which the solo instrument was the organ and in which the soloist was Handel were different in one important respect. They were conceived as ancillary to a larger scheme, at intermissions in oratorio. Therefore while the concerto relieved the tension of the oratorio plot its technical flights were projected against a particular background. Thus the divisions never ran out of control.

The organ concertos were works of maturity. Op. 4 was published in 1738; Op. 7 in 1740.[4] They accordingly carry the flexibility conspicuous in all Handel's later music. Normally they possess four movements, but the length and character of each movement varies from work to work. A significant step in the direction of poetry is indicated by the frequent tendency to emphasize the slow movements at the expense of the more or less formal allegros. It is evident that these works were approved. Hawkins leaves this tribute:

> When he gave a Concerto, his method in general was, to introduce it with a Voluntary movement on the Diapasons, which stole on the ear in a slow and solemn progression; the harmony close wrought, and as full as could possibly be expressed; the passages constructed with stupendous art; the whole, at the same time, being perfectly intelligible, and having the appearance of great simplicity. This kind of prelude was succeeded by the Concerto itself, which he executed with a degree of spirit and firmness that no one even pretended to equal. Such, in general, was the manner of his performance; but who shall describe its effects on his enraptured

[4] A third set appeared posthumously.

auditory? Silence, the truest applause, succeeded, the instant that he addressed himself to the instrument; and that was so profound, that it checked respiration, and seemed to controul the functions of nature [whatever that may mean!], while the magic of his touch kept the attention of his hearers awake only to those enchanting sounds to which it gave utterance.[5]

It remains to detail the enchantment. As for a "slow and solemn progression," there is none of greater beauty than the opening *Larghetto* of the Concerto in F major (No. 5, Set I): here is the consummation of simplicity. Of almost equal simplicity, but of more profound feeling, is this enhanced repetition of the opening bars of the *Largo, e piano* from the B flat major Concerto (No. 1, Set II), a movement which follows the sober optimism of the first Andante in the remoteness of D minor:

The preceding movement, in two sections, is a free fantasia on this commonly used bell motiv:

which serves as an impressive ground. Another interesting ground-bass treatment occurs in the G minor Concerto (No. 5, Set II), where the Olympian tread of the octave-spacing continues from beginning to end of the *Andante larghetto, e staccato,* the only relief lying in the counterpoint in the organ. That the orchestra was more than a sleeping partner becomes apparent when in the twelve-bar *Adagio* of the G minor Concerto (No. 3, Set

[5] Hawkins, v. 413.

I) a *concertino* carries more or less extravagant modulations in contrast both to the organ and the *ripieno*, when in the D minor Concerto (No. 4, Set II) veiled melancholy is enshrined thus:

or when in the last little Concerto of the first set the organ is alternative to the harp, the violins are muted, the lower strings are *pizzicato* and flutes are added to a Botticellian atmosphere of fair-weather ingenuousness. For the sake of completion it should be added that precisely what we most desire, Handel's extemporized cadenzas, are lost for ever. A concerto without its embellishments and with subsequent editorial accretions is as near the original as is a medieval church stripped of its wall paintings and made to look dismally religious by pitch pine and garish glass.

The surprising variety of orchestration suggested in the organ concertos is evident throughout Handel's larger-scale chamber works. The reason was the different conditions which prevailed when the works were written. The six *Concerti Grossi* (Op. 3), written at Hanover, at Canons or for the marriage of the princess royal in 1733, employed flutes, oboes, bassoons and strings disposed in the normally contrasting arrangement of *concertino* and *ripieno*. The open-air music, that for the *Water Music* and the *Royal Fireworks*, naturally lays more insistence on the wind. More or less experimental combinations exist in various sketches. An organ concerto with choral termination, intended for the 1737 revival of *The Triumph of Time and Truth;* a concerto for two *concertini,* each consisting of two horns, two oboes and a bassoon, and supported with the customary string ensemble; concertos for trumpets and horns and for horns and side-drums. But the crowning works in concerto form are the great set written in 1739 and published as Op. 6.

In these works it is tempting to see the peak of Handel's creative genius. Elsewhere the flame of inspiration may leap momentarily higher, but nowhere else has consistency of imaginative thought so triumphal a progress. It is generally evident that Handel was on good terms with his orchestral players (it is encouraging to find no anecdotes to suggest the contrary). Understanding their point of view—after all, Handel started life as a fiddler at Hamburg—he was able to maintain that subtle balance between all departments which pleases the players and likewise the audience. With no more than strings and *continuo* a wealth of light and shade is achieved by the subtle interplay of *concertino* and *ripieno*. Elgar follows the pattern with magnificent fidelity to Handelian ideals in the *Introduction and Allegro* and underlines the lesson of the concertos that economy in material leads to amplification of musical thought. This economy imposes one sort of unity on the *Concerti grossi:* key relationship (in allowing the principal key to dominate all the movements Handel was following Corelli); and another, larger unity: that of action or idea. This is apparent in performance where any one of the concertos impresses as a complete essay and not, as in the case of so many suites, as a series of heterogeneous items thrown into accidental contiguity. It is not quite satisfactory to contain, as Romain Rolland does, the music within objective limits by the erection of somewhat arbitrary concrete imagery. More philosophically it may be suggested that each concerto concerns itself with one facet of the pattern of life, and that what variety is apparent rises from cognate impressions associated with the central idea.

This centrality of outlook, the capacity for representing largely and truthfully one aspect of the universal, is the supreme mark of greatness, and if Handel and Beethoven are to be in any way associated, as by Beethoven's admission they should,[6] it is by referring the concertos to Bee-

[6] *Vide* p. 212.

thovenian standards of expression. Frequently in his overtures Handel leads us to suppose that the introductory slow movement is more than a conventional curtain-raiser: here are two quotations which contain in little space the conviction that the prelude was of parallel importance with its companion movements:

The tremendous rhythmic vigour here contained is urged insistently throughout the respective movements, the first declining into the mystery of this coda:

the second sweeping into spacious scale progressions cousinly to those in the first movement of Beethoven's Seventh Symphony.

Writing fugues was not Handel's forte; writing fugally was. The contrapuntist who won early respect from Mattheson spreads himself throughout the *Concerti grossi*, although not in the construction of school fugues. In the last movement of the second Concerto the subject walks briskly through its exposition until halted by the ingenuousness of:

which the *concertino* projects against a plain chordal background in the accompanying parts. The two ideas eye each other like a couple of unintroduced mongrels and finally join together in boisterous merry-making which happens to involve double invertible counterpoint. The principal subject—Handel favoured fugues with two subjects —of the *Andante* of the third Concerto has Bachian tautness and resolves its dolours into a passionate climax of great power:

The whole of this Concerto is cast in severity, the prevailing darkness of the colouring being emphasized by the delicate detail of the *Polonaise,* the bright robe of which sets off the grief of the *mater dolorosa.* The *Allegro* shows the forward-looking Handel engaged in rough violation of all the accepted clauses relating to key change:

This ellipsis is characteristic, as in the eighth Concerto the *Andante* shows:

while the *Grave* proceeds with similar brusqueness from one scene to another:

This last passage contains the clue to the process. In choral music of the older schools such abruptness had grown naturally out of the juxtaposition of unrelated triads. Handel borrowed the idea, used it frequently and with majestic effect in his choral music, and translated it orchestrally. His harmonic sense led him to pursue courses which are effective by their unexpectedness. In the fifth Concerto the pedal-points of the second movement and the nine consecutive bars of tonic seventh, dangerously near the end, in the third movement speak with picturesque accent on romanticism. Students of elementary harmony may like to take up a set of consecutive fifths from the third bar of the *Minuet* in the ninth Concerto and inquire of their tutors wherein lies the crime.

Ingenuity in harmony and counterpart should not blind us to the fact that Handel's chief blessing was a capacity for containing his text in a single line of melody. Apprenticeship to the theatre had taught that intensity of thought had more significance when memorably placed within the scope of the melodically minded listener. But melody gets pushed out to the limits. Wide intervals indicate mystery in the first movement of the ninth Concerto and wild spirits in the fifth movement of the fifth Concerto. In contradistinction, however, Handel can turn a one-note subject, as in the second section of the seventh Concerto, into a matter for jesting. This comic fugue terminates with cellos and basses wagging their bows over the diminution of minim to crotchet and crotchet to quaver.

The attention to landscape detail so familiar in the oratorios and the operas pervades the concertos, so that in the *Andante larghetto* of the eleventh Concerto this is placed after an opening of vigorous octave strides:

and a little later another corner is turned to reveal the insistent chatter of

The truth is that tunes cropped up as if by accident, and where Handel had only meant a servant-boy episode he set a Sam Weller on an irresistible career.

Chapter 12

Characterization

FROM HIS BIOGRAPHY it is clear that Handel was a realist. From his music a similar deduction, though with a certain difference in emphasis, may be drawn. In general his music had close association with the façade of life, being in seven cases out of ten concerned with more or less obvious description. From a Platonic point of view what we receive may be twice removed from reality, but despite that we conceive a fresh and vital reality of a new musical order. The purpose of music has defied the efforts of philosophy and theology to discover it. The most we may with certainty conclude is that it deals with the antithesis of ideas. In abstract music (this arbitrary term is here used on account of its relative convenience in definition), such as Bach's *Art of Fugue* or Mozart's G minor Symphony, the motivating ideas are of purely musical significance. It will be remembered that Berlioz to show his distaste for Handel dragged in a reference to a "tub of pork and beer": a phrase which intends rudeness but points complimentarily to the *nihil humani alienum puto* thesis which is the substance of this chapter. The Russian writer referred to earlier claims Handel as a people's composer. The non-ideological side of this thought will be endorsed by the least musical, who will explain that the only music which for them has significance is Handel's. The incredible influence Handel holds, ruefully we must confess by means of the one or two fragments which duly pass from school hall to parish hall and from parish hall to town hall, is indicative of a particular capacity for understanding human nature. This came from an observation not of what people wanted, but of what people were, and are. Whether Handel succeeded in passing through the stages enumerated in the *Symposium* to arrive at ultimate goodness and beauty is a matter of opinion; what is certain is his shrewd observation of the world around him. Not only was he gifted in observation, but also in narrative expression, which being easeful and friendly breeds familiarity.

There were few crimes of greater magnitude in the eighteenth century than that of unsociability; therefore the easiest way to misunderstand Handel is to regard him as a detached creature addicted to supernal communion. Romantic anecdotes, in single setting assuming alarming significance, about the tears which accompanied the parturition of the Messianic Hallelujah disguise the fact that Handel was rarely at ease with God and sought general inspiration from what was epigrammatically considered the proper study of mankind.

It has already been indicated that music in the eighteenth century had greater relevance to everyday life than has been the case since. Thus in the most typical of eighteenth-century composers we should unravel part of the intelligence of the music by consideration of this point in its most graphic expression.

Handel left no diary and only a handful of polite letters, but a solitary inscription in one of his sketch-books to be found in the Fitzwilliam Museum has some compensatory value. The psychologist may care to enlarge on its significance: here it is sufficient to draw attention to the secret of well-oiled counterpoint, to the mental contiguity of work and play, and to the bachelorly preoccupation with details of hospitality (unless we accept Brown's libellous suggestion of addiction to secret drinking) which speak through this terse memorandum:

12 Gallons Port	
12 Bottles French	Duke Street
	Meels.

Handel engaged in decanting the port, in handing it round, in genial conversation, preludes the optimistic philosophy which imbues his music with infectious confidence, good nature and tolerance. And such convivial intimacy gave precisely those opportunities for observation which, from a worldly point of view, elude the more pietistic. And then supervenes the direction of Handel's education in opera and his own natural enthusiasm for that form of expression.

An opera is a story about people and their emotions intensified through the use of music. What people happen to be called on the stage is immaterial: what they are in fact are projections of the personality and emotional excitement of the audience which attends the opera. The heroic puffs up the manly breast; the villainous attracts anger or else that sneaking affection of daring wickedness which we all entertain; beauty provokes wonderment; distress draws tears; and so we might proceed through the gamut of conventional opera types. In more senses than one audience and actor were closer together in the eighteenth century than to-day, and Handelian audiences were fully competent to rival the players in histrionic endeavour. Thus, although the horseplay would have tried the patience of the earnest, there was a directness in approach to the project of opera which by-passed academic philosophies and took all that we may lecture about as read. The main requisites were colour, novelty, hot emotion and virtuosity: the requisites in fact of any popular art whose existence is dependent on satisfaction in the box office. Handel's triumph and failure were due to his practice of achieving more than was expected from him, but because he did this he rose above his environment and left for posterity an enlargement of the better attributes of contemporary outlook. This he did by avoiding writing with deliberation for posterity and by keeping his finger on the public pulse.

FitzGerald refers to Handel as "a good old pagan at heart" and, in tacit agreement with Leigh Hunt, who makes kindly observation on his Theocritan aptitude for dropping milk and honey, puts a pen accurately on the side of truth when writing:

I think Handel never gets out of his wig, that is, out of his age: his Hallelujah Chorus is a chorus, not of angels, but of well-fed earthly choristers, ranged tier above tier in a Gothic cathedral, with princes for audience, and their military trumpets flourishing over the full volume of the organ. Handel's gods are like Homer's, and his sublime never reached beyond the region of the clouds.[1]

Bach invaded the *Himmelreich;* Handel found *Lebensraum* on earth. The fact is clear if Handel's music is regarded as a whole. Operas, oratorios and other works of cognate character form an immense portrait gallery and an inexhaustible fund of carefully catalogued human emotion. For reasons which will in due course be made apparent oratorio provided a better framework for extended psychological study, but opera was the first experimental laboratory. Unless the nature of Handel's operatic style is in some way understood the oratorios are lacking in point.

The people whom Handel was initially constrained to represent were of a conventional type. Kings and princes of a most excellent goodness, in the portrayal of whom a careful eye was cocked courtwards, for the seventeenth-century habit of incidental flattery had not entirely passed out; bad kings and princes, who were possibly Jacobites in disguise; beauty in distress; sorcerers and sorceresses whose presence was often necessary for the smooth operation of the improbabilities which had to culminate in happy endings; occasional retainers, prophets, priests and warriors. It was the greatness of Handel to turn these vehicles of varied aria—*cantabile, di portamento, di mezzo carattere, parlante, di bravura* or *d'imitazione*—and recitative into people.

If Handel's characters sometimes stand stiff-jointed and stylized, it is because such behaviour was expected and because had this connection with normality been ignored the operas would have suffered immediate relega-

---

[1] This FitzGerald wrote after seeing Macready's stage revival of *Acis and Galatea* in 1847.

tion to the realm of impracticability. As it was, differences of opinion with singers and audience led to the ill acceptance of much of the finest music. But when Handel's people pose they do so with magnificent full-blooded theatricality. The angel of *La Resurrezione* ends with Grinling Gibbons florescence the aria "Disserratevi, oh porte d'Averno!" thus:

Rinaldo strikes the heroic in what George Eliot would have called the "mechanical dramatic" manner:

Com-bat - ti da for - te, com-bat - ti da for - te, che fer-mo li mio sea

and Galatea trails self-pity behind her like a representation of Rossettian charm.

The end-stopped theatrical presentation of personality was inevitable so long as Handel referred to the conventions by which recitative, although Keiser had educated him in the dramatic possibilities latent herein, and aria fulfilled the functions of plain narration on the one hand and onomatopoeic virtuosity on the other, while the incongruity of *da capo* provided a further handicap. But despite these obstacles Handel rarely leaves his characters solely mechanical. Into his arias he pours corpuscular energy, an achievement rare in the fluent Buononcini or in any other contemporary composer. For the most part it is possible to dislike Handel's feather-brained heroines—as helpless in the grip of circumstance as any of Hardy's—but, for all their supine resignation, they are attractive in lineament, and in their decorative subordination they reflect something of the eighteenth-century attitude towards women. Representative heroines of this order are the pallid Magdalena of *La Resurrezione,* the child-like Asteria of *Tamerlano,* the vapid Queen of *Solomon* and the obedient Merab of *Saul.* In depicting these women Handel seizes on the obvious, achieves skilful and apt portraiture, but hardly touches subtlety. On a first hearing this static quality may seem to define all Handelian characters: royalty has its vocabulary of apposite dignity: the hieratic, as in Valens in *Theodora* or that impressive song of the Levite in *Solomon,* "Praise ye the Lord," its Anglo-Catholic poise of cultured superiority; while braggarts storm in the same strain of cheerful anger from Argante to Harapha. To continue this catalogue is merely to indicate that, as all Handel's characters are in some measure self-projective, a family likeness is not to be unexpected.

The excuse of narrative, whether in drama, in literature

or in dramatically conditioned music, is that emotional behaviour is naturally settled by the tendencies of plot. In the period under review the plot as such was subsidiary to the circumstances evolved by its often ductile meanderings. Sterne, Richardson, Fielding, Smollett and clearly Hogarth concerned themselves with the kaleidoscope of life, and in selecting incidents from their *milieu* endeavoured to portray faithfully what they saw, what was, rather than what they thought ought to be. This latter was left to the imagination of the beholder. Handel's music was complementary to the art of the above-mentioned, and his strength must lie in his capacity to express his sensibility to human passion. The moral purpose which he began to experience towards the end of his life was the natural outcome of extensive observation, a development of sympathy with what he described, and that attractive brotherliness which Leigh Hunt ascribed to Abou Ben Adhem.

What happened to Polissena in *Radamisto* is neither here nor there, but her anguish of soul, the result of her husband's attachment to Zenobia, is thus portrayed:

There is a universality about this which immediately makes the turgid plot development irrelevant and provokes sympathy with the victim of misfortune whoever she may be. Burney remarks somewhere that no one could use octave and unison passages with such effect as Handel. The rests, the melodic intervals, the ambiguous tonality of Polissena's opening are all symptomatic of the complex simplicity which Handel used in moments of strained emotion. In *Floridante* Orante similarly speaks agonizingly through the terseness of

This form of direct repetition links the Handelian style of musical development with that of twentieth-century practice: the fundamental idea is represented in one short and pregnant theme which then impresses the listener not by evolution in the academic way, but by stark alliteration. Of this habit no more expressive example can be found than in the accompaniment to the "Monster Atheist" of *Saul*. Accompaniment is the wrong term: the more intense Handel's thought the more coalescently vocal and instrumental parts unite in balanced symmetry. It was this insistence on the necessity for orchestral partnership which led Handel into trouble with his contemporaries, but the truth is that his vision looked forward to a new form of expression. Tolomeo's "Stille amare," for instance, is not so much a song as a tone-poem the opening of which

leaves in the unsubstantial terms of pure music what Tolomeo endeavours, in inchoate mixture of recitative and aria and with death on his lips, to put into coherence.

On the side of tragedy Dejanira's "Where shall I fly," in *Hercules,* Samson's "Total Eclipse" and Orlando's mad scene are the most penetrating and awe-inspiring examples of Handel's capacity for uncovering the raw nerve-centres of mental agony. Sheer despair, haunting and spectral fear, mad desires translate the personality from humanity to bestiality or to primeval chaos. Dejanira expels her evil spirits. Orlando passes the region of reclamation except for the intervention of magic. Once again bare octaves suffice to carry the voice; once again the music is peremptorily occupied in reiteration; and for the first time in history the time-signature 5–8 appears. The catastrophic passage, so frequent in reference and so rare in appearance, stands thus:

Was it prevision of personal misfortune or simply the observation of kindled imagination which prompted this anachronistic *scena?* The craft is superb. Mental affliction crosses recitative and aria, ebbs to exhaustion through the healing influence of the "Vaghe pupille" gavotte and finally reposes Orlando in troubled sleep over the time-honoured motif of chromatically descending ground-bass. The return to sanity is achieved through the mediation of Zoroaster. Necromancy plays its superficial part, but the emotional picture is larger than the obvious limits of opera allow. Handel comes near, at this juncture, to the fundamental and unanswerable problems of life and death. Both in matter and manner there is an occasional tinting of Elgar. While Orlando is tossed into unhappy uncertainty the beneficent powers are arranging his release from suffering, the high priest officiates pontifically with solemn appeal to the unknown gods:

and supernatural agents bring restorative to the shadowy beauty of this soothing interlude:

The music for this scene is, perhaps, the most profound essay in characterization in the whole of Handel. But one point remains abundantly clear: Handel judged not his fellow men, but extended to them the full warmth of his sympathy. It is this sympathy, coupled with an abiding affection, which embraces all the moods in which we find the figures of opera and oratorio. Old age in mellowed serenity in the "Nel riposo" of *Deidamia* or in the Manoah music of *Samson;* spirited chaperonage in the two Irenes of *Tamerlano* and *Theodora;* leafy amorousness in Dorinda's music at the beginning of the second act of *Orlando;* the bucolic jollity of *Hercules;* the apt representation of Ben Jonson's bluster in *L'Allegro;* even the *sic semper tyrannis* of Haman in *Esther* or of Tiridate in *Radamisto;* and the below-stairs comedy of *Serse* and *Almira.* The grateful antidote to the commonplace thesis that Handel principally enjoyed pious occupation in the production of endless Hallelujahs for the faithful is Elviro's Mozartian (albeit the cries of London exude in springtime vivacity) flower-selling song from *Serse:*

The student of Handel will be readily able to add to this list of varied character studies and in so doing he will realize Handel's kinship with the diarist. But Handel was not only a diarist, he was a dramatist, and drama depends on the relationship evolved between one character and another. Because he was not satisfied in leaving his people in splendid isolation Handel proceeded to bring them into a psychological relationship typical of Mozart and to divest the opera of its more obvious function of providing a concert in fancy dress. Love-making, for the benefit of those who read autobiography in every bar, did not rouse Handel to considerable enthusiasm. But when jealous suspicion and possible infidelity appear the music warms up to the pitch of painful realism evident in the duets between Porus and Cleosida or Samson and Delilah. In *Rinaldo* and *Teseo* there are masterly contrasts between the two women in each opera, who respectively duel with each other over the possession of the men. In *Hercules* Iole and Dejanira are similarly brought together, but with greater subtlety, and their unsought rivalry is projected against a more significant background wherein the mutability of human nature and the vicious turns of inexorable fate are tragically intermingled. And at the climactic moment the shadow overhanging the scene takes recognizable shape as the chorus, that element which Handel required to fulfil his dramatic intentions with complete fidelity, after the foreboding of an octave introduction utters:

One more example of Handel's psychological insight must suffice. It is in that scene in *Solomon* where the two women appear: impudent harlotry and rich motherhood can rarely have had such representation.

This counterpoint of ideas is turned into triple counterpoint by the presence of Solomon, whose judicial behaviour at this point is perfect. To present three or more strands of thought simultaneously is the most involved problem in musical drama. Handel achieved the trio in *Acis and Galatea,* the quartets in *Radamisto, Semele* and *Jephtha,* all of which would appear superb at any period, but incredible in an age when such extravagantly truthful demonstrations of human frailty and perplexity were regarded as improper interpolations in an evening's enjoyment.

The libretti with which Handel had to deal were frequently of infuriating puerility, but they served as incentive to the composer to recreate from his imagination the types of personality there collected. Characters and situations were so arranged in Handel's capacious and orderly mind that they were ready for any contingency: hence the speed of execution receives additional sanction. The operas were often episodic—the plots were to blame for this; the oratorios hardly ever. In general the texts on which he worked for oratorio composition possessed a singleness of direction never evident in the complex organizations of the eighteenth-century opera; moreover, and this will receive amplification in a later chapter, the introduction of the chorus enabled additional matter relevant to the argument and impossible of mention by the principal characters to be adduced. The main difference between opera and oratorio lies in the capacity of the latter form to show not only isolated moments of inspired characterization but continuity in emotional development. Samson remains Samson through all vicissitudes and is musically recognizable at any given moment. Nicotris, like Storge in *Jephtha,* adjusts herself to whatever situation may arise, but stands perpetually fixed in an incredible pattern of grief, righteousness and forbearing motherhood. And in those late works *Theodora* and *Jephtha* Handel takes youth in hand with consummate understanding, leading Theodora and Iphis from the feckless innocence of newly awakened love through anxiety, bred of principle on the one hand and devotion on the other, to certainty in the value of values and to the uncommon climaxes of death in the one case and conventual immuration in the other. Their name should be Cordelia.

Chapter 13

"Tonmalerei"

IF THERE IS one aspect of Handel which reveals him more than any other as sharing the traditional philosophy of the English it is his outlook on nature. The revival of romanticism belonged to his period, as the preoccupation of music with details of illustration—itself an inevitable outcome of the development of instrumental technique—the realistic essays in scenic adventure and the transition of poetic thought all indicate. "What this increased interest in nature signified," writes Professor Ifor Evans,

> is difficult to record. Part of it was a delight in "prospects," in scenes which a painter might use. Now that roads were improving, gentlemen and ladies could look out from their carriages on the views, and many of them they found good. Some even constructed "views" on their own estates and parklands. The delight was often not for the pretty and regular design, but for the more wild and rugged aspects of nature. It was as if the human mind were in revolt against the increasing rationalism of the century.[1]

In isolating Handel's approach to nature emphasis is once again laid on his genius for expressing the motions of eighteenth-century thought and equally on his genius for transcending the commonplace and rising superior to his contemporaries by integrating fragmentary facets of imaginative exploration into unity. It is not uncommon to note that Handel conscribed a company of frogs, lice and

[1] B. Ifor Evans, *A Short History of English Literature* (Pelican Books), p. 39.

locusts and that he brought down hailstones and fire from heaven for the discomfiture of Pharaoh's hosts, that he emulated Marvell's "green thought in a green shade" in *Semele,* that he commanded thunder and lightning in *Riccardo I* and *Joshua,* that he shared with the Almighty the governance of the sea in the Chandos anthem "The Lord is my Light" and in *Israel in Egypt,* and that in a hundred other instances he demonstrated powers of observation such as rarely find so adequate an expression. But it is less frequent to observe that Handel not only contemplated nature picturesquely, but also with a conviction that the mind of man and the operations of nature were of a piece in the universal design. Handel was by no means lacking in religious faith, but his faith of an elementary and practical order left ample room for the expansion of a free will into those realms of speculation uncongenial to the theologically dogmatic.

From a technical point of view Handel invented nothing: he merely did what other people did, but generally better. Many eighteenth-century composers were exploring the possibilities of realism. Vivaldi had written seasonable music, in concerto form, to illustrate spring, summer, autumn and winter. Kuhnau had put sections of the Old Testament into sonatas. Werner had produced the detailed preciosity of an *Instrumental-Kalender* and Telemann had invested opera and oratorio with large portions of elementary scene-painting. Such experiments served a double purpose: on the one hand the freedom of music was safeguarded against the encroachments of pedantry, and on the other the theatre was saved from operatic atrophy. In any form of drama continual adjustment of the scales is necessary for the preservation of true balance or rather, since drama has never fixed itself in absolute equipoise, for a semblance of true balance. Elizabethan drama accommodated itself to the inn-yard by expressing the scenic setting in the text. Eighteenth-century opera overcame the disadvantage of a tale told in an alien tongue by rendering narrative superfluous by elegance in backcloths, by extravagance in properties, by conventional plot-arrangement (one opera being very much the same as any other in the number of persons employed and in the order and function of the various types of aria enumerated on page 163) and by the transference of antithesized ideas from the medium of words to that of music. In this latter respect the particular of verbal expression was losing itself in the universal of musical exegesis. In the meantime, however, music was going half-way to meet the situation by embracing particularity. By nineteenth-century standards, which set opera religiously enthroned in the ultimate theories of Wagner, the eighteenth century was lacking in sense. Opera as an entertainment, opera as a diversified concert, opera without action (singers as a rule quitted the stage after each appearance) was all wrong, but only by the arbitrary standards of later generations. Viewed objectively the opera of Handel's day should be regarded as a necessary stage in the development of aesthetic perception. It was the training-ground of singers and orchestral musicians. It may be that, looking backwards, Debussy, Mussorgsky, Wagner, Meyerbeer, Berlioz, Mozart and Gluck were chief agents in the evolution of opera; but what they in turn achieved was at least hinted at by Handel.

Handel's delineation of character was exact and meticulous. He threw on his canvas universal types of men and women such as we find elsewhere defined in the works of Memling. It happened that Memling's types were dressed as Flemish citizens, Handel's as heroes or heroines of classical or Hebraic tradition. Behind both sets was placed the background of nature. Memling's countryside shone in jewelled beauty and contrast; Handel's implied, Hardy-like, an influence over the characters it supported. Solomon, in the oratorio of that name, is a study not so much of a ruler skilled in jurisprudence as of a naturalist turning pantheist. *Acis and Galatea* is an essay less in personal than in landscape charm, and the metamorphosis of Acis into a river appears a proper sort of poetic justice. In the opening scene of *Orlando* Zoroaster stands majestically on his mountain-side, and whether the music directs attention to the one or on the other it is impossible to decide. Burney was sensitive to something strange and new when he referred to the scene as having "a wild grandeur in it of a very uncommon kind."[2]

In the second act of *Orlando* the summer lightness of Dorinda's "Quando spieghi:

and the whole murmurous nature of the forest music exert an influence on the musical progress of the opera by throwing Orlando's later madness into the most poignant relief. Wherever we look the presence of nature as a separate, subtle and enveloping personality is evident. The *Nachtmusik* of *Floridante* and *Amadigi* combines Schumann and Weber in a sensuous blend of mingled starlight and feminine charm; the garden path, up which most of us are led and beyond whose end we seldom explore, presents the tree prospect of "Ombra mai fu"; moonshine reflects in the nocturnal intermezzo of *Ariodante; Susanna* is a gossip piece interlaced with the sounds and sights of village life; sunrise and sunset inspire the loveliest of the arias in *Theodora* and *Samson; L'Allegro* has the vivacity of a seventeenth-century *genre* painting, but also the more fragile poetry of Constable.

The intention of theoreticians was that music should, as Avison suggests, depict nature; but the operations of emotional behaviour were also considered to be susceptible of direct expression. Mattheson wrote that

> One can represent all the passions of the heart by simple harmonies and their concatenation, without words, so that the hearer grasps and understands the development, the meaning and the ideas of the musical utterance as though it were in actual spoken utterance.[3]

To this philosophy was linked the whole of Handel's achievement, and viewed in this light his music dissolves into a profounder heart-search than modern conditions of performance allow. The majestic, leonine Handel is but part of an immeasurably greater whole. The subtlety of theatrical chiaroscuro and the subtlety of life in general drew from him a new orchestral technique. This has been discovered already in incidental music which reveals something more than mere appositeness and suggests that the composer saw, in part at any rate, the substance which casts the shadow on the wall of the cave. This intensity of contemplation shows up again in the overtures which preface opera and oratorio. Starting from the original curtain-raising function of such music they proceeded to vary in outline (the outline bequeathed from Lully through Steffani) as the needs of the whole work decreed and even to summarize the emotional direction of the plot. The overture to *Messiah,* greyly contrasting its E minor with the E major of the first aria, holds Advent in its sober dignity and refrains from anticipating festivity by omitting the customary third movement in minuet form; that to *Saul* foretells the opening *epinicion* by turning into an organ concerto; that to *Deborah* presents Baalites and Israelites in immediate antipathy by quoting their particular thematic material from the later stages of the oratorio; that to *Esther* preludes obviously the tyranny, despair and triumph which furnish the life of the plot. The overture

[3] Mattheson, *Die neueste Untersuchung des Singspiels,* 1744.

to the *Occasional Oratorio* is so familiar that its military zest needs no emphasis. In the overture to *Serse* the comedy is drawn out in the humour of the fugue subject:

and in the playfulness of its succeeding dialogue:

Alcina was a combination of opera and ballet and preludes its *élan* in an overture of fitting vivacity. The lines of the minuet:

epigrammatize the sparkling quality of this work and recall Mrs. Delany's exclamation that "whilst Mr. Handel was playing his part I could not help thinking him a necromancer in the midst of his own enchantments."

From orchestral we may turn to choral *Tonmalerei*. And here it would appear necessary to discuss the general principles which influenced Handel in his choral technique. This is always impeccable, and because the approach to the orchestra is at apparent variance with that of later schools and the balance of choir and orchestra has in large-scale performances altered to the disadvantage of the latter an undue emphasis is laid on the magnificence of those exceptional choral movements which appeared to justify their performance in the Crystal Palace. Handel himself was accustomed to small and relatively capable companies of singers for his choral movements which initially, except for works written for ecclesiastical use exclusively, were incidental. In opera and oratorio the eighteenth century followed in the wake of the seventeenth and aptly produced a chorus for the representation of crowd effects. Soldiers, sailors and attendants formed the basis of secular and observant congregations of faithful Christians of sacred choralism. Handel enjoyed crowds, appreciated the effectiveness of combined voices as an addition to orchestral colour, lived among people whose pleasure often led to the conviviality of collective singing, and accordingly expanded choral music into greater significance than hitherto. But the intention was not to exclude the orchestra at any time: it was to treat the one with the other on equal terms just as in later times the woodwind or the brass *ensemble* came to a reciprocal understanding with the strings. The Handelian view of the function of chorus is illustrated more simply in the operas than in the oratorios, where other considerations supervene.

In *Il pastor fido* may be noted the minuet pleasantry of the final chorus (choruses as finales were *de rigueur* in the system) "Quel ch' il cielo" which, if not remarkable, is at all events fitted with the airy Arcadianism apt for pastoral drama. The Athenians have a cheerful welcome song for Theseus in the second act of *Teseo*. Burney observes of "Ogn' un acclami" that it is not like the oratorio choruses, for an evident reason:

> In these the subject being generally solemn, and in the church style, should partake of choral complication; whereas an opera chorus, being in action, and committed to memory, must necessarily be short, easy and dramatic.[4]

The importance of the choral writing, whether in opera or oratorio, lies not so much in complexity or in lack of complexity as in its dramatic situation. The short bursts of choral observation in *Messiah,* in *Israel in Egypt,* in the *Funeral Anthem* are simple in process but momentous in setting. In general this is true of Handel's music as a whole, and we cannot but deplore the practice of cutting

[4] Burney, *History,* iv. 241.

amiable patterns for public offering while ignoring the texture to which the patterns belong. There is a chorus in *Alcina* which runs thus:

Larghetto

Ques - too il cie - lo di - con - ten - ti -

This has lately been put into the trimness of high-school uniform. It belongs to the naughty ravishment of Alcina's palace, Alcina being another of Handel's seductive heroines who combined the functions of princess and sorceress for the bewitchment of Ruggiero. There is no doubt that if some headmistresses were aware of Handel's mind-picture as he wrote "Questo il cielo," with what effectiveness can only properly be deduced from the score, the purified school song would be banned forthwith. This is not a complaint against the practice of encouraging the young to sing Handel so much as an objection lodged against the refusal, on the part of those who should know better, to take Handel seriously when he intended seriousness of artistic purpose. Of all the opera choruses that which is most telling is the "Viva, viva il nostro Alcide," with which *Giulio Cesare* opens. Here we have the tremendous exhilaration which infects the festive crowds of *Deborah, Solomon* and *Saul* and sets in immediate view the hot heroism of romanticized royalty. The oratorio choruses, possessed of a larger significance than those of the operas, will be treated in greater detail, but it must be urged that they too had their origins in dramatic propriety.

Chromatic harmony is another weapon in the dramatic armoury, and reference must be made to Handel's dependence thereon in particular moments. The chromatic ground-bass usage, as in *Orlando, Poro* and in the magnificent petitionary pessimism of the Israelites' "How long O Lord" in *Susanna,* follow familiar models: Purcell, in fact, is immediately recalled. Where, however, there is no ground-bass to impose a regulated course, Handel breaks the bonds of conformity and allows the urge of inspiration to dive into uncharted waters. In *Israel in Egypt* there is the "He sent a thick darkness" chorus, of whose modulations Tovey has to say that

> they are as expressive as the modulations in Bach's Chromatic Fantasia, inasmuch as they traverse most of harmonic space. On the other hand, they differ profoundly from the Chromatic Fantasia, and from Handel's own Passion recitatives in *The Messiah,* because they are not enharmonic—that is to say, each step is known as far as it goes, but there is no general aim and the end of the groping is incalculably remote.[5]

Herein we may emphasize "each step is known as far as it goes"—a dictum applicable to the whole range of Handel's technical accomplishment and indicative of the perplexity in which we so frequently find ourselves, discovering how much we know of Handel and, at the same time, how little. As in the chorus of darkness Handel intrudes deep mystery into "How are the mighty fallen" and "Their bodies are buried in peace" in the *Funeral Anthem.* In twenty bars or so an immense profundity is stirred, by means which are perfectly obvious save in one respect. That is in the ellipticism of modulation already mentioned in connection with the *Concerti grossi* which takes us from key to key with this degree of suddenness:

The feeling is seventeenth-century[6] and on this form of behaviour the eighteenth-century modernists no doubt looked deprecatingly. It savoured of archaism. When, however, school logic conflicted with emotional tension Handel preferred to follow the latter. In respect of this

[5] Tovey, *Essays in Musical Analysis,* v. 97.
[6] Op. cit., p. 98.

we may look at the second part of "Tyrants now no more shall dread," a chorus from *Hercules* which produces

> *Horrid forms of monstrous birth*
> *Again shall vex the groaning earth;*
> *Fear of punishment is o'er,*
> *The World's avenger is no more.*

These words, provoked by the death of Hercules under signally unfortunate circumstances, were sufficient to set Handel on a course symbolic of the bewilderment of the leaderless:

which terminates thus:

It is passages such as this to which we may like to think Cowper points.[7] It is in passages like this that Handel shows his complete mastery of technique and his intellectual capacity for psychological interpretation.

We have all had our Handelian training in church, and the perfect church-going mood is one of pure ab-

---

[7] Cowper, *The Task*, book vi:
> *Remember Handel? Who, that was not born*
> *Deaf as the dead to harmony, forgets,*
> *Or can, the more than Homer of his age?*

stract reverence. A mood of active intelligence would be scandalous. Thus we get broken in to the custom of singing Handel as if he meant nothing; and as it happens that he meant a great deal, and was tremendously in earnest about it, we know rather less about him in England than they do in the Andaman Islands, since the Andamans are only unconscious of him, whereas we are misconscious.[8]

The misconsciousness arises from a misconception that Handel was more interested in God than in man. The reverse is the truth. If this is by now established we may turn to the oratorios with clearer vision.

[8] Shaw, *Music in London 1890–4,* i. 110.

Chapter 14

The Oratorios

—So INVOLVED ARE the motions of human thought that what is entertainment to some is instruction to others and what passes as amusement to one generation serves the next with didactic purpose. In music the difficulty of appreciation lies in the fact that the component elements are of both orders simultaneously, so that the last quartets of Beethoven or the operas of Mozart are at once fit for philosophic scrutiny on the one hand and plain enjoyment on the other. Handel's purpose was primarily to amuse, to embellish life with leisurely occupation—how leisurely it was is clear from the inability of subsequent admirers to survive uncut masterpieces—but he also had in mind the enigmatic capacity of art for ethical interpretation and direction. He spoke out on this point to Lord Kinnoul. This being the case, sympathy may be extended both to those who treat *Messiah* sacramentally and to those who, ignoring doctrinal implications, surrender themselves to an orgy of aural titillation. That the pious and the hedonistic sit side by side at such performances of Handel's "sacred" music as are familiar is not, as they so often consider it, a tribute to them, but to Handel's vast instinct for universal companionship. This sense of fraternity would be better understood if the whole of Handel's output were known; even, if we accept the point of view that the operas are unperformable (which they are not), were the whole of the oratorios known.

If choral societies were filled with initiative and with versatile singers and took it upon themselves to produce works of such diversity as the Passion of 1716, *Saul*,

Theodora, Susanna and *Jephtha—Israel in Egypt* is only here excluded because it is relatively familiar—it would be seen that Handel, so far from being among the Lord's anointed, which is where idolatry places him, is very mortal in his approach to immortality. At home with the elemental passions of men and women, he fails to get nearer to God than do most of us who have no special claim to spiritual superiority. Bach imposes humility, seeming so frequently to see into eternity; Pergolesi inspires ardour because he is burnt up with the heat of his Mariolatrous devotion; Palestrina implies, almost Jesuitically, the logic of God; Byrd details philosophy. Handel does none of these things. He stands before the unknown in bewildered sorrow at suffering, in joy at virtue triumphant, in anger, of a particular paternal and sympathetic order, at moral turpitude, in simple wonder at whatever is incomprehensible. He shouts "Hallelujah" from pure *joie de vivre,* sings praises with the robust vigour of a prosperous churchwarden and prays with the variable intensity of those who look to supernaturalism under stress of despair. The Handelians may complain that this undervalues Handel. On the contrary, it indicates his special claim to supremacy. He understands human nature in its strength and in its weakness with more acuteness than any other of the great composers. This is why there can be no division between opera and oratorio in his case. The concern of both is with human affairs.

The pedigree of oratorio takes us back inconveniently far to trace in detail. In any case the normal encyclopaedists can present it with ramified exactitude. Here it may be recapitulated that towards the end of the sixteenth century opera, sanctified solely by verbal indication, was impressed into the service of the Counter-Reformation with due caution by Filippo Neri, a priest whose behaviour matched his birth in nobility and led to his canonization. Neri's intention was to make intelligible to the illiterate youth of Rome the mysteries of theology by their presentation in terms of drama and music. His innovation, which in view of medieval religious drama was not really an innovation, stimulated Italian composers of the seventeenth century to issue many works of this kind. Thus from Cavalieri to Scarlatti a steady flow of picturesque essays in dramatic-musical form appeared to grace varied episodes of ecclesiastical association, from the *mater dolorosa* to the life-story of St. Philip himself. Among the vast array of oratorios and contatas then composed those of Giacomo Carissimi were particularly significant, blending recitative, aria and chorus into narrative interest suitable for ecclesiastical performance. Hawkins expresses an opinion which immediately directs attention to the Handelian contact: "Carissimi excelled in imitating the inflexions of the human voice, and in uniting the charms of music with the powers of oratory."[1] As the score of *Jephte* is easily accessible the Handelian student is urged to take the opportunity of making contact with this precursor of later oratorio. Handel knew his Carissimi sufficiently well to adapt "Plorate filiae Israel" for the chorus "Hear Jacob's God" in *Samson*.

The style of Carissimi was, however, outmoded when Handel lived in Italy. Its severity hardly commended itself to the worldlings who, opera having been prevented in the theatre by edict of Pope Innocent XII, dictated that oratorio should select such episodes from holy writ as would stimulate eroticism in the operatic tradition. Hence such pleasing subjects as Susanna and Bathsheba and the secularity of Handel's first contribution to oratorio in Italy.

It is to be regretted that *La Resurrezione* is no more than a library curiosity. Completely operatic, with a lovable Lucifer (Handel could never find the heart thoroughly to dislike villainy and shared the modern belief that sinners in general are victims of causality), a sweet-voiced little Magdalene, an agreeable—if somewhat Tennysonian —St. John, an angel of pleasant virtuosity, and with delicious water-coloured orchestration, this *oratorio sacro* imbues religious exercise with an easefulness which may be reprehensible to the austere, but which suggests a degree of comfort in heaven not to be despised by the world-weary. Renaissance painters believed less in heaven on

[1] Hawkins, iv. 92.

earth than in earth, that well-fed and well-housed earth represented by the cardinals' standards of living, in heaven. The only improvements possible were in sanitation.

Germany countered Italy with religious music of different significance. The social history of Reformation and Thirty Years War, together with the natural consequences of a northern climate, induced deeper reflection on the problems of suffering and of pain. Therefore there arose the tradition of setting the story of the Passion with its concentration of congregational interest in, and not merely on, the subject by the employment of chorales. Before Bach the representative names were Schütz and Keiser, but Handel wrote two Passions, of which one, that of 1716, deserves consideration. It is interesting in that it demonstrates how de-germanized Handel had become by long residence abroad, yet, in contrast, how strongly he endeavoured to construct his music so as to be acceptable in the place of its presentation. The framework is German, but not the content. Chorales appear in severe unemotion. A daughter of Zion shows herself, but with little concern for the tragedy she witnesses. St. Peter is present in unseemly high spirits; Judas in obvious contrition which rings with little conviction in empty roulades:

Flames, chas-tize _____ me

and Christ. Here we may pause and consider in greater detail Handel's reaction to the central figure of the Crucifixion. The part of Christ redeems this Passion from the charge of complacency, which otherwise, and with propriety, might be directed at it. But Christ is the Man of Sorrows, with manhood as Handel's exclusive wonder. We view Him pictured with dignity, virility and affection as a companion of men sacrificed as a man on the altar of uncertain and extraneous circumstantial operation. The consecration of bread and wine is portrayed with massive simplicity:

and with a tenderness redolent of Handel's quick intensity of emotion before the shrine of friendship. "Lo! I will smite the shepherd" is angry with the vigorous integrity which sweeps through "Why do the nations" in the face of wilful disobedience and with the same breadth of arpeggio-fired inspiration. The Agony in the Garden produces the awe-laden sympathy of:

This is scrupulous portraiture, but lacking in the larger hope which sees not so much immolation of manhood as the triumph of the godhead. Thus Handel shows how his vision suffers general limitation in incomprehension of deep theology, but also he displays it limitless in human understanding.

It was fortunate for the subsequent history of oratorio that during his years of Burlington-Chandos patronage opportunities occurred for conversations with Pope, Gay and the surrounding constellation of wits and worthies. Human affairs are so frequently set in motion by accidents of companionship that it is safe to assume that had Handel not been on amiable terms with practitioners of arts other than his own *Esther* would not have appeared. Had this not happened, the possibilities of an English variant of *oratorio sacro* would have remained latent.

It may be imagined that Racine's *Esther*[2] came into conversation by chance, that Pope considered it an attractive proposition for translation, that Handel was sufficiently interested in what he had overheard to borrow a copy of the work, and that after reading it he suggested its further possibilities as a libretto. Here it may be interposed that he would have acknowledged in Racine a reflection of many of the ideas which were also his own. Racine was a dramatist whose strength lay in humanizing the conventional figures of classical mythology. Therefore he emphasized matter at the expense of form and acquired a solidity of expression in the same way as did ultimately Handel. It is further worthy of mention that not only Racine's *Esther,* but also his *Athalie* prompted music by Handel.

Esther (Handel's *Esther*) is an uneven work. Its principal defect is that it lacks the cohesion which marks the later oratorios. The solo music is tentative, except where Handel in Haman's cataclysmic opening looks prophetically forward through the years:

and much is in fact transferred from the Passion. The choruses similarly vary in quality so that the first with its ingenuous contrapuntal interjections and its anthem derivation carries not very much of personal conviction. The mannered use of the ♩♩ idiom in "Shall we of servitude complain" is also symptomatic of conscious adaptation to English usage. Passing by "Ye sons of Israel, mourn," which has a histrionic plaintiveness akin to that of the coeval funereal chorus in *Acis and Galatea,* and the handsome jingle of "Hallelujah" (an Italian "Hallelujah"[3] whose coruscations are a relief from the lumber-

---

[2] An English version of *Esther* was done in 1715 by Thomas Brereton, a graduate of Brasenose College, Oxford, and a "gentleman of Cheshire."

[3] Borrowed from the brilliantly attractive motet *Silete venti.*

ing of later choruses to this text) as possessing potentialities of extreme effectiveness in performance, we must draw up in astonishment at the final, cantata-like "The Lord our enemy has slain," which, with its *canto fermo* to crown the concluding "for ever blessed," is magnificent.

The years passed, and Handel forgot the existence of *Esther*. In 1732 it was without his foreknowledge revived. In that same year Aaron Hill inscribed his plea for opera in the vernacular. Handel witnessed the success of the revival, took note of his friend's admonition and called Humphreys into consultation. It may be that further incentive to oratorio came from the publication four years earlier of John Ernest Galliard's *Morning Hymn of Adam and Eve,* a slender cantata, but a hint that Milton was a possible source of libretto inspiration. However, Milton does not just yet come into the Handel field. In 1733 it was Humphreys's version of the story of Deborah which called his attention. With the best will in the world it is difficult to arouse very much enthusiasm for this work, and the point of view of those who complained at the increased prices must be considered reasonable. In *Deborah,* however, Handel did discover the effectiveness of contrast between two choirs representing different philosophies: his Israelites unfortunately are possessed of an inapt docility which dulls their music and which enlists support for the Baalites who, if obtuse, are spirited in utterance. Dramatically, despite its apparent unification by the introduction of *Leitmotive, Deborah* is a poor sequel to *Orlando* which appeared at about the same time. It is seldom that Handel really touches banality, but when the priests of Baal can do no better than this:

the palm for heathen exaltation must temporarily rest with Mendelssohn.

In *Athaliah* Handel reverts more happily to his operatic vein, and while Baalites and Israelites again present a background of conflict, with more subtlety defined in extravagances of languor and charm, the personalities of Athaliah, a character tied up with Storge and Dejanira in a primitive state of subjection to irrational projections from the fearful dream-world, Josabeth, Joash and Joad (a knowledgeable sort of person) play in the forefront parts of attractive individuality. Up to this point there is, if one may ever say it of Handel, an immaturity in the disposition of oratorio: in each there is a specialized interest but no real fusion of the disparate elements such as is met with, after a space of two years, in *Saul*.

Saul is one of Handel's most extensive studies of human nature in primitive form. It holds the stylized libretto in contempt and deals in the same terms of epical eloquence with a story of heroic proportions as does the writer of the book of Samuel. Jennens was neither better nor worse than most of the poetasters who constructed libretti to order, but the fiery clash of ancient arms defeated his decorous transcription. However—and here a case may be made out for texts which in this way are incomplete —there was scope for Handel to revivify the dry bones. Handel went back to the Authorized Version and made an oratorio the music of which carried the same dignity, poetry and ripeness as the seventeenth-century words. Interest starts with the people of the plot, people delineated with the exactness of photogravure. But while we study the gnawing deceit of Saul, the pert independence of Merab (who puts ideas into her father's head by refusing to marry one "of poor, plebeian parents born"), the pretty romanticism of Michal, the somewhat evirated mutual affection of Jonathan and David, the witch of Endor and the prophetic apparition of Samuel, the chorus saves itself for more or less abstract commentary. It is true that the chorus is also participant in the drama, with what effect is manifest in the opening chorus, but its detachment from the immediate scene is adroitly controlled so that the strictures laid on Saul by his subjects and in his presence have no incongruity. In this respect actionless oratorio has the advantage over opera, and *Saul* produces the choruses which are neither fit for opera, being too prodigious, nor for church, because too unkempt, but entirely proper to their intended setting: the theatre during Lent. "Envy, eldest born of Hell" and "O fatal consequence of rage" are terrible in their particular and in their universal application. The decadence of Saul as described in the latter is presented in terms which bear superficial resemblance to a not dissimilar mood survey in the *Schicksalslied* of Brahms. Thus the chorus follow the demented turmoil of the mind of Saul:

The affection possessed by Handel for Saul raises that monarch to the full heroic stature necessary for tragedy —"a man who is not eminently good and just, yet whose misfortune is brought about not by vice or depravity, but by some error or frailty."[4] Saul is kept free from exaggeration, and when he displays anger it is anger redolent of quick temper and free from unspoken malignity of thought. "A serpent in my bosom warmed" is illustrative of this point and also of the further point that Handel treated formal considerations with scant courtesy when it suited his dramatic purpose. This aria terminates abruptly in G minor, without a *da capo,* as Saul hurls his javelin at a too agile David. The anger becomes uncontrollable, and as jealousy mingles with despair there comes the sudden impulse to invoke the powers of darkness. Thus Saul, whose recitatives are dramatically the most cumulative

[4] Aristotle, *Poetics,* xiii.

in tension in the whole range of oratorio, turns the corner
to final moral dissolution:

The soldierly death of Saul calls from David, hitherto
an exemplar of sickly virtue, his best song, "In sweetest
harmony they lived," and treachery passes out of the picture as the maids of Israel are reminded that it was to
Saul's indulgent care they owed the scarlet and gold they
wore. The oratorio should end with the chorus "O fatal
day," but the necessity for a cheerful finale imposed on
Handel the task of setting "Go on," at least twenty times
repeated, which the Israelites shouted at David together
with sundry exhortations and guarantees of divine favour
as he girded on his sword for the next campaign.

The companion work to *Saul* was *Israel in Egypt*. Here
is simply the story of a people in their progress from
adversity to victory, epically related in what is to all in-
tents and purposes a choral symphony. Whether Handel
borrowed other men's ideas or not is not so important
as the thankfulness to God, nowhere else so patent, which
infuses the music, leads to the overwhelming impact of
the ageless paean which prefaces the final chorus, and
symbolizes the recovery of Handel himself from illness,
the triumphant passage of the Children of Israel and,
more than this, that of all peoples who have come through
the darkness of oppression and subjugation. This is music
of which it might truly be said that "the touch of life has
turned to truth." The first chorus, in which the tremendous effect of the withheld bass part when it sets the earth
rumbling with its cry to God should be noted as born

of genius, is the representation of Europe as I remember it in 1941.[5]

—Why in 1741 Handel forsook his natural field of dramatic and heroic narrative for the solemn libretto of *Messiah* is difficult to decide. That it was entirely due to evangelistic zeal is improbable. The possibility is that the cause was more personal. At a period when disillusionment preyed on his mind his thoughts took flight to happier times, and the memory of his dead sister came back to him. And with her memory came that of her favourite text—"I know that my Redeemer liveth." Therefrom possibly sprung the conception of a commemorative work—a *Trauerode,* which however should see death swallowed up in victory. Handel could see death in no other way.

The first triumph in *Messiah* is the text. Here one wonders at the felicity of extraction—in one detail the mixture of Job and Corinthians in the text above mentioned is so happy that it passes even the learned unnoticed—and whether Jennens really possessed the devotion to Holy Writ to produce so masterly an abstract of Christian thought. It has reasonably been suggested[6] that the text owed to Nonjuror practice (Jennens being a Nonjuror), but one reflects also that Handel once observed over the selection of words for the coronation music: "I have read my Bible very well and shall choose for myself." Accordingly it may be presumed that Handel had a good deal to do with the textual compilation of *Messiah*. This is

[5] A letter eulogizing *Israel in Egypt* appeared in the *London Daily Post,* dated 18th April 1739. The following extract indicates the writer's approval of my thesis. I apologize to my Catholic friends for the particular example of evil. They will, I am sure, judge the writer charitably and allow his comments validity in essence while making allowances for the prejudices of the period:

"Did such a Taste prevail universally in a People, that People might expect on a like Occasion, if such Occasion should ever happen to them, the same Deliverance as those praises celebrate; and Protestant, free, virtuous, united, Christian England need little fear, at any time hereafter, the whole Force of slavish, bigotted, united, unchristian Popery, risen up against her should such a conjuncture ever hereafter happen."

[6] "The Text of *Messiah*," Geoffrey Cuming, in *Music and Letters,* July 1950, p. 226 et seq.

supported by the fact that the central figure of the work appears only in the background. Partly this may have been due to subservience to public feeling, but partly to Handel's lack of ease in the neighbourhood of divinity. Thus the music bears an impersonality, an eighteenth-century and Protestant quality as Handel throws aside, except for the "He trusted in God" chorus, the intense passion and fire of *Saul* and *Israel in Egypt*. A Wren-like monument is the result: a temple of marble on which Mozart was later to hang stucco ornaments.

Messiah is a careful and awe-inspired work. The scoring is indicative of this in its ferial nature. More thrilling choruses may be found in *Israel in Egypt* or in *Belshazzar,* finer arias in *Samson* or *Theodora*, recitative of greater musical significance in *Saul* or *Jephtha,* but nowhere else is there a firmer homogeneity. This is due to Handel's evocation of ceremonial dignity. And this in turn explains the English affection for *Messiah:* it represents what, since the Reformation, they have generally felt obliged to feel about God in public. Because it is representative of a nation's thought *Messiah* is a notable work, but also, inevitably, it is not Handel at his greatest. Jennens expressed an opinion that Handel might have done better with the subject. Jennens was wrong. Handel could have done no more with *Messiah,* but with a different text and with a less abstract theme he could have written music which, considered on its own merits and without the subtle influence of familiar words of acknowledged genius and specific religious association, was more intrinsically poetic.

The confirmation lies in the next oratorio—*Samson,* where music once again runs into the familiar channels of heroic narrative. Here we have an anthology of Milton, ingeniously doctored by Newburgh Hamilton,[7] running

---

[7] Newburgh Hamilton was related to (the relationship may be guessed at) and lived with the Duke of Hamilton. Before his association with Handel his fame had precariously rested on *The Doating Lovers, or The Libertine Tamed* and *The Petticoat Plotter* (Thomas Winchop, *Scanderbeg*). It looks as though Handel selected his text for those works which had Hamilton's collaboration. In the first codicil to his will it is stated: "I give to Mr. Newburgh Hamilton, of Old Bond Street, who has assisted

into the full tide of Handel's inspiration. The constant comparison of Handel with Homer has fullest significance in attachment to this oratorio, in which the clash of personalities is developed amid the tumult of many voices, both human and divine. There is also evident that particular capacity of Handel for living with the ancients and at the same time for placing both them and us, the listeners, in the same timeless pattern. Thus the priests of Dagon and those of Jehovah, well matched in strenuous earnestness, champion all the characters who immortalize the eternal struggle between the powers of darkness and of light. The choral writing which enshrines this metaphysical duality is sublime in picturesqueness and inflexibility. The voices move with the sinuous grace of strings, a quality not so consistently achieved by Handel until he wrote *Samson,* and yet in so doing lose nothing of the mountainous grandeur apparent twenty years before. The urgency of "Awake the trumpet's lofty sound," the expression of plea and counter-plea in "Fix'd in His everlasting seat"—with this exalted exploitation of rests to suggest astonished contemplation:

the extension of *da capo* formality to "With thunder arm'd," with insight into the minds of those who reinforce the humility of prayer with more vigorous methods of advising the Almighty, the contrapuntal genius which contains a nation's grief in the twelve bars of "Weep, Israel,

---

me in adjusting words for some of my compositions, one hundred pounds." Which was a hundred pounds less than Morell received. *Samson* borrows from *Samson Agonistes,* the odes "On the Nativity," "On the Passion," "On Time," "At a solemn Musick," the "Epitaph on the Marchioness of Winchester" and the translations from the Psalms.

weep" and the finality of the concluding hymn of praise are tokens of the complete mastery of choral technique.

In *Samson,* however, the emancipation of the chorus is not at the expense of the solo singers. Far from it. Each has his or her personality tightly packed into recitatives and arias in which untidy ends of virtuosity no longer trail about deprived of dramatic point. Samson with his tragic strength, Manoah with the virility of his paternal affection, Harapha, who stamps through the score with superb ὕβρις, and Dalila, whose truculent amorousness is implied as much as stated, are among the most heroic of all the persons of opera or oratorio.

The athletic quality of *Samson* leaves *Joseph and his Brethren* immobile and generally unattractive, but the old barbaric spirit returns in full glory in *Belshazzar,* an oratorio in which the contrast between vicious pleasure and God-inspired virtue, appropriately armed with effective weapons of offence, is demonstrated in the plain manner of an old morality play with keen emphasis on the inevitable wages of sin. Despite the coloured pageant of riotous living centred in the carousal music, *Belshazzar* holds a greater sense of personal obeisance before the divine will than do many of the other oratorios. The keynote is sounded initially by Nicotris, a tragic queen of immense power and courage on whom Handel lavished music of unsurpassable quality, in an extensive *recitativo accompagnato,* whose subject is the decline and fall of empires. The "sprung rhythm" of Jennens's verse at this point momentarily attaches him to poets of greater fame. Handel's treatment of the closing bars of this recitative may be quoted as demonstrating the richer implications of his tone-painting faculty:

runs the same shad-ow-y round of fan-cied

A further instance of this developed symbolism occurs in the scene during which Daniel interprets the writing on the wall:

The perfect dramatic setting of the chord of the diminished seventh.

The *Occasional Oratorio* served its ardent purpose by collecting contributions from earlier works: the overture survived the occasion and may still be enjoyed by those who like sublimated bellicosity. *Judas Maccabaeus* has little to commend it (Handel disliked a story devoid of love interest) and *Joshua* is fairly dull. "See the conquering hero," text by Morell out of Dryden,[8] provoked a dialogue which may be taken to heart by those who neglect the greater works of Handel. Sir John Hawkins was asked by Handel how he liked this chorus. "Not so well as some things I have heard of yours." Then said Handel: "Nor I neither, but, young man, you will live to see it a greater favourite with the people than my other fine things."

Alexander Balus, the third of the conscious tributes to

[8] Cf. *Alexander's Feast:*
> The jolly god in triumph comes!
> Sound the trumpets, beat the drums!

Jewry, was less popular than either *Judas Maccabaeus* or *Joshua.* This may be ascribed to the inability of the oratorio public, which by 1748 was setting up limited piety and prudery as standards of criticism, to reconcile themselves to a love story, albeit with biblical sanction, arrayed in the persuasive delicacy of Longus. Lest, however, it should be thought that Handel was indulging in unhealthy fancies, it should be duly noted that *Alexander Balus* is a bright celebration of conjugal fidelity and, while an influx of brigandage affords some excellent and dramatic relief, the central theme of matrimonial propriety is responsible for Cleopatra's sweet songs and for the cheerful connubiality of the epithalamium chorus "Hymen fair, Urania's son." *Susanna* is a companion monument to chastity. The artlessness of this charming work is epitomized in:

Ask if yon da-mask Rose be sweet, that scents the am-bient Air

a ballad strain which might have come from Somerset. The decline of the elders into senile maudlinity is consummately portrayed and the etching of "Away, away, ye tempt me both in vain," a trio for Susanna and the two elders, is perfect. Behind the plot stands the awful severity of "How long, O Lord," a magnificently contrived prayer expanded over a ground-bass, the mystical union of the brute passions of man and of nature in "The torrent that sweeps in its course," and the rustic backchat of village gossips. The theme of the work is summarized hopefully in the final operatic and four-square chorus which emphasizes that

> *A virtuous wife shall soften fortune's frown,*
> *She's far more precious than a golden crown.*

Public morality, if affected at all by works of art, is less likely to be disturbed by *Susanna,* whose title has kept it immured for the private delectation of scholars, than by *Solomon,* in which the dalliance of Solomon with the Queen of Sheba contrasts violently with his relationship with his own vapid queen. *Solomon* has a considerable number of double choruses of great splendour, but their omnipresence is inclined to add an overplay of sententiousness to a work of uneven quality.

Regarding *Theodora* there remains evidence of Handel's private opinion. Handel possessed a rare perspicuity in self-criticism, and his judgment should be respected. He, so Morrell wrote,

> valued it more than any performance of the kind, and when I once asked him, whether he did not look upon the Grand Chorus in *The Messiah* as his masterpiece? "No," says he, "I think the chorus at the end of the second part in Theodora far beyond it, 'He saw the lovely Youth.'"

Theodora has the maturity and the same mellowed courtesy that Shakespeare displays in *The Winter's Tale*. A Christian story, a rare choice for Handel, *Theodora* looses the gloom from eighteenth- and nineteenth-century religion by seizing on the attractiveness of the first Christians—an attractiveness which embraced courage. In the springtime of the faith the devout had not forgotten the pleasances of paganism. The geniality of "Come, mighty Father" is worship of a more affectionate order than that to which the more ecclesiastical choruses in other oratorios admit us and springs in refinement from the rites of Venus and Flora, which also find eloquent expression in this work. There is in *Theodora* a contemplative quality and an intimacy revealing old Handel detached personally from the conflict of life, but in complete sympathy with the victims of catastrophe.

Finally there comes *Jephtha:* the *summa summarum*. The greatness of *Jephtha* reposes in Handel's philosophic absorption in the vast problem propounded by the plot—the obedience of man to the legislation of eternity. The abstract philosophy is carried by the chorus whose utterances, nine of them, lie rooted in the earthly actions of Jephtha, but offshoot towards the universal. The climactic, quadripartite "How dark, O Lord, are Thy decrees," placed (let it be noted) after Jephtha's desperate "Deeper and deeper still," contains the human acknowledgment of divine supremacy, achieved only after mystified and even angry protestation against the uncertainty of the pilgrimage. Handel, with blindness imminent (indeed, it was the above-mentioned chorus which suffered interruption on this account), had reason to follow his argument closely, for he knew himself to be in the inexorable grasp of destiny. The averting of a tragic denouement is accomplished in *Jephtha* by the intermission of an *angelus ex machina*, but the low-level drama of Jephtha, Iphis, Storge and Hamour is of small consequence beside that traced by the finger of God. Against the severity of the Almighty, however, Handel places a tranquillity in heaven which draws peace over the final stages of life. The opening of the "Cherub and seraphim," with its arpeggio-wrought effulgence, first cousin to the opening of *Zadok the Priest*, paints a picture which finds reflection in the lambent beauty of "Waft her, angels," the serene token of Jephtha's ultimate acceptance of the beneficence of divine governance, and in the music with which Iphis prepares to leave the world.

It is easy and natural to have talent at twenty; to have talent still at forty, that is the best; to keep it until old age, when it has been enriched by the experience of a lifetime, that is to be something more than a man of talent. Genius is always rare, and always admirable; but most admirable when it has matured into something that is uniquely personal.[9]

What Handel wrote at twenty and at forty may be easily discovered. What he wrote after the age of sixty reveals the unique genius of the man, and no work more than *Jephtha*, which secretes immortality in an awareness of spiritual adventure, in the hopefulness of perennial youth, and in the expression of the experience of a full life.

[9] R. C. Trevelyan, *Windfalls*.

Chapter 15

A Miscellany

BEYOND THE PALE of oratorio lies a sequence of works, neither opera nor oratorio, though related to both, which may only be ignored at the risk of falling victim to the Chadband-Handel myth. We move round the periphery which bounds the familiar terrain to discover a variety of entertainment reminiscent more of the spontaneity of the seventeenth than of the sophistication of the eighteenth century. The boundary between one age and another or between one form of art and another—Quiller-Couch's analogy with the limits which administratively settle where one county ends and the next begins may aptly be remembered—only assumes *raison d'être* when a certain distance from the arbitrary dividing line is covered on one side or the other. In respect of Handel rigid categorization, except where the cataloguer orders his lists, is impossible. Difficulties were early encountered. *Acis and Galatea* was variously described as a serenata (*Daily Journal*, 5th June 1732), which term also belonged to the earlier *Aci, Galatea e Polifemo,* as a pastoral (*Daily Journal*, 13th March 1731), as a pastoral opera (*Daily Post*, 2nd May 1732) and as a "Mask" in Walsh's edition of 1730. Twenty-six years later the last term reappeared. The *Norwich Mercury* of Saturday, 28th February 1756 recorded:

> Cambridge, Feb. 26. On Thursday night the Mask of Acis and Galatea was performed at Trinity Coll: Hall before a very numerous audience and was conducted by Dr. Randall, Professor of Music in this University.

From masque, the thoroughbred seventeenth-century stock, came the ideals of English opera. English opera, that is, as it was to develop under Purcell and receive its most extensive, elegant, odd and moving expression in *The Fairy Queen*. Masque entailed poetry—how exquisite may be judged from reference to the occasional offerings of Ben Jonson, Campion, William Browne of Tavistock and others of their courtly order. And it was poetry incapable of affiliation with the necessary music for the glamorous atmosphere of the public theatre. Masque also entailed dancing, the culmination of whose music was in *The Fairy Queen,* and the painting of scenery. The backcloths of Inigo Jones are the finest things of this sort in the history of the English stage. The place for masque was at court on the occasion of a royal wedding, a coronation, the visit of a foreign potentate or a royal coming-of-age. Some pearls were produced, but as they were cast before swine they were disallowed by the Cromwell regime. To be fair to the Puritans it should be admitted that Inigo Jones's landscapes concealed many scenes of lechery. The idea of the masque, however, never died, so that Purcell depended on it, as later did Rich in his pantomimes (with music by Galliard) and Arne in *Alfred,* which properly fitted a garden party given by the Prince of Wales. Handel caught the spirit and when first presented with a piece of really lyrical poetry inscribed the music of *Acis and Galatea*.

Appropriateness, according to Dionysius of Halicarnassus, is the chief source of beauty. This thought may be applied justly to whatever Handel wrote, but in the particular instance of *Acis and Galatea* it will be seen that his appreciation of Gay's poetry—an echo of the whimsy of Jonson's *Oberon*[1] and a Jonsonian transmutation of classical into English country scenes—a feeling of affection for a legend which may at one time have impinged on a classical education, plus the knowledge that his finished work would adorn a *fête champêtre,* produced a masterpiece of Arcadianism, refined yet mixed with a

[1] Which masque was used by Arne in 1771 as the basis of *The Fairy Prince*.

natural zest which kept the music free from preciosity. The whole thing, excepting that voluminous "Wretched lovers" chorus, catches at the heart like a memorable verse by Chaucer. *Acis and Galatea* is no oratorio, nor should it be performed like an oratorio. Put it on a sunny lawn on a summer's day.

Holst wrote of *Acis and Galatea* and that even sunnier companion work *L'Allegro*: "Why didn't the old chap write more of that sort of thing?" He did. He wrote notably *Semele*. Congreve designed *Semele* as an opera libretto in 1710. The year is perhaps worth noting and it may be speculated whether Handel, possibly knowing Congreve through his other literary associates, was on the point of treating this promising theme when the Academy project came to monopolize his attentions. However that may be, *Semele* remained untouched until 1744. Then it served as an antidote to piety. It was, said Mainwaring, "after the manner of an oratorio an English opera, but called an oratorio"—a pretty jugglery with nomenclature. But whatever *Semele* may be called it is, as the argument indicates in the word-book, a characteristic Renaissance flirtation with paganism.

After Jupiter's amour with Europa, the daughter of Agenor, king of Phoenicia, he again incenses Juno by a new affair in the same family, viz., with Semele, niece of Europa, and daughter to Cadmus, king of Thebes. Semele is on the point of marriage with Athamas, a prince of Boeotia; which marriage is about to be solemnized in the temple of Juno, goddess of marriages, when Jupiter, by ill omens, interrupts the ceremony, and afterwards transports Semele to a private abode prepared for her. Juno, after many contrivances, at length assumes the shape and voice of Ino, sister to Semele; by the help of which disguise, and artful insinuations, she prevails with Semele to make a request to Jupiter, which, being granted, must end in her ruin.

The surprise is that this was allowed in English, and in Lent.

Semele has its moments of tension, as in the lengthy recitative of Cadmus, "Ah wretched Prince," which culminates in the terse description of the seizure of Semele by Jupiter, with versatility appearing here as an eagle, and in the aerial ascent of raped and raper to the "Waft her, angels" formula; in Juno's magnificent "Awake Saturnia"; in the concluding scene which grows out of Semele's request and Jupiter's oath. But the same diversionary air overhangs the music as in *Acis and Galatea*. The story, indicates Handel, is a fable of no consequence, so what he allows to remain freshest in the memory is a distillation of nature's charms. "Where'er you walk" in fact is the perfect summary.

A year later Handel once again retreated into classical antiquity. *Hercules,* done from Sophocles (*The Women of Trachis*) by the Rev. T. Broughton,[2] in contrast to *Semele,* is a work accurately described by its first advertisement as "a new musical drama." Like *Saul, Hercules* is a study in jealousy. It is also, like *Saul,* a commentary on human impotence. Dejanira's murder of her husband (one may agree with her in her judgment of Hercules's motives in bringing back captive the beautiful Iole from Oechalia) illustrates this impotence in simple form. Hercules is done to death painfully, and after cremation, a process warmly described in "Oh Jove! What land is this?" lands safely among the senior deities with easy access to nectar and ambrosia. Dejanira, however, wins more sympathy than Saul. She is richer in portraiture, more heroic and defeated by a problem which might beset any woman passing the prime of her beauty and encountering an apparent rival of Iole's calibre. The whole of Dejanira is contained in the honest-to-goodness scolding of "Resign thy club" (a title which should not be misinterpreted): an upright woman with a rasping tongue and a malignant impetuosity. Iole is a fitting foil to the older woman; graceful in movement, dignified in rebuttal of the false charges laid against her, sympathetic to Dejanira when she should have forfeited all claims to sympathy and courageous in grief. Iole is the ripest of Handel's

[2] A well-known scholar and translator of *Don Quixote*.

young women, and marriage with Hyllus, son of Hercules, is (we may hope) a deserved reward for virtuous living under conditions of difficulty. Hercules himself is a bluff soldier with equal zest, if we read the music aright, for battle, murder and sudden death (provided that he is the dispenser) and bucolic sports. He also has a simplicity of character which places him immediately within the environs of sympathy.

The chorus appropriately holds a Greek position in abstract commentary. The quality of the individual choruses is uniformly high and, as in *Samson,* there is a pervasive flexibility. Thus a passage in doubled sixths illuminates the festivities which, at the end of Act I greet the returning Hercules:

And thus with subtle insinuation comment is made on the affection of Hyllus for Iole:

The uniqueness of *Hercules,* however, rests not so much on high technical competence as on the sensitive response of the music to changes of mood in the drama. Dejanira holds tragedy in mind in her first aria. Anxiety for her lord and master is the immediate source of melancholy, but deeper lies the intensity of the unknown grief. Notice the chromatic suspense—and Handel used such effects only rarely:

Parallel with this is the acridity of Iole's lament for her father:

with which dissonant discomfiture Handel points the despair which resolves itself in the anaesthetic resignation of "Peaceful rest." One more illustration must suffice to indicate the dramatic integrity of *Hercules*. During Act II Dejanira recalls that she has possession of a robe, dipped in the blood of Nessus which

> *boasts a wondrous virtue, to revive*
> *The expiring flame of love: so Nessus told me,*
> *When dying to my hand he trusted it—*
> *I will prevail with Hercules to wear it,*
> *And prove its magic force—*

So Dejanira in good faith endeavours to overcome her fears of infidelity (that her fears were groundless heightens the dramatic tension) and the chorus respond with delicious satisfaction at so happy a denouement:

Love and Hy-men, hand in hand, Come, re - store the nup-tial band!

This completes the second act. From such a climax of contentment Act III immediately plunges us into disaster. The robe was poisoned. Act III is a drama within a drama. Hercules dies in agony: Dejanira maddens as Handel lashes her with the snakes of Alecto, with the vision of "Megaera fell, and black Tisiphone" in an aria which carries the unearthly impress of terror Blake understood. But from the trough of despair all are led by Jupiter, who sends his messenger to terminate the drama. An inevitable conclusion, but more appropiate to this excursion into antiquity than to the oratorios. That is if art and philosophy must be bounded by theology.

Another classical adaptation, the *Alcestis* (*Alcides* in the edition of Arnold), was arranged for Handel by Smollett. This English opera was metamorphosed into *The Choice of Hercules,* as for some reason or other Rich's projected performance never came off. With the minor works of attractive parts must be placed the incidental music to Ben Jonson's *The Alchymist* which, although reduced from *Rodrigo* in some part, has an antique simplicity in its airs and dances:

recalling the flavour of Lupo or Coperario, intimates of Jonson's and his particular composers, and pioneers whose honour has been neglected. Then there is the *Terpsichore* music which Arnold, with an eye unconsciously directed at the progenitors of so much music of the class, again designated "A Masque."

There are a hundred or so Italian cantatas and duets, whose composition at various times provided exercise in conventionality and ephemeral pleasure for the eclectic. The cantatas, after the manner of operatic scenes, and the duets, after the model of Steffani, were easy carriers of mellifluence. Their influence was ubiquitous.

The genius of Handel was so pervasive that no work of his may entirely be ignored and we must be reluctant to draw the line at any point short of the complete pilgrimage. Yet here it must be done. This chapter was designed to segregate fine secularity and to free Handel from the eternal curse attached by the sentimental to a "sacred" musician. The final conclusion is that in Handel there is neither Jew nor Gentile, neither bond nor free: there is a corpus of integrated membership, which, transcending critical definition, can only be comprehended by those who believe in the final independence of music and are willing to lay aside the dark glass of prejudice and pedantry to see the music—and the man—face to face.

Chapter 16

L'Envoi

"There, Sir, is the portrait of the inspired master of our art; when I open my eyes in the morning, I look upon him with reverential awe, and acknowledge him as such, and the highest praise is due to your country for having distinguished and cherished his gigantic genius."[1]

So GLUCK, IN his bedroom, delivered his private thoughts to Michael Kelly as they stood before a rich-framed painting of Handel. A man may be judged from the quality of his friends, and Handel's represent a catholic assortment. The tributes of those who followed the same vocation may be considered, not because they are of necessity the most valuable, but because they display a degree of unanimity unusual in artists. The man commanded universal respect and indeed affection, but so too did his art. So much so that Handel was regarded by his greatest successors as the *fons et origo* of music and the tutelary genius of musicians. Intellectual genuflection was first made by Gluck. The gesture was impressive in that his reception by Handel in London—in 1747—was brusque and hardly encouraging.

"You have taken too much trouble over your opera," said the old man, having eyed the score of *La caduta*

---

[1] Kelly, *Reminiscences*, i. 255. One assumes that Gluck meant England and not Ireland, although it would be attractive to think that Gluck regarded an Irishman as an Irishman and not as an Englishman, and that he intended some tribute to the politeness of the generous nation which welcomed Handel in 1742.

dei giganti. "Here in England that is mere waste of time.
What the English like is something they can beat time to
[Charles II was, according to Evelyn, the founder of the
pulsatory school of appreciation], something that hits
them straight on the drum of the ear."[2] Which is, after
all, a legitimate and homely interpretation of a fundamental of musical expression. If there was one lesson
taught by Handel to posterity, and to Gluck according to
Burney, it was that periphrasis is anathema.

An early and notable victim of Handel's straight-hitting
faculty was Haydn. After hearing "The nations tremble"
from *Joshua* he told Shield that "He had long been acquainted with the music, but never knew half its powers
before he heard it, and he was perfectly certain that only
one inspired author ever did, or ever could, pen so
sublime a composition."[3] On another occasion Shield
complimented Haydn on the quality of his recitatives in
Il ritorno di Tobia. "Ah!" exclaimed Haydn with that engaging habit of his of self-denigration, "'Deeper and
deeper,' in *Jephtha*, is far beyond that."[4] The obvious influence of Handel on Haydn produced *The Creation*, the
text for which had been lying about since before Handel's
death. Haydn undertook this work after having experienced a Lenten season of Handel in 1794.

Mozart's counterpoint frequently reflected that of the
master whose music he recollected having to read at sight
under the critical eye of George III. An imitative fugue
(the fugues of Handel were frequent companions to his
studies) and the re-orchestrations of *Acis and Galatea,
Messiah, Alexander's Feast* and the *Ode for St. Cecilia's
Day* betokened affection. It was these versions which started the canard about Handel's impotence in orchestration.
The responsibility was van Swieten's, who in enthusiasm
ordered the new scoring. Handel might have cursed van
Swieten for his effrontery, but he would have complimented Mozart on his acceptance of a welcome commission. Handel, unlike many who profess to be Handelians,

[2] Schmid, *C. W. von Gluck*, p. 29.
[3] Shield, *Rudiments of Thorough Bass*, p. 69.
[4] Ibid.

deplored indigence among artists and considered that it was the duty of a composer to undertake the particular tasks set by his patrons. Gottfried van Swieten introduced Handel to Vienna, having heard works by the master in Berlin. The credit for the German revival that was strong in Hamburg, Leipzig, and Berlin, is due to Michael Arne who first directed *Alexander's Feast* and The *Messiah* privately in Hamburg, in 1771 and 1772; to C. P. E. Bach, who gave the first German version of The *Messiah* in 1775; and to the German translators, Klopstock and Eberling.[5] Through this pioneer work came the enthusiasm behind Chrysander's great undertaking, and the fruitful labours in more recent times of scholars and conductors in Göttingen and Halle.

Of his peers Beethoven was perhaps the most generous in his appraisal of Handel. "He was the greatest composer that ever lived. I would uncover my head, and kneel before his tomb."[6] And again, when forty volumes of Arnold's edition came to him on his deathbed: "There is the truth."

Handel was never so much alive as when he was dead. For this there were two principal reasons. The first was George III; a discriminating music-lover and consistently generous in his promotion of Handel's posthumous fame. He supported the commemoration performances of 1784 —that mammoth progenitor[7] of all musical festivals and choral constipation—encouraged Arnold's edition and was graciously pleased to accept from Christopher Smith those manuscripts which now glorify the royal collection. But with George III there was more to it than mere monarchic patronage. He could pen a critical memorandum to Burney's account of the commemoration:

> Dr. Burney seems to forget the great merit of the choral fugue "He trusted in God," by asserting that the words would admit of no stroke of passion. Now

[5] *Vide: Über die ersten Messias-Aufführungen in Deutschland,* Walther Siegmund-Schultze, in *Händel-Jahrbuch,* Vol. VI, 1960.

[6] *Vide: Beethoven and Handel,* Donald MacArdle, *Music and Letters,* January 1960, p. 33 *et seq.*

[7] Upwards of five hundred musicians participated.

the real truth is, that the words contain a manifest presumption and impertinence, which Handel has, in the most masterly manner, taken advantage of. And [this observation throws interesting light on Handel's methods of extemporization] he was so conscious of the moral merit of that movement, that, whenever he was desired to sit down to the harpsichord, if not instantly inclined to play, he used to take this subject; which ever got his inspiration at work, and made him produce wonderful capriccios.

It may be suspected that the court grew a little weary of the subject of Handel. When the king left off, Mrs. Delany, a royal pensioner, would lapse into fond reminiscence.

On a memorable day in 1789 Fanny Burney ran into the king in the gardens at Kew. Fanny was terrified. The king was not well and under restraint. On this morning, however, an interval of tired sanity prevailed. The king called to Fanny, kissed her cheek, and "What a conversation followed! When he saw me fearless, he grew more and more alive, and made me walk by his side. . . ." The conversation eventually turned to Dr. Burney and the *History*.

> This brought him to his favourite theme, Handel; and he told me innumerable anecdotes of him, and particularly that celebrated tale of Handel's saying of himself, when a boy: "While that boy lives, my music will never want a protector." And this, he said, I might relate to my father.
>
> Then he ran over most of his oratorios, attempting to sing the subjects of several airs and choruses, but so dreadfully hoarse that the sound was terrible.[8]

The second principal to Handel's immortality was the revivification of religious fervour. The Catholic church in its wisdom affords ample opportunity for emotional exultation, both in its liturgy and its furniture. The Protestant creeds, having renounced these riches, were obliged

[8] Fanny Burney, *Diary*, 2nd February 1789.

in the course of time to find compensation in other ways. Hence the inauguration of romantic hymnody in the eighteenth century. Handel had written a chorus which had brought even a king to his feet. If it were necessary to summarize the religious character of the English people during the late eighteenth and early nineteenth centuries one word would suffice—Hallelujah. Hallelujah, which split the establishment, opened the eyes of the blind, brought sinners to tearful repentance, lit the ceremonial fires on Mow Cop, inspired the erection of a thousand conventicles and sent Handel rampaging the country like one of his Old Testament heroes. When a rich sequence of Hallelujahs was discovered to belong to a work entitled *Messiah* the terminology caught at the imagination of those whose spiritual pabulum was the Old Testament. It was part of Handel's misfortune, and part too of his glory, that his music should readily have become an integral part of the Englishman's religion. Anecdote was useful in supporting the position. There were memories of the aged and beloved Handel presiding in his latter days over performances for the benefit of the foundlings, of the constant worshipper at St. George's, Hanover Square, of the visionary who was reported to have seen the opened heavens in the white heat of inspiration, of the sublime deathbed and of the last wish that he might die on Good Friday "in hopes of meeting his good God, his sweet Lord and Saviour on the Day of His Resurrection." The Great (and Good) Mr. Handel was born in 1759.

Thus the subsequent public history of Handel is that of *Messiah* and fitting excerpts from a limited number of other oratorios. In the *Chester Courant* for 9th June 1772 appeared a notice which will serve to show what stimulus Handel gave to the provinces both in religious and in musical development. Many who remembered Handel's encounter with the saucy Johnson (precisely entered by one treasurer of the cathedral as Ap John) thirty years before would have been provoked to reminiscence by the following:

On Tuesday, the 16th instant will be performed in

the Broad Isle of the Cathedral, of this City, the Oratorio of

"MESSIAH"

On Wednesday Evening, the 17th, will be performed in the Exchange,

A Miscellaneous Concert of Select Pieces of Music, Vocal and Instrumental, the particulars of which will be expressed in the bills of the day.

The principal vocal parts by Miss Linley, Miss M. Linley, Messrs. Norris, Price, Matthews, etc.

The Instrumental by several of the most eminent performers from different parts of the Kingdom.

On Thursday the 18th, will be performed, the Oratorio of

"SAMSON"

And on Friday, the 19th, will be performed the Oratorio of "JUDAS MACCHABAEUS." No person to be admitted without tickets, which may be had at Messrs. Smith and Green's offices, opposite the White Lion, and all the Book Sellers' shops; where likewise may be had Books of the Several Oratorios.

N.B. The South Door and the Cloister Door of the Cathedral will be opened each morning at Ten o'clock, and the performance will begin exactly at Eleven.[9]

And that, more or less, has been going on ever since. Occasionally the higher powers showed their approval by contributing to the orchestration. Once Jupiter capped Handel's thunderbolt. It was during a performance in 1791 at York of *Israel in Egypt* that a storm burst. Michael Kelly related how

[9] The history of Handel at Chester is admirably told in Dr. J. C. Bridge's "The Organists of Chester Cathedral": *Journal of the Architectural, Archaeological and Historic Society* (Chester), vol. xix, and in R. V. H. Burne's *Chester Cathedral*, London 1958, p. 200 et seq.

never before or since did I behold such a tremendous night,—such bursts of Heaven's artillery, and such sheets of fire, combined with the sacred words and the majestic music of the mighty master, were altogether appalling and magnificent.[10]

Religion and Handel were not confined to cathedral churches. There were the new foundations of the Methodists to which a hitherto musically disfranchized class were gradually drawn. Singing brought vision into the new squalor of industrial England and dignity to the singers. Handelian choruses levered latent talent into operation and became the priceless property (via the tonic sol-fa class) of the factory workers of Lancashire and Yorkshire, the potters of Staffordshire and the miners of Wales. Handel, who had among his early friends an unashamed coalman from Clerkenwell, would have been pleased. Here we may tread out of music into sociology to contemplate our grandparents escaping from the muck of Manchester to the vision of the glory of the Lord as revealed to them by Handel. Here the cynic stands dumb. We have heard what Gluck, Mozart, Haydn and Beethoven said about Handel. What they did in the Potteries may be remembered as a greater tribute. In 1892 the Hanley Glee and Madrigal Society received an invitation to sing Gaul's *Israel in the Wilderness* at the Crystal Palace. The invitation was declined because the choir preferred to stay at home to practise *Israel in Egypt*.[11]

Almost without noticing it we have traversed a hundred years in a couple of paragraphs. A hundred years during which the settlement of oratorio left as well as its positive aspect a negative legacy. Under the impact of the newly cultivated vice of respectability—a quality which in the eighteenth century was literally laughed out of court—the Victorians lost the vivacity of Handel (nor has it yet been regained) and let choral singing deteriorate to the stand-

[10] Kelly, op. cit., ii. 8.

[11] The subject of the Handel cult in the English provinces is fully discussed by me in a contribution to the *Händel-Jahrbuch* of 1960.

ards of community singing: they habituated themselves, as Bernard Shaw puts it, to "lumbering along with Hallelujah as if it were a superior sort of family coach."[12] Worse than that, they welcomed the fitful enlightenment of the twilight corybantic Christianity by the lucubrations of repressed academists. Israel went with Gaul to the Wilderness and stayed there for a long time. The enemies of sacred music are not the religious but the religiose.

Rejecting an excellent book a friend commented the other day: "There's too much imagination about this. I like facts." Which is a fair and concise exposition of the artistic creed mistakenly believed by the English to be the one they follow. The truth is that our imagination proceeds from a pragmatic terminus. But as we look at the world around us we allow a fertilization of fancy. Thus poetry exudes from common things. Unconsciously we take the validity of poetry for granted and therefore tend to deny its existence. Because he too starts from earthly phenomena and from commonplace actions and invests them with the imagery of poetic aspiration Handel finds house-room with us. This is the secret of his genius.

Matthew Arnold preached that poetry should be a criticism of life. It is not clear that he knew precisely what he meant himself. We may, however, approximate to his idealism if we contemplate the uniqueness of Handel. He was, above almost all other composers, lively because he was full of life. His music, moreover, is a part of life. The least literate among music-lovers will appreciate this. Epping Forest on a summer's day recalls a song from *Semele,* or perhaps from *Serse;* the Thames at Richmond the *Water Music;* civic or military festivity the march from *Rinaldo;* athletic victory a chorus from *Joshua;* surpliced choir-boys an air from *Theodora;* the burial of the dead a march from *Saul.* No other music serves in quite the same intimate and yet universal way. No other music, so far as we are concerned, is so oblivious of time. Handel, like Shakespeare and Dante, wrote for his audience:

---

[12] Shaw, op. cit., i. 110.

their glory is that they have outlasted the conditions they observed. Yet it was by observing them that they gained the world's ear. Let us, who are less than they, beware of seeming to belong to our own time.[13]

Handel was a Londoner, the musician laureate of the *beau monde*. But into the stifling air of the city he brought the fragrance of the country. Not all his time was spent in Brook Street. This is too often forgotten. The eye of fancy follows the coach routes. Handel views the garden of Kent, stands on the spaciousness of Salisbury Plain, looks at the royal antiquities of Chester and dreams by the Dove. Did they tell him about Izaak Walton? At Calwich, in the freshest country in England, they put a monument to Handel—an eighteenth-century pavilion. They call it still—Bernard Granville's house is gone, but the pavilion remains in quiet testimony to the fragrance of a near-forgotten friendship—with divided dedication the Temple of Handel and of fishing.

Handel was a Londoner, but he loved England. He became an Englishman, but he loved Europe. The story of this book is of a lover of humanity, of one who understood his fellow men and wrote their character with affection and optimism in the imperishable terms of great music. Manly music which springs from the contemplation of man. Is that not the source of the philosophy of the Augustans?

They wrote of him after his death:

Such was Handel, in whose character whatever there was wrong there was nothing mean; though he was proud his pride was uniform; he was not by turns a tyrant and a slave: a censor in one place and a sycophant in another; he maintained his liberty in a state in which others would have been vain of dependence: he was liberal even when he was poor, and remembered his former friends when he was rich. . . .[14]

[13] Quiller-Couch, *On the Art of Writing*, p. 44.
[14] *Gentleman's Magazine*, May 1760.

Appendix A

CALENDAR

(*Figures in brackets denote the age reached by the person mentioned during the year in question.*)

Year	Age	Life	Contemporary Musicians
1685		Georg Friedrich Händel born Feb. 23, at Halle, son of Georg Händel (63), district surgeon and barber.	Bach born, March 21; Scarlatti (D.) born, Oct. 26. Abaco aged 10; Albinoni 11; Ariosti *c.* 25; Blow 37; Böhm 24; Buononcini 13; Buxtehude 48; Caldara *c.* 15; Campra 25; Charpentier *c.* 50; Clarke *c.* 25; Corelli 33; Couperin 17; Croft 7; Desmarets 23; Destouches *c.* 13; Durante 1; Eccles *c.* 22; Fux 25; Geminiani 5; Keiser 11; Kerl 57; Kuhnau 25; Lalande 28; Legrenzi *c.* 60; Lotti 18; Lully 53; Muffat (sen.) *c.* 40; Pachelbel 32; Pasquini 48; Pepusch 18; Purcell 26; Rameau 2; Reinken 62; Scarlatti (A.) 26; Steffani 31; Telemann 4; Vivaldi *c.* 15.
1686	1		Marcello born, July 31/Aug. 1; Porpora born, Aug. 19.

Year	Age	Life	Contemporary Musicians
1687	2		Graupner born, Feb.; Lully (55) dies, March 22; Senaillé born, Nov. 23.
1688	3		Fasch (J. F.) born, April 15; Foggia (84) dies, Jan. 8.
1689	4		
1690	5		Carey born (approx.); Legrenzi (c. 65) dies, July 26; Muffat (jun.) born, April; Vinci born.
1691	6		d'Anglebert (63) dies.
1692	7	Learns to play the clavichord. His father (70) has no intention of encouraging a musical career.	Tartini born, April 8; Vitali (G. B.) (c. 48) dies, Oct. 12.
1693	8	Visit to court at Weissenfels, where he plays the organ so well that the duke advises his father (71) to let him have competent tuition. To this no objections are raised.	Kerl (65) dies, Feb. 13; Locatelli born; Sammartini (G.) born (approx.).
1694	9	Begins to study under Zachau (31). He progresses on the clavier and organ, and takes up the violin and oboe. His general education proceeds at the Gymnasium.	Daquin born, July 4; Leo born, Aug. 5.
1695	10	Makes great progress and begins to compose. 6 Sonatas for two oboes and bass.	Greene born; Purcell (36) dies, Nov. 21.
1696	11	Visit to Berlin, where he plays at court. An offer of assistance in respect of advanced	

Year	Age	Life	Contemporary Musicians
		musical tuition is refused by his father (74), who wishes him to take up legal studies. The boy returns to Halle.	
1697	12	Death of H.'s father (75), Feb. 11. He continues musical studies and writes a number of church cantatas and organ pieces.	Leclair born, May 10; Quantz born, Jan. 30.
1698 1699 1700	13 14 15	Composes much in his spare time.	Francœur born, Sept. 28. Hasse born, March 25. Strungk (60) dies, Sept. 23.
1701	16	First contact with Telemann.	Graun born, May 7; Sammartini (G. B.) born.
1702	17	Enters Halle University as a law student, Feb. 10. Leporin, who makes a habit of defaulting, is dismissed from the cathedral and H. is appointed organist, March 13. Large number of church cantatas composed.	
1703	18	Ends his University studies and resigns his organist's post, spring. Meets Steffani at Hanover (?). He goes to Hamburg, where Mattheson (22) assists him to become known as organist and clavier player, and he becomes second violin at the Opera under the management of Keiser (29). Visit to Lübeck,	Lampe born.

Year	Age	Life	Contemporary Musicians
		Aug., to see if the succession to Buxtehude (66) can be secured; but as this means marrying Buxtehude's daughter, Anna Margreta (28), both H. and Mattheson refrain from applying for the succession. Return to Hamburg.	
1704	19	Passion according to St. John performed, Lent. Opera, *Almira*, begun. Quarrel with Mattheson (23) over the playing of the continuo in the latter's opera, *Cleopatra*, Dec. 5, and reconciliation, Dec. 30.	Biber (60) dies; Charpentier (*c.* 69) dies, March; Muffat (sen.) (*c.* 59) dies, Feb. 23.
1705	20	*Almira* produced at Hamburg, Jan. 8. It is very successful, and is repeated some twenty times. Second opera, *Nero*, produced, Feb. 25. The Hamburg Opera begins to deteriorate under Keiser (31). H. dissociates himself from it and takes pupils.	
1706	21	Many songs, harpsichord pieces and cantatas composed, also (approx.) the operas *Florindo* and *Daphne* (originally one work, but divided because of its length). Departure for Florence. Secular	Galuppi born, Oct. 18; Martini born, April 24.

Year	Age	Life	Contemporary Musicians

cantatas composed there. He is introduced to Prince Ferdinando de' Medici at Pratolini, near Florence, and (?) meets Alessandro Scarlatti (47) there, Sept.

1707 22 Leaves Florence for Rome, Jan. (approx.). Psalms, *Dixit Dominus, Laudate pueri* and other Latin church music composed there. Return to Florence, July, where his first Italian opera, *Rodrigo,* is produced with great success. Visit to Venice, autumn.

Buxtehude (70) dies, May 9; Clarke (*c.* 47) dies, Dec. 1.

1708 23 Meeting with Lotti (41), Steffani (54), Gasparini (40) and Earl of Manchester in Venice and friendship with Domenico Scarlatti (23). Return to Rome, early spring, where he is received by the Arcadians. There he meets Corelli (55), Marcello (22) and Pasquini (71). He is also received by Prince Ruspoli and Cardinal Pietro Ottoboni (40). Oratorio, *La Resurrezione,* and cantata, *Il Trionfo del tempo e del disinganno,* com-

Blow (60) dies. Oct. 1.

Year Age	Life	Contemporary Musicians

posed in Rome, also secular cantatas to words by Cardinal Benedetto Pamfili (55), including *Apollo e Dafne* and *Fillide ed Aminta*. Departure for Naples, end of June. French canzonets in the style of Lully composed there. Meets Donna Laura. Pastoral play, *Aci, Galatea e Polifemo,* composed.

1709 24 Meeting with Cardinal Vincenzo Grimani, who commissions an opera for Venice from H. Third visit to Rome, spring. H. hears Calabrian shepherds sing and play their Christmas songs, end of year. Second visit to Venice for the carnival. Opera, *Agrippina*, produced there, Dec. 26.

Benda (F.) born, Nov. 25; Colasse (60) dies, July 17; Duni born, Feb. 9; Richter (F. X.) born, Dec.

1710 25 There he is encouraged by English and Hanoverian visitors, including Prince Ernest of Hanover and Baron Kielmansegge, to go to London. He makes the journey by way of Hanover, where he goes with Steffani (56), who resumes his duties at the electoral court there. He is appointed musical director by the

Arne born, March 12; Avison born (approx.); Bach (W. F.) born, Nov. 22; Boyce born, Feb. 7; Pasquini (73) dies, Nov. 22; Pergolesi born, Jan. 3.

Year	Age	Life	Contemporary Musicians
		Elector Georg Ludwig (50) and the visit to England is postponed until the autumn, when (?) he visits his mother at Halle and leaves for London. He is presented to Queen Anne (45), and Aaron Hill (25), manager of the King's Theatre, suggests an opera, *Rinaldo,* to him, which he composes, to an Italian libretto by Rossi, in a fortnight, using many earlier pieces.	
1711	26	Production of *Rinaldo,* Feb. 24. It is given fifteen times before the opera season closes on June 2. H. appears at Thomas Britton's (*c.* 67) musical club, meets Babell (*c.* 21), who arranges harpsichord lessons on airs from *Rinaldo,* and influential amateurs. Return to Hanover, early summer, after another visit to Düsseldorf. Visit to Halle, June. Steffani (57) shows him much kindness and influences him musically. Chamber duets composed for Princess Caroline of Ansbach. Oboe Concertos and 12 cantatas.	Holzbauer born.

Year Age	Life	Contemporary Musicians
1712 27	Asks leave of Georg Ludwig (52) for a second visit to England. It is granted on condition that he return within a reasonable time. Arrival in London, late autumn. Production of the opera, *Il pastor fido*, at the King's Theatre, Nov. 22. Opera, *Teseo* finished, Dec. 19.	Zachau (49) dies, Aug. 14.
1713 28	Production of *Teseo* at the King's Theatre, Jan. 10. The manager, Owen MacSwiney, fails and decamps, leaving H. and the singers unpaid; but they continue to give the opera at their own risk. *Te Deum* for the Peace of Utrecht finished, Jan. 14. Uncertain whether a work by a foreigner will be sung at the peace celebrations, H. writes a birthday ode for Queen Anne (48), which is sung, with one by Eccles (*c.* 50), Feb. 6. The queen is so delighted with it that she commands H. to have the *Te Deum* and a *Jubilate* ready for the celebrations. These take place at St. Paul's Cathedral, July 7. Anne is too ill to	Corelli (60) dies, Jan. 10; Dauvergne born, Oct. 4; Krebs born, Feb. 10; Terradellas born, Feb.

attend, but hears the
works privately later,
granting H. a yearly
salary of £200. The
Te Deum is modelled
on one by Purcell.
The Earl of Burling-
ton (18) invites H. to
live at his house in
Piccadilly and intro-
duces him to society.
Meeting with Pope
(25), Gay (28) and
Arbuthnot (46).

1714 29 Opera, *Silla,* (?) com-   Bach (C. P. E.) born,
posed and performed   March 8; Gluck born,
at Burlington House.   July 2; Homilius born,
Accession of the Elec-   Feb. 2; Jommelli born,
tor Georg Ludwig of   Sept. 10.
Hanover (54) to the
English throne as
George I.

1715 30 Opera, *Amadigi*, pro-   Alcock born, April 11;
duced at the King's   Nares born, April; Wag-
Theatre, May 25.   enseil born, Jan. 15.
Geminiani (35) intro-
duces H. (who for
obvious reasons had
kept out of the king's
way) to court by in-
sisting on being ac-
companied at the
harpsichord by him.

1716 31 Departure for Hanover in the suite of
George I (56), July.
Visit to Dresden in
search of singers for
London. Composition
of a Passion Oratorio
by Brockes (36). Vis-
its to Hamburg, Ans-
bach and Halle. Re-

Year Age	Life	Contemporary Musicians
	turn to London, end of year. *Concerto grosso,* F major (Op. 3, No. 4), composed for the benefit of the opera orchestra.	
1717 32	After revivals of *Rinaldo* and *Amadigi,* the opera season closes without any prospect of renewal, end of June. Music by H. played to the court on the Thames (*Water Music*), July 17.	Nichelmann born, Aug. 13; Purcell (Daniel) (*c.* 57) dies, Nov.; Stamitz (J. W.) born, June 19.
1718 33	The Earl of Carnarvon (45) invites H. to take up his residence at Canons, near Edgware, in succession to Pepusch (51). He is to conduct the band, play the organ and compose the *Chandos Anthems.*	Vitali (T. A.) (*c.* 53) dies (approx.).
1719 34	A Royal Academy of Music formed for the production of opera, Feb. The Earl of Carnarvon (47) created Duke of Chandos, April. H. goes to Germany in search of singers. He finds one at Düsseldorf. Letter to Burlington. Summer spent at Hanover. Visit to Dresden, July-Sept. There he secures several Italian singers for the London season of 1721, meets Lotti (52) again and plays	

before the Elector
Frederick Augustus I
(49) of Saxony. Visit
to Halle, autumn,
where his sister, Doro-
thea Sophia Michael-
sen, has died in 1718.
Return to London.
Composition of the
pastoral cantata *Acis
and Galatea,* the poem
by Gay (34).

1720 35 Italian opera season   Agricola (J. F.) born,
under the auspices of   Jan. 4.
the Royal Academy
of Music opens at the
King's Theatre under
H.'s direction, April 2.
Opera, *Radamisto,*
produced there, April
27. The masque, *Ha-
man and Mordecai*
(*Esther,* H.'s first English oratorio), per-
formed at Canons,
Aug. 29. First book
of Suites for harpsi-
chord published, Nov.
14. Opening of the
second Royal Acad-
emy season with
Astarto by Buononcini
(48), who comes to
London, Nov. 19.
Most of the *Concerti
grossi* (Op. 3) com-
posed at Canons.

1721 36 Production of the op-   Kirnberger born, April.
era, *Muzio Scevola,* at
the King's Theatre,
April 15. The third
act is by H., the sec-

ond by Buononcini (49) and the first either by Ariosti (*c.* 61) or by the cellist Filippo Mattei. The public begins to be divided in its adherence to H. or Buononcini. The latter gains the upper hand after the opening of the third Royal Academy season, Nov. 1, the public, unsettled by the bursting of the South Sea Bubble, favouring lighter entertainments. Production of the opera, *Floridante*, Dec. 9.

1722 37 H.'s popularity diminishes. Opening of the fourth Royal Academy season, Nov. 7. The opera, *Ottone*, on a libretto by Nicola Haym, is postponed until the arrival of Francesca Cuzzoni (*c.* 22), which has been delayed. She arrives end of Dec., but proves extremely obstinate, refusing to sing the aria "Falsa immagine" until H. seizes her and threatens to throw her out of the window.
Benda (G.) born, June 30; Kuhnau (62) dies, June 25; Nardini born; Reinken (99) dies, Nov. 24.

1723 38 *Ottone* produced at the King's Theatre, Jan. 12. It does much to reinstate H. in the
Gassmann born, May 4.

public favour. But
Flavio, produced May
14, has no great suc-
cess. Fifth Italian sea-
son opens, Nov. 27.

1724 39 Ariosti's (*c.* 64) op-   Theile (78) dies, June.
era, *Vespasiano,* pro-
duced Jan. 14, proves
such a failure as to
threaten the existence
of the Italian Opera.
H., to save the situa-
tion, hastily finishes
Giulio Cesare, which
is produced Feb. 20.
He plays the organ at
St. Paul's Cathedral
before the Princesses
Anne and Caroline,
his pupils, Aug. 24.
Sixth Royal Academy
season opens, Oct. 31.
Buononcini (52) has
been dismissed. Pro-
duction of the opera
Tamerlano, Oct. 31.

1725 40 Opera, *Rodelinda,* pro-   Krieger (J. P.) (76) dies,
duced at the King's   Feb. 6; Scarlatti (A.)
Theatre, Feb. 13. It   (66) dies, Oct. 24.
has an immense suc-
cess. Seventh Italian
season opens, Nov. 30.
Ariosti's (*c.* 65) en-
gagement is not re-
newed. John Christo-
pher Smith (Schmidt)
(13), son of H.'s treas-
urer, becomes his
pupil.

1726 41 H. becomes a natural-   Lalande (69) dies, June
ized Englishman, styles   18; Philidor born, Sept. 7.
himself George Frid-
eric Handel and is

Year	Age	Life	Contemporary Musicians

created, next to Croft (48), Composer of Musick to the Chapel Royal. Opera, *Scipione*, finished March 2 and produced March 12. Production of the opera, *Alessandro*, in which Faustina Bordoni (33), who has been newly engaged, appears as well as Francesca Cuzzoni (*c.* 26), May 5. A dangerous rivalry between the two singers develops.

1727 42 Eighth season of Italian opera opens at the King's Theatre, Jan. 7. Opera, *Admeto*, produced, Jan. 31. There is much disturbance, the public having split into two parties supporting either Bordoni (34) or Cuzzoni (*c.* 27). Opera, *Riccardo I*, finished, May 16. The two prima donnas engage in a hand-to-hand fight, to the delight of the audience, on the stage during a performance of Buononcini's *Astianatte*, which brings the season abruptly to a close, June 6. Coronation of George II (44), at which H.'s Coronation Anthems are sung, Oct. 11. Ninth opera

Croft (49) dies, Aug. 14; Traetta born, March 30.

Year Age   Life   *Contemporary Musicians*

season opens, Sept. 30. H. is now sole musical director, but the Royal Academy of Music is so disorganized by intrigues among the singers, and the public so discouraged by the violent demonstrations for and against the artists, that it is impossible to secure enough subscriptions. *Riccardo I* is produced, Nov. 11.

1728 43 Opera, *Siroe*, produced at the King's Theatre, Feb. 17, and *Tolomeo*, April 30. The King's Theatre closes, June 1, and the Royal Academy of Music in its original form is wound up. The public is tired of Italian opera and transfers its affection to Gay's (43) satire on it, *The Beggar's Opera*, which, with music arranged by Pepusch (61), has had an enormously successful run since its production on Jan. 29. A New Royal Academy of Music is formed for the production of Italian opera, summer, with Heidegger as manager and H. as musical director.

Hiller (J. A.) born, Dec. 25; Lœillet (*c.* 53) dies; Marais (72) dies, Aug.; Piccinni born, Jan. 16; Steffani (74) dies, Feb. 12.

1729 44 H. goes to Italy to hear new operas and engage singers, Jan. He visits

Monsigny born, Oct. 17; Sarti born, Dec. 1.

Florence, Milan, Venice, Rome and other cities and hears works by Porpora (42), Vinci (38), Hasse (29) and Pergolesi (18). He also becomes acquainted with the librettos of Metastasio (30). At the conclusion of his Italian tour, H. goes to Halle, where he finds his mother blind and infirm, June. Bach (44), who is ill at Leipzig, sends his son Wilhelm Friedemann (19) to Halle to invite H. to go and see him, but H. is unable to do so. Return to London, end of June. The new Italian season opens at the King's Theatre with the production of the opera, *Lotario,* Dec. 2. It has no great success and the new prima donna, Anna Strada del Pò, does not please.

1730 45   Opera, *Partenope,* produced at the King's Theatre, Feb. 24. Second New Royal Academy season opens with a revival of *Scipione,* Nov. 3, in which Senesino (*c.* 50) reappears.

Aylward born; Jackson born, May 29; Senaillé (43) dies, Oct. 15.

1731 46   Opera, *Poro,* set to Metastasio's (33) *Alessandro nell' Indie,*

Cannabich born.

Year Age   *Life*   *Contemporary Musicians*

produced, Feb. 2.
Stage performance
without choruses of
Acis and Galatea at
John Rich's (*c.* 49)
theatre in Lincoln's
Inn Fields, March 26.
Third New Royal
Academy season
opens, Nov. 13.

1732 47 Operas, *Ezio* and *So-*   Haydn born, March 31/
sarme, produced at   April 1; Linley born.
the King's Theatre,
Jan. 15 and Feb. 15.
Performance of the
oratorio, *Esther*, at
the house and under
the direction of Ber-
nard Gates (*c.* 47),
on H.'s birthday, Feb.
23. It is repeated at
the "Crown and An-
chor" under the aus-
pices of the Academy
of Ancient Music and,
May 2, at the King's
Theatre under H.'s
own direction. Inci-
dental music to Ben
Jonson's *The Alchy-
mist*, produced by
John Rich (*c.* 50) at
Covent Garden,
March 7. It is mainly
an adaptation of the
dance tunes from
Rodrigo of 1707.
Stage performance of
Acis and Galatea with
choruses, May 17.
Arne (22) conducts
and his sister, Susanna
Maria (18), sings the

	part of Galatea. H. himself gives another performance at the King's Theatre with a mixed cast of English and Italian artists, June 10. Some numbers of the earlier Italian version of 1708 are used. Fourth New Royal Academy season opens, Nov. 4. Opera, *Orlando*, finished, Nov. 20. A series of Sonatas for violin, flute or oboe and harpsichord (Op. 1) begun.	
1733 48	*Orlando* produced at the King's Theatre, Jan. 27. Oratorio, *Deborah*, produced there, March 17. H. dismisses Senesino (*c.* 53), who succeeds, with the help of his noble admirers, in opening a rival Italian opera in Lincoln's Inn Fields. Several singers forsake H., and the Prince of Wales's side of the court adheres to Senesino. Porpora (47) is engaged as musical director. Visit to Oxford, where he gives several performances and finishes the oratorio, *Athaliah*, which is produced there, July 10. He declines the title of Mus. D. offered him by the	Couperin (65) dies, Sept. 12.

university. Visit to
Italy to engage sing-
ers, including Cares-
tini (*c.* 28). Opera,
Arianna, finished, Oct.
5. H. opens his season
of Italian opera before
his opponents are
ready, Oct. 30. 6 Son-
atas for two violins,
flutes or oboes with
harpsichord (Op. 2)
published by Roger
(Amsterdam) and re-
printed by Walsh, who
also brings out a pir-
ated edition of a sec-
ond series of Suites
for harpsichord, con-
sisting of "lessons" for
Princess Anne.

1734 49 Opera, *Arianna*, pro-   Ayrton born; Carter born;
duced at the King's   Cooke (B.) born; Gossec
Theatre, Jan. 26. H.'s   born, Jan. 17; Sacchini
undertaking, being pa-   born, July 23.
tronized by the un-
popular court in op-
position to the adher-
ents of the Prince of
Wales, is deserted by
many members of so-
ciety, in spite of the
momentary success of
Carestini (*c.* 29).
First performance of
a new version of *Il
pastor fido* (*see*
1712), May 18. H.
quits the King's The-
atre, the lease of
which is at once dis-
posed of to the rival
company by Heideg-

ger. H. makes an arrangement with Rich (c. 52) to produce Italian opera alternately with English Drama at Covent Garden at popular prices, summer. The season opens in Lincoln's Inn Fields, Covent Garden not being ready, Oct. 5. Covent Garden opens with *Il pastor fido*, preceded by a ballet, *Terpsichore*, composed by H. at the request of Rich, who wishes Mlle Sallé to dance on this occasion, Nov. 9. 6 *Concerti grossi* (Op. 3) published, Dec. 7.

1735 50 Opera, *Ariodante*, produced at Covent Garden, Jan. 8, and *Alcina*, April 16. During Lent H. gives a series of fourteen concerts, at which he performs various oratorios and for which he composes two organ Concertos. Farinelli (30) being now attached to the rival company, H.'s losses become alarming and the season closes on July 2. After a cure at Tunbridge Wells, he retires from public life, autumn, and composes a version of

Bach (J. C.) born, Sept. 5; Eccles (c. 72) dies, Jan. 12; Krieger (J.) (83) dies, July 18.

Dryden's *Alexander's Feast* by Newburgh Hamilton. 6 Fugues for harpsichord published by Walsh.

1736 51 *Alexander's Feast* finished, Jan. 17, and first performed at Covent Garden, Feb. 19. Wedding Anthem performed at the marriage of the Prince of Wales, April 27. Opera season opens at Covent Garden, May 5. Production of the opera, *Atalanta,* in honour of the royal wedding, May 12. Farinelli's (31) success at the rival house is rapidly waning, and Fielding's (29) satirical play, *Pasquin,* deals a serious blow to Italian opera. Operas, *Arminio* and *Giustino,* finished, Oct. 14 and 20. Another season opens at Covent Garden, Nov. 6, and the rival company opens, Nov. 23, under the direction of Hasse (37), who has taken the place of Porpora (50).

Anfossi born (approx.); Caldara (*c.* 66) dies, Dec. 28; Fasch (C. F. C.) born, Nov. 18; Pergolesi (26) dies, March 17.

1737 52 Production of the operas, *Arminio,* Jan. 12, and *Giustino,* Feb. 16. During Lent H. gives performances of *Esther, Alexander's Feast*

Mysliveček born, March 9. Carey (*c.* 47) and Lampe (34) produce *The Dragon of Wantley,* a parody of *Giustino,* Oct. 26.

Year	Age	Life	Contemporary Musicians
		and a new version of *Il Trionfo del tempo* of 1708, also several new concertos for organ and other instruments. Worn out by financial cares and excess of work, he has a stroke which paralyses his right arm, April 13. Production of the opera, *Berenice,* May 18. H. undergoes a cure at Aix-la-Chapelle, late summer. He returns to London in better health, Nov. Heidegger, collecting the remains of the two failing Italian opera companies, opens a season at the King's Theatre on his own account, Oct. 29. He invites H. to write two new operas and a pasticcio. Funeral Anthem for Queen Caroline sung in Westminster Abbey, Dec. 17.	
1738	53	Production of the opera, *Faramondo,* at the King's Theatre under Heidegger's management, Jan. 7, of the pasticcio, *Alessandro Severo,* Feb. 25, and of the opera, *Serse,* April 15 (?). Concert at Vauxhall, where Roubiliac's (42) statue of H. is unveiled, May 2. First	Battishill born, May; Murschhauser (75) dies, Jan. 6.

meeting of the Royal Society for the Support of Decayed Musicians founded by Greene (43) and Festing, of which H. becomes a member, April 19. Arne (28), Boyce (28), Carey (*c.* 48) and Pepusch (71) are present. Oratorios, *Saul* and *Israel in Egypt,* finished, Sept. 27 and Nov. 1. 6 organ Concertos (Op. 4) published by Walsh, Oct. 4. 7 Sonatas for two violins, flutes or oboes and harpsichord (Op. 5) composed.

1739 54 Oratorio, *Saul,* produced at the King's Theatre, Jan. 16, and *Israel in Egypt,* April 4 and 11. Italian opera being now almost completely obliterated, H., who is now at the theatre in Lincoln's Inn Fields, adds oratorios, serenades and odes to his repertory. Composition of Dryden's *Ode for St. Cecila's Day* finished, Sept. 24. 12 *Concerti grossi* for strings (Op. 6) composed, Sept. 29–Oct. 30. First performance of the *Ode for St. Cecilia's Day* at Lincoln's Inn, Nov.

Dittersdorf born, Nov. 2; Keiser (65) dies, Sept. 12; Marcello (53) dies, July 24; Rust born, July 6; Wanhal born, May 12.

		22. H., like Hogarth (42), takes an active interest in the Foundling Hospital just founded by Captain Coram (71).	
1740	55	First performance of *L'Allegro, il Penseroso ed il Moderato* for solo voices, chorus and orchestra, at the theatre in Lincoln's Inn Fields, Feb. 27. Opera, *Imeneo,* finished Oct. 10 and produced Nov. 22, without a suitable Italian company and without success. His last opera, *Deidamia,* finished, Nov. 20. 12 *Concerti grossi* (Op. 6) and 6 organ Concertos (Op. 7) published by Walsh.	Arnold born, Aug. 10; Böhm (79) dies (approx.); Lotti (73) dies, Jan. 5; Webbe born.
1741	56	Production of the opera, *Deidamia,* Jan. 10. It is given only three times, Italian opera being now definitely out of fashion. H., utterly discouraged and financially ruined, decides to retire from his public activities and gives a farewell concert, April 8. Oratorio, *Messiah,* begun Aug. 22 and finished Sept. 12. Oratorio, *Samson,* finished, except two numbers, Oct. 29.	Arne (Michael) born; Desmarets (79) dies, Sept. 7; Fux (81) dies, Feb. 13; Grétry born, Feb. 8; Naumann born, April 17; Paisiello born, May 9.

Year	Age	Life	Contemporary Musicians
		Messiah rehearsed at Chester. H. arrives in Dublin, where he has been invited by the Duke of Devonshire, who is Lord Lieutenant of Ireland, Nov. 18. Series of subscription concerts opened in Dublin, Dec. 23. 6 orchestral Concertos by H., Tartini (49) and Veracini (*c.* 56) published by Walsh.	
1742	57	*Hymen*, an English concert version of *Imeneo* (*see* 1740), produced March 24. Production of *Messiah* in Dublin, April 13, and repeated, June 3. Return to London, Aug. 13. Oratorio, *Samson*, completed, Oct. 12.	Abaco (67) dies, July 12.
1743	58	Production of *Samson*, at Covent Garden, Feb. 18. First London performance of *Messiah*, at Covent Garden, March 23. Secular oratorio, *Semele*, finished, July 4. Oratorio, *Joseph and his Brethren*, finished, Sept. *Te Deum* and Anthem for the victory of Dettingen performed in the Chapel Royal, Nov. 27.	Boccherini born, Feb. 19; Carey (*c.* 53) dies, Oct. 4; Vivaldi (*c.* 73) dies.
1744	59	Production of *Semele* at Covent Garden, Feb. 10, and of *Jos-*	Campra (84) dies, June 29; Leo (50) dies, Oct. 31.

Year	Age	Life	Contemporary Musicians
		eph and his Brethren, March 2. Secular oratorio, *Hercules*, finished, Aug. 17. Oratorio, *Belshazzar*, finished, autumn (approx.). H. again takes the lease of the King's Theatre, autumn.	
1745	60	Production of *Hercules* at Haymarket, Jan. 5. Production of *Belshazzar* at one of H.'s subscription concerts at the King's Theatre, March 27. H. is again ill. He is again obliged to give up the performances at the King's Theatre, which his opponents have done their best to damage, April. Meeting with Gluck (31) on his visit to England, autumn. Loyalty of H. during the "1745."	Albinoni (71) dies (approx.); Dibdin born, March 4.
1746	61	Production of the *Occasional Oratorio*, specially written for the Covent Garden season, which again proves unprofitable, Feb. 14. H. appears with Gluck (32) at a concert and plays a Concerto of his own, March 25. Oratorio, *Judas Maccabaeus*, finished, Aug. 11.	Hook born, June 3; Stamitz (C.) born, May 7.
1747	62	In Lent H. again takes	

Year Age	*Life*	*Contemporary Musicians*
	Covent Garden Theatre for a series of subscription concerts. The season is more successful and *Judas Maccabaeus*, produced April 1, is repeated five times. Oratorios, *Alexander Balus* and *Joshua*, finished, July 4 and Aug. 19.	
1748 63	*Joshua* and *Alexander Balus* produced at Covent Garden, which Handel has again taken for a series of Lenten Concerts, March 9 and 23. Oratorios, *Solomon* and *Susanna*, finished, June 13 and Aug. 24.	Shield born, March 5.
1749 64	*Susanna* and *Solomon* produced during Lent at Covent Garden, Feb. 10 and March 17. Music written for the fireworks to be held in Green Park in celebration of the Peace of Aix-la-Chapelle, April 27. H. offers the governors of the Foundling Hospital the proceeds of a concert. The concert held in the chapel of the hospital, May 27, and an Anthem composed for the occasion performed. Oratorio, *Theodora*, finished, July 31.	Cimarosa born, Dec. 17; Destouches (*c*. 77) dies (approx.); Vogler born, Jan. 15.
1750 65	H. finishes music to	Bach (65) dies, July 28;

Year	Age	Life	Contemporary Musicians
		Alcestis, a dramatic piece by Smollett (29), to be staged by Rich (*c.* 68) at Covent Garden, Jan. 8. It is withdrawn, and he uses nearly all the music for the interlude, *The Choice of Hercules,* which is finished, July 5. *Theodora* produced at Covent Garden without success, March 16. H. for the first time plays the organ presented by him to the Foundling Hospital, and conducts *Messiah* there, May 1. Elected a governor of the Foundling Hospital, May 9. He pays his last visit to Germany, summer. Coach accident in Holland.	Buononcini (78) dies (approx.); Salieri born, Aug. 19; Sammartini (G.) (*c.* 57) dies (approx.); Veracini (*c.* 65) dies.
1751	66	*The Choice of Hercules* produced at Covent Garden, March 1. H. visits Cheltenham to take the waters, the symptoms of his illness of 1737, recurrent ever since, making themselves strongly felt, spring to June 13. His eyesight begins to fail. Oratorio, *Jephtha,* finished, Aug. 30. On seeking medical advice, H. finds that blindness is imminent, winter.	Lampe (48) dies, July 25; Terradellas (38) dies, May 20.

Year Age	*Life*	*Contemporary Musicians*
1752 67	Production of *Jephtha* at Covent Garden, Feb. 26. His Lenten seasons there now enjoy universal recognition. Unsuccessful operation on his eyes, May 3.	Clementi born, (?) Jan.; Pepusch (82) dies, July 20; Reichardt born, Nov. 25; Zingarelli born, April 4.
1753 68	Is now almost totally blind. John Christopher Smith (41), acts as his amanuensis.	Dalayrac born, June 13; Viotti born, May 23.
1754 69	Unable to write new works, he is able, with the help of Smith (42), to revise and add to old ones. He also appears at concerts occasionally, playing harpsichord and organ from memory or extemporizing.	Kozeluch born.
1755 70		Durante (71) dies, Aug. 13; Winter born.
1756 71		Mozart born, Jan. 27; Umlauf born.
1757 72	Production of *The Triumph of Time and Truth,* a new version of *Il Trionfo del tempo* of 1708 and 1737, produced at Covent Garden, March 4, with additional numbers dictated to J. C. Smith (45).	Pleyel born, June 1; Scarlatti (D.) (72) dies; Stamitz (J.) (40) dies, March 30.
1758 73	His health deteriorates. Towards the end of the year his appetite leaves him and he has premonitions of his approaching end. But	Dagincourt (74) dies; Zelter born, Dec. 11.

Year Age   *Life*   *Contemporary Musicians*

    he still appears at some concerts.

1759 74 In spite of his failing health, H. attends a performance of *Messiah* on March 30. He is seized with faintness afterwards and has to take to his bed.

    Handel dies in London, April 14.

Graun (58) dies, Aug. 8. Agricola (J. F.) aged 39; Alcock 44; Anfossi *c*. 23; Arne (T. A.) 49; Arne (M.) 18; Arnold 19; Avison *c*. 49; Aylward 29; Ayrton 25; Bach (W. F.) 49; Bach (C. P. E.) 45; Bach (J. C.) 24; Battishill 21; Benda (F.) 50; Benda (G.) 37; Boccherini 16; Boyce 49; Cannabich 28; Carter 25; Cimarosa 10; Clementi 7; Cook (B.) 25; Dalayrac 6; Daquin 65; Dauvergne 46; Dibdin 14; Dittersdorf 20; Duni 50; Fasch (J. F.) 71; Fasch (C. F. C.) 23; Francœur 61; Galuppi 53; Gassmann 36; Gazzaniga 16; Geminiani 79; Gluck 45; Gossec 25; Graun 58; Graupner 72; Grétry 18; Hasse 60; Haydn 27; Hiller (J. A.) 31; Holzbauer 48; Hook 13; Jackson 29; Jommelli 45; Kirnberger 38; Kozeluch 5; Krebs 46; Leclair 62; Linley 27; Locatelli 66; Martini 53; Monsigny 30; Mozart 3; Muffat (jun.) 69; Myslivecek 22; Nardini 37; Nares 44; Naumann 18; Nichelmann 42; Paisiello 18; Philidor 33; Piccinni 31; Pleyel 2; Porpora 73; Quantz 62; Rameau 76; Reichardt 7; Richter (F. X.) 50; Rust 20; Sacchini

Year Age   Life

Contemporary Musicians
25; Salieri 9; Sammartini
(G. B.) *c.* 58; Sarti 30;
Shield 11; Stamitz (C.)
13; Tartini 67; Telemann
78; Traetta 32; Umlauf 3;
Viotti 6; Vogler 10;
Wagenseil 44; Wanhal 20;
Webbe 19; Winter 4; Zel-
ter 1; Zingarelli 7.

Appendix B

CATALOGUE OF WORKS[1]

OPERAS

Admeto (1727) (73).

Agrippina (1709), Vincenzo Grimani[2] (57).

Alcina (1735) (86).

Alessandro (1726), Antonio Rolli (72).

Almira, Königin von Castilien (1704), Friedrich Keustking and Lope de Vega (55).

Amadigi (1715), Heidegger (62).

Arianna (1734), Francis Colman (83).

Arminio (1737) (89).

Ariodante (1735), Antonio Salvi (85).

Atalanta (1736) (87).

Berenice (1737) (90).

Deidamia (1741), Rolli (94).

Ezio (1732), Metastasio (80).

Faramondo (1738), Apostolo Zeno (91).

Flavio (1723), Nicola Haym (67).

Floridante (1721), Rolli (65).

Giulio Cesare (1724), Haym (68).

Giustino (1737), Count Beregani (88).

Imeneo (1740) (93).

Lotario (1729), Matteo Noris (77).

[1] The numbers of the appropriate volumes in Chrysander's Händelgesellschaft edition are given in brackets. HHA after a title signifies the new, definitive Hallische Händel-Ausgabe (Bärenreiter of Kassel and Deutscher Verlag für Musik, of Leipzig). Works shown thus * are in preparation; otherwise full scores and performing material are available. The name of the editor is also given in each case. With each work, and published separately, is a critical commentary.

[2] Names given after the dates are those of the librettists.

Muzio Scevola (1721), Rolli (third act only by Handel) (64).

Orlando (1733), Braccioli (82).

Ottone (1723), Haym (66).

Partenope (1730), Silvio Stampiglia (78).

Pastor fido, Il (first version, 1712). Giacomo Rossi (59).

Pastor fido, Il (second version, 1734) (84).

Poro (1731), Metastasio's *Alessandro nell' Indie* (79).

Radamisto (1720), Haym (63).

Riccardo primo, re d'Inghilterra (1727), Rolli (74).

Rinaldo (two versions, 1711 and 1731), Rossi (58).

Rodelinda (1725), Haym (70).

Rodrigo (1707) (56).

Scipione (1726), Rolli (71).

Serse (1738) (92); HHA, ed. Rudolph Steglich.

Silla (1714) (61).

Siroe (1728), Haym, after Metastasio (75).

Sosarme (1732), Noris (81).

Tamerlano (1724), Haym (69).

Teseo (1713), Haym (60).

Tolomeo, re d'Egitto (1728), Haym (76).

Lost Hamburg Operas:

    Daphne (c. 1706), Hinsch.

    Florindo (c. 1706), Hinsch.

    Nero (1705), Feustking.

Advertised in 1739, but probably never performed:

    Jupiter in Argos (MS. in the Fitzwilliam Museum, Cambridge).

Unperformed and unpublished:

    Alfonso primo.

    Flavio Olibrio.

    Honorius.

    Tito.

    Unnamed Opera (MS. in the Fitzwilliam Museum).

Recitatives to 11 Pasticcios compiled by Handel from works by various composers (1730–47).

BALLET

Terpsichore (1734) (84).

INCIDENTAL MUSIC

Alceste (1750), Tobias Smollett (46).

Alchymist, The (1732), Ben Jonson.

SERENATAS, MASQUES, PASTORALS, ODES AND INTERLUDES

Aci, Galatea e Polifemo (two versions, 1708 and 1732) (95).

Acis and Galatea (1719), John Gay (3).

Alexander's Feast (1736), Dryden (12); HHA, ed. Konrad Ameln.

Allegro, il Penseroso ed il Moderato, L' (1740), Charles Jennens, after Milton (6); HHA, ed. J. S. and M. V. Hall.

Choice of Hercules, The (1751) (18); HHA, ed. Walther Siegmund-Schultze.*

Haman and Mordecai (first version of *Esther*) (1720), ? Pope, after Racine (40).

Hercules (1745), Rev. T. Broughton (4).

Hymen. English concert version of the opera *Imeneo* (1742).

Ode for the Birthday of Queen Anne (1713) (46); HHA, ed. Walther Siegmund-Schultze.

Ode for St. Cecilia's Day (1739), Dryden (23).

Parnasso in festa, Il (1734) (54).

Praise of Harmony (c. 1739), Newburgh Hamilton.

Semele (1744), after Congreve (7).

ORATORIOS

Alexander Balus (1748), Rev. Thomas Morell (33).

Athaliah (1733), Samuel Humphreys (5).

Belshazzar (1745), Charles Jennens (19).

Deborah (1733), Humphreys (29).

Esther (second version of *Haman and Mordecai*, 1732), Humphreys (41).

Israel in Egypt (1739), words from the Bible (16).

Jephtha (1752), Morell (44).

Joseph and his Brethren (1744), Rev. James Miller (42).

Joshua (1748), Morell (17).

Judas Maccabaeus (1747), Morell (22).

Messiah (1742), words from the Bible (45); HHA, ed. John Tobin.*

Occasional Oratorio (1746), ? Morell (43).

Resurrezione, La (1708) (39).

Samson (1743), Newburgh Hamilton, after Milton (10).

Saul (1739), Jennens (13); HHA, ed. Percy M. Young.

Solomon (1749), ? Morell (26).

Susanna (1749) (1); HHA, ed. Bernard Rose.*

Theodora (1730), Morell (3).

Trionfo del tempo e del disinganno, Il (1708 and 1737), Benedetto Pamfili (24).

Triumph of Time and Truth, The (1757) (20).

Passion Music

Der für die Sünden der Welt gemarterte und sterbende Jesus (1716), Barthold Heinrich Brockes (15); HHA, Karl G. Fellerer.*

Johannespassion (1704), Gospel of St. John and arias by Wilhelm Postel (9); HHA, ed. W. Schröder.*

Church Music

Ach Herr, mich armen Sünder, Church Cantata (*c.* 1696).
Chandos Anthems (1716–18) (34–5):
  1. *O be joyful in the Lord.*
  2. *In the Lord I put my trust.*
  3. *Have mercy upon me.*
  4. *O sing unto the Lord a new song.*
  5. *I will magnify Thee.*
  6. *As pants the hart.*
  7. *My song shall be alway.*
  8. *O come, let us sing.*
  9. *O praise the Lord with one consent.*
  10. *The Lord is my light.*
  11. *Let God arise.*
  12. *O praise the Lord, ye angels of His.*
Coronation Anthems (1727) (14):
  1. *Zadok the Priest.*
  2. *The King shall rejoice.*
  3. *My heart is inditing.*
  4. *Let Thy hand be strengthened.*
Dettingen Anthem (1743) (36).
Dettingen *Te Deum* (1743) (25).
Dixit Dominus (1707) (38); HHA, ed. Eberhard Wenzel.
Foundling Hospital Anthem (1749) (36).
Funeral Anthem for Queen Caroline (1737) (11).
Gloria Patri (1707).
Haec est Regina virginum (*c.* 1707–8).
Hymns. Rev. C. Wesley (MS. in the Fitzwilliam Museum):
  O Love divine, how sweet thou art.
  Rejoice, the Lord is King.
  Sinners, obey the Gospel Word
  Kyrie Eleison (incomplete, 1707).
Lobe den Herrn meine Seele (1719).
Laudate pueri, F major (1702) (38).

Laudate pueri, D major (1707) (38).

Magnificat (1707?).

Nisi Dominus (1702–7) (38).

O praise the Lord, anthem (36).

Salve Regina, G minor (1707) (38).

Seuiat tellus inter vigores (1707).

Silete venti, motet (1729?) (38).

Te Deum, A major (*c.* 1727) (37).

Te Deum, B flat major (1716–18) (37).

Te Deum, D major (*c.* 1714) (37).

Utrecht *Te Deum* and *Jubilate* (1713) (31).

Wedding Anthem for Princess Anne (1734) (36).

Wedding Anthem for the Prince of Wales (1736) (36).

VOCAL CHAMBER MUSIC

6 *Alleluias* for voice and harpsichord (*c.* 1735–45) (38).

Venus and Adonis, cantata for soprano (words by John Hughes).[3]

72 Italian Cantatas for one or two voices and instruments (50–3).

7 Italian Cantatas (MSS. in the Fitzwilliam Museum).

20 Italian Duets with continuo (1707–8, 1741–5) (32):

    1. *Caro autor di mia doglia.*

    2. *Giù nei Tartarei regni.*

    3. *Sono liete, fortunate.*

    4. *Troppo cruda, troppo fiera.*

    5. *Che vai pensando.*

    6. *Amor gioie mi porge.*

    7. *Va, speme infida.*

    8. *A mirarvi io sono intento.*

    9. *Quando in calma.*

    10. *Tacete, ohimè, tacete.*

    11. *Conservate, raddoppiate.*

    12. *Tanti strali al sen.*

    13. *Langue, geme, sospira.*

    14. *Se tu non lasci amore.*

    15. *Quel fior che all' alba ride.*

    16. *No, di voi non vo' fidarmi.*

    17. *No, di voi non vo' fidarmi.*

    18. *Beato in ver.*

    19. *Fronda leggiera.*

[3] Discovered in anonymous MS. in British Museum by William C. Smith and performed at Handel Festival, Halle, 1962.

20. *Ahì, nelle sorti umane.*
2 Italian Trios with continuo (32):
   1. *Se tu non lasci amore.*
   2. *Quel fior che all' alba ride.*
7 French canzonets (1708).
3 *Deutsche Lieder* (pub. Breitkopf and Härtel, 1933).
9 *Deutsche Arien* (pub. Breitkopf and Härbel).

INSTRUMENTAL CHAMBER MUSIC

Hornpipe for the Concert at Vauxhall (1740) (48).
8 *Sinfonie diverse* (48).
15 Solos for a German flute, oboe or violin and continuo, Op. 1 (*c.* 1724) (27).
Sonata for 2 violins, bass and organ, G minor (48).
Sonata for *viola da gamba* and cembalo, C major (*c.* 1705) (48).
3 Sonatas for flute and cembalo (*c.* 1710) (48).
9 Sonatas for 2 violins, oboes or flutes and continuo, Op. 2 (1733) (27).
7 Sonatas for 2 violins or German flutes and continuo, Op. 5 (1738) 27).
6 Sonatas or Trios for two oboes and continuo (1696) (27).
11 Sonatas for flute and continuo, HHA, ed. Hans-Peter Schnitz.
6 Sonatas for violin and continuo, HHA, ed. J. P. Hinnenthal.

ORCHESTRA

6 *Concerti grossi,* for flutes, oboes, bassoons and strings, Op. 3 (1729) (21); HHA, ed. Frederick Hudson.
   1. B flat major-G minor. 2. B flat major. 3. G major.
   4. F major. 5. D minor. 6. D major-minor.
12. *Concerti grossi,* for strings, Op. 6 (1739) (30); HHA, ed. Adolf Hoffman and Hans F. Redlich.
   1. G major. 2. F major. 3. E minor. 4 A minor.
   5. D major. 6. G minor. 7. B flat major. 8. C minor.
   9. F major. 10. D minor. 11. A major. 12. B minor.
Concerto, C major, for 2 oboes, bassoon, 4 horns, strings and continuo (47).[4]
Concerto, D major, for 2 oboes, bassoon, 4 horns, 2 trumpets, drums, strings and continuo (47).[4]

[4] These two works are identical, and both are used in the *Fireworks Music.*

Concerto, F major, for 2 oboes, bassoon, 2 horns, strings and continuo (47).

Concerto grosso, C major, for 2 oboes and strings (21).

Concertos:

1. B flat major, for oboe and strings (21).
2A. B flat major, for oboe and strings (21).
2B. F major, for 2 horns and strings (21).
3. G minor, for oboe and strings (21).
4. (Sonata) B flat major, for solo violin, oboes and strings (21).

Double Concerto (*a due cori*), E flat major (? 1740–50) (47).

Double Concerto, F major (? 1740–50) (47).

Fireworks Music (1749) (47).

Overture for the pasticcio, *Alessandro Severo* (1738) (48).

Overture for the pasticcio, *Oreste* (1734) (48).

Overture in B flat major (48).

Water Music (*c.* 1717) (47).

ORGAN AND ORCHESTRA

6 Concertos, Op. 4 (1738) (28):

    1. G minor. 2. B flat major. 3. G minor. 4. F major.
    5. F major. 6. B flat major.

6 Concertos, Op. 7 (1740) (28):

    1. B flat major. 2. A major. 3 B flat major. 4. D minor.
    5. G minor. 6 B flat major.

5 Concertos (48):

    1. F major. 2. A major. 3. D minor. 4. D minor. 5. F major.

HARPSICHORD MUSIC

Capriccio, F major (2).
Capriccio, G minor (2).
Chaconne, F major (2).
Courante e due Minuetti, F major (2).
Fantasia, C major (2).
6 Fugues (*c.* 1720) (2).
Lesson, A minor (2).
Preludio ed Allegro, G minor (2).
6 Short Fugues (48).
Sonata, C major (2).
Sonata, C major (2).
Sonatina, B flat major (2).
Suite, D minor (2).

Suite, G minor (2).

Suites (or Lessons) (1720) (2):

1. A major. 2. F major. 3. D minor. 4. E minor.
5. E major. 6. F sharp minor. 7. G minor. 8. F minor. HHA, ed. Rudolph Steglich.

Suites (or Lessons) (1733) (2):

1. B flat major.[5] 2. G major. 3. D minor. 4. D minor.
5. E minor. 6. G minor. 7. B flat major. 8. G major.
9. G major (*Chaconne*).

Various Suites (48).

There was a tradition that, during his 1737 visit to Aix-la-Chapelle, Handel wrote a *Jubelkantate* for the city of Elbing in East Prussia, and that the music was subsequently lost. The facts are that for the fifth centenary of the foundation of the city a libretto was compiled by one Seiler, headmaster of the Gymnasium, and that music was arranged for it by Johann Jeremias du Grain. The work was entitled *Hermann von Balcke*. The recitatives were supplied by du Grain and the arias, some of which were also by du Grain, were in part adapted from Handel's *Partenope, Riccardo I, Ottone, Admeto, Scipione* and *Alessandro*. Handel himself was unaware of this pasticcio, at any rate before its performance. The MS. was discovered at Elbing by Irmgard Leux (*vide Archiv für Musikwissenschaft*, vol. vii, pp. 441–51). *Hermann van Balcke* was broadcast from Königsberg in 1933.[6]

[5] Containing the air (with variations) on which Brahms wrote variations of his own for piano.

[6] I am indebted to Professor O. E. Deutsch for permitting me to use this information.

Appendix C

PERSONALIA

Abaco, Giuseppe dall' (1709–1805), Italian cellist, born in Brussels, son of the violinist Evaristo dall' Abaco. He worked at Bonn, London, Vienna and elsewhere, and composed cello sonatas.

Albinoni, Tommaso (1674–1745), Venetian violinist and composer.

Ariosti, Attilio (born *c.* 1660), Italian operatic composer, who produced his first opera, *Dafne,* at Venice in 1686.

Arne, Cecilia. See Young.

Arne, Susanna Maria. See Cibber.

Avison, Charles (*c.* 1710–70), organist at Newcastle-on-Tyne. Pupil of Geminiani and author of *An Essay on Musical Expression,* in which Handel is sometimes adversely criticized.

Avolio (or *Avoglio*), *Signora,* Italian soprano singer of whose career nothing is known apart from its coincidence with that of Handel.

Baldassari, Benedetto, Italian tenor singer, in London 1720–2.

Banister, John (died 1735), English violinist and teacher of his instrument, composer for the theatre, son of John Banister (1630–79).

Beard, John (*c.* 1717–91), English tenor singer, chorister at the Chapel Royal under Gates (q.v.) in his boyhood, appeared first as a mature singer in works by Handel in 1736.

Bernacchi, Antonio (1685–1756), Italian male soprano singer and teacher, first heard in London in 1716.

Berselli, Matteo, Italian tenor singer, who came to London with Senesino (q.v.) in 1720.

Bertolli, Francesca, Italian contralto singer, first heard in London in 1729.

Bordoni, Faustina (1693–1783), Italian mezzo-soprano singer, made her first appearance in Venice in 1716 and came to London ten years later. Married Hasse (q.v.) in 1730.

Boschi, Giuseppe, Italian bass singer, member of St. Mark's, Venice; (?) sang Polyphemus in Handel's *Aci* in Naples, 1709. First appeared in London in 1711.

Boyce, William (1710–79), English composer and organist, boy chorister at St. Paul's Cathedral in London and later pupil of Greene (q.v.), whom he succeeded in 1755 as Master of the King's Band. Organist of the Chapel Royal from 1758. Published a collection of English *Cathedral Music* 1760–78.

Brade, William (1560–1630), English string player and composer who worked in Germany. In 1618 he was in Halle and his daughter Magdalene married a surgeon to whom Handel's father was apprenticed.

Brockes, Barthold Heinrich (1608–1747), poet and important official in Hamburg.

Buononcini (or *Bononcini*), *Giovanni Battista* (born 1672), Italian opera composer, son of Giovanni Maria Buononcini (*c.* 1640–78), whose pupil he was and whom he succeeded as chapel-master of the church of San Giovanni in Monte at Modena, his birthplace. Attached to the court of Vienna in 1692 and of Berlin in 1696; produced his first operas in Rome in 1694. Vienna and Italy, 1706–20; London, 1720–32.

Burney, Charles (1726–1814), composer and historian. His Handel comments are valuable in that he had played the violin in Handel's orchestra.

Buxtehude, Dietrich (1637–1707), Swedish composer and organist, settled in Denmark and from 1668 organist of St. Mary's Church at Lübeck.

Campra, André (1660–1744), French composer of Italian descent. He became musical director at Notre-Dame in Paris, but was also famous as an opera composer.

Caporale, Andrea (died *c.* 1756), Italian violoncello player who came to London in 1734 and joined Handel's opera orchestra in 1740.

Carestini, Giovanni (*c.* 1705–*c.* 1759), Italian male soprano singer, afterwards a contralto. Came out in Rome in 1721 and made his first London appearance in 1733.

Carey, Henry (*c.* 1690–1743), English poet, composer and dramatist, pupil of Roseingrave (q.v.) and Geminiani (q.v.).

Carissimi, Giacomo (? 1604–74), Italian composer who cultivated the forms of oratorio and cantata in their early stages.

Castrucci, Pietro (1679–1752) and *Prospero* (died 1760), Italian violinists, who came to London in 1715, Pietro becoming leader of Handel's opera orchestra and Prospero a member of it.

Cervetto, Giacomo (1682–1783), Italian violinist and composer, who settled in London in 1728. He wrote violin and chamber music.

Cibber, Susanna Maria (née Arne) (1714–66), English contralto singer and actress, sister of Thomas Augustine Arne. She first appeared on the London stage in 1732 and married Theophilus Cibber in 1734.

Clari, Giovanni Carlo Maria (1677–1754), Italian composer. He was chapel-master in turn at Pistoia, Bologna and Pisa.

Clayton, Thomas (*c.* 1670–*c.* 1730). English composer and adapter, who set Addison's opera, *Rosamond*, in 1707, and for whom Pope wrote his *Ode for St. Cecilia's Day* in 1713.

Clegg, John (1714–*c.* 1750), English violinist of outstanding gifts, who became insane in 1744.

Coperario, Giovanni (John Cooper) (*c.* 1570–1627), English lutenist, violist and composer who worked under an assumed Italian name after his studies in Italy, whence he returned to England *c.* 1604.

Croft, William (1678–1727), English organist and composer, pupil of John Blow at the Chapel Royal, organist at St. Anne's, Soho, from 1700 and organist with Jeremiah Clark at the Chapel Royal from 1704; Master of the Children there from 1715.

Cuzzoni, Francesca (*c.* 1700–70), Italian soprano singer, first appeared in Venice in 1719 and in London in 1722.

Defesch, William (died *c.* 1758), Flemish organist, violinist and composer, who settled in London in 1731, having been organist at Antwerp cathedral.

Dieupart, Charles (died *c.* 1740), French violinist, harpsichord player and composer settled in London.

Dubourg, Matthew (1703–67), English violinist, pupil of Geminiani (q.v.), for many years in Dublin and towards the end of his life in London, his birthplace.

Durastanti, Margherita (born *c.* 1695), Italian soprano singer, who came to London in 1720 and again in 1733. The text of a cantata sung by her at a benefit concert was by Alexander Pope.

Ebner, Wolfgang (c. 1610–65), German organist and composer who worked in Vienna, both at St. Stephen's Cathedral and in the court chapel.

Épine, Francesca Margherita de l' (died 1746), Italian or French singer, who first came to England in 1692, remaining there until her death and marrying Pepusch (q.v.) in 1718.

Erba, Dionigi, Italian composer, chapel-master at the church of San Francesco, Milan, in 1692.

Fabri, Annibale Pio (1697–1760), Italian tenor singer also known under the name of "Balino," who first came to England in 1729. He was also a composer.

Farinelli (Carlo Broschi) (1705–82), Italian male soprano singer, made his first appearance in Rome in 1722, when he had already acquired some fame in southern Italy, and went to Vienna in 1724. His first appearance in London was in 1734.

Ferrabosco, Alfonso (c. 1575–1628). English composer of Italian descent, educated at Queen Elizabeth's expense. He became a musician at the court of James I.

Festing, Michael Christian (died 1752), English violinist and composer for his instrument in London, pupil of Geminiani (q.v.). Made his first appearance about 1724 and became a member of the king's private band in 1735. Musical director of Ranelagh Gardens from 1742.

Frasi, Giulia, Italian singer, who first appeared in London in 1743.

Froberger, Johann Jacob (c. 1617–67), German organist and composer. He was a pupil of his father at Halle, court organist in Vienna in 1637–57, visited Italy and England, and died in France.

Galliard, John Ernest (c. 1687–1749), German composer, settled in England c. 1706. Oboist, composer of pantomimes, anthems and cantatas.

Galuppi, Baldassare (1706–85), Venetian composer, who produced his first opera at Vicenza in 1722. He was in London in 1741–3, became vice chapel-master at St. Mark's in Venice in 1748 and chapel-master in 1762.

Gasparini, Francesco (1668–1727), Italian composer, pupil of Corelli and Pasquini (q.v.), chorus master at the Ospedale di Pietà in Venice, and appointed chapel-master of St. John Lateran in Rome in 1725.

Gates, Bernard (1685–1773), English theorist, singer and composer, Gentleman of the Chapel Royal from 1708 and Master of the Children some time before 1732.

Gaul, Alfred (1837–1913), English organist and composer, pupil of Zachariah Buck at Norwich Cathedral and later organist at various churches in Birmingham.

Geminiani, Francesco (1667–1762), Italian violinist and composer, pupil of Corelli in Rome, came to England in 1714 and lived in London, Dublin, Paris and again in Ireland until his death.

Giardini, Felice de (1716–96), Italian violinist and composer. He studied at Milan Cathedral and with Somis at Turin, played in various Italian opera orchestras, visited Germany and settled in London, where he succeeded Festing as leader of the Opera orchestra in 1752.

Gizziello (Gioacchino Conti) (1714–61), Italian male soprano singer, who first appeared in Rome in 1729 and made his first London appearance in 1736.

Graun, Karl Heinrich (1704–59), German singer and composer. Studied at Dresden, went into the service of the court at Brunswick and later worked at that of Frederick II of Prussia, first at Rheinsberg and after the king's accession at Potsdam and Berlin.

Greene, Maurice (1695–1755), English organist and composer in London, chorister at St. Paul's Cathedral as a boy, where he became organist in 1718. In 1727 he succeeded Croft (q.v.) as organist and composer to the Chapel Royal.

Grimaldi. See Nicolini.

Haberman, Franz Johann (1706–83), Bohemian composer, who published six masses in 1747.

Harington, Henry (1727–1816), English physician and an amateur musician. He was a doctor at Bath and composed vocal music, including probably the familiar setting of Ben Jonson's "Drink to me only."

Hasse, Johann Adolph (1699–1783), German composer of Italian operas, born near Hamburg, where he came out as tenor at Keiser's (q.v.) Opera. Afterwards sang at Brunswick, where he produced his first opera in 1721. Then went to Italy to study dramatic music under Porpora (q.v.) and Alessandro Scarlatti. Appointed musical director and manager of the royal opera at Dresden in 1731. Married Faustina Bordoni (q.v.) in 1730.

Heintz, Wolff (fl. c. 1540), organist at Halle.

Keiser, Reinhard (1674–1739), German composer, studied

under Schelle at St. Thomas's School in Leipzig. Went to the court of Brunswick in 1692 and to Hamburg two years later, where he made the Opera the most distinguished in Germany for a time and composed 116 works for it. He also wrote church music, including oratorios and a Passion according to St. Mark.

Kelway, Joseph (died prob. 1782), organist of St. Martin's-in-the-Fields, harpsichordist to Queen Charlotte. Devoted to the music of Scarlatti.

Kerl (or *Kerll*), *Johann Caspar* (1627–93), German organist and composer, born in Saxony, but settled early in Vienna as a pupil of Valentini. Then studied in Rome under Carissimi (q.v.) and probably the organ under Frescobaldi.[1] In the service of the Elector of Bavaria in Munich, 1656–74. Went to Vienna as private teacher and was appointed court organist there in 1677.

Krieger, Johann Philipp (1649–1725), German organist and composer. Studied at Venice and became chamber musician to the Duke of Saxe-Weissenfels.

Kuhnau, Johann (1660–1722), German organist, clavier player, composer and writer on music, cantor at Zittau, went to Leipzig in 1682, became organist at St. Thomas's Church in 1684 and cantor in 1701, in which post he preceded Bach.

Lampe, John Frederick (*Johann Friedrich*) (1703–51), German bassoon player and composer at Brunswick; came to England about 1725 and settled in London, but went to Dublin in 1748 and to Edinburgh in 1750.

Leveridge, Richard (*c.* 1670–1758), English bass singer in London, who made his first appearance before Purcell's death in 1695 and sang until a few years before that of Handel, his last recorded appearance being in 1751. He was also a composer of songs and theatre music.

Linley, Elizabeth Ann (1754–92), English soprano singer, daughter of Thomas Linley of Bath, where she sang as a child. She made her first important appearance at the Worcester Festival in 1770 and married Sheridan in 1773.

Linley, Mary (1759–87), English singer, sister of the preceding. She sang in oratorio and at festivals until her marriage to Richard Tickell.

Locke, Matthew (*c.* 1630–77), English composer. He was a choir-boy under Edward Gibbons at Exeter Cathedral and

---

[1] But Kerl was only sixteen when Frescobaldi died.

settled in London c. 1650, becoming an important stage and chamber composer.

Lœillet, Jean Baptiste (1680-1730), Flemish flautist, oboist and composer. He settled in London in 1705 and joined the orchestra at the King's Theatre. Later he went to Munich as chamber musician to the Elector of Bavaria, but returned to London some time after 1725.

Lotti, Antonio (c. 1667-1740), Venetian composer, singer in the Doge's chapel as a boy, produced his first opera at the age of sixteen. Became second organist at St. Mark's, Venice, in 1692 and first in 1704. He was at Dresden in 1717-19.

Lupo, Thomas (16th-17th century), English lutenist, singer and composer, member of a large family of musicians of Italian origin.

Mainwaring, Rev. John (1724-1807), rector of Church Stretton, Salop, and Professor of Divinity at Cambridge. Author of many theological works and (for no very obvious reason) Handel's first biographer. He was thirty-six and not, as is frequently stated, twenty-five, when he wrote his biography.

Mattei, Filippo, Italian violoncellist and composer at the Opera in London.

Mattheson, Johann (1681-1764), German writer on music, organist and composer, first sang female parts at the Hamburg Opera, then composed two operas (1699 and 1704), became cantor at Hamburg Cathedral in 1715, wrote several books on music, the most important being *Das neu eröffnete Orchester* (1713), *Der vollkommene Capellmeister* (1739) and *Grundlage einer Ehrenpforte* (1740).

Merighi, Antonia, Italian contralto singer, who first appeared in London in 1729.

Montagnana, Antonio, Italian bass singer, who first appeared in London in 1731.

Muffat, Gottlieb (1690-1770), German composer, pupil of Fux in Vienna, where he became court organist and music master to the imperial children.

Nicolini (Nicola Grimaldi) (born c. 1673), Italian male soprano singer, later a contralto, made his first appearance in Rome, about 1694. First came to England in 1708.

Pasquali, Francesco (16th-17th century), Italian composer who studied and worked in Rome.

Pasquini, Bernardo (1637-1710), Italian composer, who as

a young man became organist of Santa Maria Maggiore in Rome.

Pepusch, John Christopher (Johann Christoph) (1667–1752), German composer and theorist born in Berlin, appointed to the Prussian court at the age of fourteen, emigrated first to Holland and came to England about 1700, where he settled in London for the rest of his life. Married Margherita de l'Épine (q.v.) in 1718.

Pescetti, Giovanni Battista (c. 1704–c. 1766), Italian composer, pupil of Lotti at Venice. He lived in London from c. 1737 to shortly after 1750 and then worked at St. Mark's in Venice.

Porpora, Niccola Antonio (1686–1767), Italian composer, theorist and singing teacher, came to London as Handel's rival in 1729.

Porta, Giovanni (c. 1690–1755), Italian composer. Having been in the service of Cardinal Ottoboni in Rome, he lived in London in 1720–36 and then went to Munich.

Quantz, Johann Joachim (1697–1773), German flautist and composer. He studied at Dresden and Vienna, worked at the Saxon-Polish court at Dresden and Warsaw, travelled in France and England, taught the flute to Frederick II of Prussia, to whose court at Potsdam and Berlin he was attached from 1741.

Ramondon, Lewis (died c. 1720), English or French bass singer and composer, who sang in London until c. 1711 and then made a success as a song composer.

Randall, John (1715–99), English organist and composer, pupil of Gates (q.v.) at the Chapel Royal, organist of King's College, Cambridge, from 1743 and professor there in succession to Greene (q.v.) from 1755. Possibly encouraged Mainwaring (q.v.) to write a biography of Handel.

Robinson, Anastasia (c. 1698–1755), English singer, made her first stage appearance in 1714 and retired ten years later, having married the Earl of Peterborough in 1722.

Roseingrave, Thomas (1690–1766), English or Irish composer and organist, son of Daniel Roseingrave (c. 1650–1727). Organist of St. George's, Hanover Square, London, 1725–38.

Scheidt, Samuel (1587–1654), organist and composer at Halle, and one of the important figures in German music. His acquaintance with English music is shown in variations on a theme of John Dowland. In Halle he was for a time a colleague of William Brade.

Schütz, Heinrich (1585–1672), German composer. Studied at Cassel and Marburg University, also with G. Gabrieli at Venice. He returned to the court of Hesse-Cassel, but in 1614 was appointed musical director to the Elector of Saxony at Dresden.

Senesino (Francesco Bernardi) (c. 1680–c. 1750), Italian male soprano singer, attached to the court opera at Dresden in 1719 and there invited by Handel to London, where he first appeared in 1720.

Shield, William (1748–1829), English violinist and composer. Pupil of his father and of Avison at Newcastle-on-Tyne. He went to London in 1772 to join the Opera orchestra as second violin and the following year became principal viola. He composed stage pieces and in 1817 became Master of the King's Music.

Smith, John Christopher (1712–95), English organist and composer of German descent, son of Johann Christoph Schmidt of Ansbach, who came to England as Handel's treasurer and copyist.

Snow, Valentine (died 1770), English trumpeter, appointed Trumpeter to the King in 1753 in succession to John Shore (died 1752).

Stanley, Charles John (1713–86), English organist, blind from the age of two, pupil of Greene (q.v.), later organist of several London churches.

Steffani, Agostino (1654–1728), Italian composer and diplomat, who spent much of his time in diplomatic missions at German courts, but was a remarkable composer as well as a scholar and priest.

Strada del Pò, Anna, Italian soprano singer, who first appeared in London in 1729.

Stradella, Alessandro (c. 1645–82), Italian composer of noble birth who appears to have held no regular musical appointments, and what is known of his career seems to be based more on legend than on fact.

Strungk, Nikolaus Adam (1640–1700), German violinist, organist and composer, who opened an opera-house at Leipzig in 1693.

Swieten, Gottfried van, Baron (1734–1803), Austrian diplomat, physician and musical amateur in Vienna.

Telemann, Georg Philipp (1681–1767), German composer, studied at the University of Leipzig 1700–4, was appointed organist to the New Church there and founded a Collegium musicum. After holding various posts at Sorau, Eisenach and Frankfort, he was appointed cantor of the Johanneum and musical director to the five principal churches at Hamburg, posts which he held until his death.

Tesi-Tramontini, Vittoria (1700–75), Italian mezzo-soprano singer, who made her first stage appearance at a very early age. In 1719 she was at Dresden, where Handel met her, but did not engage her.

Turini, Francesco (c. 1595–1656), Italian composer. He studied in Prague, Venice and Rome, became chamber musician to the Emperor Rudolph II in Prague and later cathedral organist at Brescia.

Urio, Francesco Antonio, Italian composer at Milan, whose first published work, a set of motets, appeared in 1690.

Valentini (*Valentino Urbani*), Italian male contralto singer, afterwards a counter-tenor, who first came to London in 1707.

Veracini, Francesco Maria (1690–c. 1750), Italian violinist and composer. Studied with his uncle, Antonio Veracini, and with Tartini, lived in London in 1714–17, then worked at the Saxon court at Dresden, went to Prague in 1723 and returned to London c. 1735.

Vivaldi, Antonio (c. 1675–1741), Italian violinist and composer. Studied under his father and under Legrenzi at Venice, where he held various posts all his life, except for visits to Mantua and Vienna.

Waltz, Gustavus, German bass singer, who was (?) for a time Handel's cook.

Weideman, Charles (*Carl Friedrich Weidemann*), German flute player, settled in London about 1726.

Werner, Gregor Joseph (1695–1766), Austrian composer. He was appointed director to the Esterházy family in 1728, being Haydn's predecessor at Eisenstadt.

Whichello, Abiel (died c. 1745), English organist and composer. He was organist at a London church, taught the harpsichord and appeared at Thomas Britton's concerts.

Young, Cecilia (1711–89), English singer, married Arne (1710–78) in 1736.

Zachau, Friedrich Wilhelm (1663–1712), German composer, theorist, and organist at Halle, first teacher of Handel.

Appendix D

BIBLIOGRAPHY

Arbuthnot, John, "Harmony in an Uproar." (London, 1732.)

Avison, Charles, "An Essay on Musical Expression." (London, 1752.)

Bairstow, E. C., "Handel's Oratorio 'The Messiah.'" (Oxford and London, 1928.)

Bayne-Powell, Rosamond, "Eighteenth Century London Life." (London, 1937.)

Bingley, W., "Musical Biography." (London, 1714.)

Bishop, John, "Brief Memoirs of George Frederick Händel." (London, 1856.)

Bredenförder, Elisabeth, "Die Texte der Händel-Oratorien: eine religions geschichtliche und literar-soziologische Studie." (Leipzig, 1934.)

Brenet, Michel, "Haendel." (Paris, 1912.)

Burke, Thomas, "The Streets of London." (London, 1940.)

Burney, Charles, "A General History of Music." (London, 1776–89.)

——"An Account of the Musical Performances in Westminster Abbey and the Pantheon in Commemoration of Handel." (London, 1785.)

Carey, Henry, "Poems." Edited by F. T. Wood. (London, 1930.)

Carse, Adam, "The Orchestra in the XVIIIth Century." (Cambridge, 1940.)

Chrysander, F., "G. F. Händel." 3 vols. (unfinished). (Leipzig, 1858–67.)

Cibber, Mrs. Susannah Maria, "The Life of" (London, 1887.)

Clark, Richard, "Reminiscences of Handel, the Duke of Chandos, etc." (London, 1836.)

Coxe, J. C., "Anecdotes of G. F. Händel and J. C. Smith." (London, 1799.)

Delany, Mary, "Autobiography and Correspondence of Mary Granville, Mrs. Delany." Edited by Lady Llanover. (London, 1861–2.)

Dent, Edward J., "Handel" ("Great Lives" Series). (London, 1934.)

Deutsch, Otto Erich, "Handel, a Documentary Biography." (London, 1955.)

Flower, Newman, "George Frideric Handel: his Personality and his Times." (London, 1922; new ed. 1948.)

Förstemann, Karl Eduard, "G. F. Haendels Stammbaum, nach Originalquellen und authentischen Nachrichten." (Leipzig, 1844.)

Franz, Robert, "Ueber Bearbeitungen älterer Tonwerke, namentlich Bachscher und Händelscher Vokalmusik." (Leipzig, 1781.)

——"Der Messias, unter Zugrundelegung der Mozartschen Partitur." (Leipzig, 1884.)

Hall, James S., "G. F. Handel: the story of his Life and Works."

——"Handel among the Carmelites," in *Dublin Review* (July 1959).

Handel, G. F. Letters and Writings. Edited by Erich H. Müller. (London, 1935.)

——"Messiah." Edited from the Original Sources by J. M. Coopersmith. (New York, 1947.)

Händel-Ehrung (Halle, 1959), "Konterenz bericht," (Leipzig, 1961.)

Handel-Festschriften, (Halle, 1922), (Gottingen, 1953.)

Händel-Jahrbuch. Herausgegeben von Rudolf Steglich. (Leipzig, 1929, etc.)

Hawkins, John, "A General History of the Science and Practice of Music." (London, 1776 and 1853.)

Heinrich, E., "G. F. Händel, ein deutscher Tonmeister." (1884.)

Hoyle, John, "Dictionarium Musica." (London, 1770.)

Ireland, John, "Hogarth Illustrated." (London, 1806.)

Irving, W. H., "John Gay's London." (Harvard, 1928.)

Larsen, J. P., "Handel's 'Messiah.' " (London, 1957.)

Leichtentritt, Hugo, "Händel." (Stuttgart, 1924.)

Loewenberg, A., "Annals of Opera: 1597–1940." (Cambridge, 1943.)

Lysons, Rev. D. (and others), "Annals of the Three Choirs." (Gloucester, 1895.)

Mainwaring, J., "Memoirs of the Life of the late G. F. Handel." (London, 1760.)

Mattheson, Johann, "Grundlage einer Ehrenpforte." (Hamburg, 1740; Berlin, 1910.)

——"G. F. Händels Lebensbeschreibung." (Hamburg, 1761.)

Milnes, Keith, "Memoir relating to the Portrait of Handel by Francis Kyte." (London, 1829.)

Müller-Blattau, J., "Georg Friedrich Händel." (Potsdam, 1933.)

Musical Times, Handel Bicentenary Number (London, April 1959.)

Nichols and Wray, "The History of the Foundling Hospital." (Oxford, 1935.)

Nkarintsev, "Pictures from the Life of Handel." (Moscow, 1937.)

Prout, Ebenezer, "The Orchestra of Handel." (Proceedings of the Musical Association, Leeds, 1885-6.)

Reichardt, J. F., "Georg Friedrich Händels Jugend." (Berlin, 1785.)

Robinson, J. R., "The Princely Chandos." (London, 1893.)

Robinson, Percy, "Handel and his Orbit." (London, 1908.)

Rockstro, W. S., "Life of Handel." (London, 1883.)

Rolland, Romain, "Haendel." (Paris, 1910.)

——"Handel." Translated by A. Eaglefield Hull. (New York, 1923.)

Rosenberg, Alfred, "Georg Friedrich Händel." (Berlin, 1938.)

Rudolph, Johanna, "Händelrenaissance Eine Studie (I)." (Berlin, 1960.)

Sasse, Konrad, "Das Händelhaus in Halle." (Halle, 1958.)

Schoelcher, Victor, "The Life of Handel." (London, 1857.)

Schultz, W. E., "Gay's Beggar's Opera." (New Haven, 1923.)

Siegmund-Schultz, Walther, "Georg Friedrich Händel." (Leipzig, 1959.)

Smith, William C., "Handel: A Descriptive Catalogue of the Early Editions." (London, 1961.)

Squire, W. Barclay, "Catalogue of the King's Music Library: Vol. I, Handel's MSS." (London, British Museum, 1927.)

Stevens, D. H., "Some Immediate Effects of the Beggar's Opera." (Chicago, 1923.)

Streatfeild, R. A., "Handel." (London, 1909.)

——"The Case of the Handel Festival." (London, 1897.)

Taut, Kurt, "Verzeichnis des Schrifttums über Georg Fr. Händel. (Leipzig, 1934.)

Taylor, Sedley, "The Indebtedness of Handel to Works by Other Composers." (Cambridge, 1906.)

Townsend, Horatio, "An Account of Handel's Visit to Dublin." (1852.)

Uffenbach, Zacharias von, "London in 1710 from the Travels of." Translated by W. H. Quennell and Margaret Mare. (London, 1934.)

Ward, Ned, "The London Spy." Edited by A. L. Hayward. (London, 1927.)

Weinstock, Herbert, "Handel." (New York, 1942.)

Weissebeck, J. M., "Der grosse Musikus Händel im Universalruhme." (Nuremberg, 1809.)

Weissenborn, B., "Das Händelhaus in Halle." (Berlin, 1938.)

Williams, Maelwyn I., "Did Handel visit Cardiganshire?" in *Ceredigion, Journal of the Cardiganshire Antiquarian Society*. (1959, pp. 337–43.)

Winchop, Thomas, "Scanderbeg—with a List of all the Dramatic Authors, etc." (London, 1747.)

Appendix E

HANDEL'S FINANCES

RECORDS RELATING TO the banking account of "George Frideric
Handel [the signature in the Firm Book], in Brooke Street
Hanover Square" are still extant in the Record Office of the
Bank of England (fo. 97/2674). With the exception of a
period from 28th March 1739 to 14th February 1743 a
fairly complete statement is available from 2nd August 1732
until 21st March 1758. As details of payments are sparse
("By Cash" on the one side and "To Cash Him" on the
other have little helpful significance), an extract is only given
to cover the alleged bankruptcies. It will be clear that Handel
was not at any rate insolvent either in 1737 or 1745–6.

1734					1732		
June 26 To Cash Him				£1300	Aug. 2 By Cash		£2300
1735							
June 30	"	"	"	300			
Sep. 15	"	"	"	100			
Dec. 8	"	"	"	50			
1736							
Aug. 20	"	"	"	150			
Sep. 28	"	"	"	200			
1737							
Sep. 1	"	"	"	150			
1739							
Mar. 28 yᵉ balance				50			
				£2300			£2300

1743				1743			
Feb. 21	To Cash		650	Feb. 14	By Cash		650
	Chambers[1]			Mar. 6	"	"	250
1744				1744			
Apr. 5	"	do.	226.5.6	Nov. 3	"	"	500
17	"	Him	23.14.6	9	"	"	100
Jan. 19	"	do.	200	Dec. 11	"	"	50
May 4[2]	"	Robinson[3]	210	Jan. 5	"	"	50
May 11	"	Francesina[4]	400	Feb. 1	"	"	150
13	"	Jordan[5]	140				
				1745			
				May 9	"	"	100
			£1850				£1850

1747			1746			
Apr. 29	To Cash Him	1000	Feb. 28	By Cash		400
			Mar. 7	"	"	100
			21	"	"	100
			1747			
			Apr. 9	"	"	250
			24	"	"	150
		1000				1000

These are the only payments specified in the whole of the banking account.

In addition to this series of statements concerning his account at the Bank there are other documents indicative of Handel's shrewd financial sense.[6] Between 4th June 1728 and 22nd June 1732 he bought and sold South Sea Annuities[7] (1751) to the value of £4,622 (fo. 71/124). Between 6th May 1748 and 9th November 1749 his turnover

[1] Possibly Robert Chambers of Hackney (d. 1761), with whom Handel had dealings in 1752.

[2] Obviously 1745.

[3] Fees to Miss Robinson, daughter of John Robinson, organist of Westminster Abbey, and of Mrs. Turner Robinson. Miss Robinson (Hawkins, v. 182) sang in *Hercules* and other oratorios.

[4] Alias Mlle Duparc who, having left the opera, "attached herself to Handel, was first woman in his oratorios for many years." (Burney, *History*, iv. 667).

[5] ? Abraham Jordan, the organ-builder.

[6] Or that of his advisers.

[7] All these loans were managed by the Bank of England.

in 4% Annuities (1748) (fo. 877) was £7,750 and between 10th April 1744 and 6th May 1748 3% Annuities (1743) (fo. D. 1468) involved him to the extent of £3,000. By 2nd January 1753 he held £12,000 in 4% Annuities (1746) (fo. 874). Handel had commenced an interest in these on 22nd February 1749 with an investment of £7,700, which would appear to have come from the sale of the 1748 Annuities. On 2nd January 1753 the £12,000 were transferred to Reduced 3% Annuities. By 1759 these savings grew to £17,500. (fo. D.2646 M.2583).

In the Register Office Book A–K 1348 we read:

> MEMORANDUM that GEORGE FRIDERIC HANDELL of Brooke Street Hanover Square, Esq. in the Probate late of the Parish of St. George Hanover Square In the County of Middx. Esq. died possessed of SEVENTEEN THOUSAND FIVE HUNDRED POUNDS Reduced Annuities at £3 per cent & by his last Will and Testament dated 1st June 1750 appointed JOHANNA FRIDERICA FLOERCKEN Sole Executrix with four Codicils respectively dated the 6th. Aug. 1756, 22nd. March 1757, 4th. Aug. 1757 & 11th. April 1759 wherein he appoints GEORGE AMYAND Esq. Co Executor making no mention of the said Anns. they are at the disposal of the said George Amyand Esq. he only having proved the Will.
>
> Power reserved to make the like grant to Johann Friderica Floercken Wife of ⸻ Floercken the Neice of the said decd. & Executrix named in the said Will when she shall apply for the same.
>
> Probate dated at Doctrs. Comm. 26 April 1759
Regd. 30th. April 1759

The final story of the disposal of Handel's fortune in Reduced 3% Annuities is told in the following statement (D.2646 M.2583). It will be seen that the legatees mentioned hereunder did better than the terms of the will specify.

1759	£	2 Jan. 1753. By Anns.	£
2 May. To Christopher Smith[8] of Dean St. Soho, Gent.	2470	1746 Con'	12000
John Duburk of Hanover Sq., Gent.[9]	600	19 July 1754. Benjamin Jones of Bow, Gent.	1500

---

[8] Was left £2,000 in the will.
[9] Was left £500 in the will.

16 May. Peter Gallier, senior. C h r i s t i a n Reich of Westminster. Gents. Thomas Wood, Gent. of St. Giles in the Fields } 1254

25 May. To William Delacreuse of Castle Street, Esq. 400

Henry Monk of Dublin, Esq. 100

8 June. William Prevost, jnr. of Shad., Thames, Gent. 500

27 June. Edward Shewell of Lombard St. Goldsmith 500

28 June. James Smyth[10] of New Bond St. Perfumer 700

11 Oct. Johanna Friderica Floercken Wife of Johan Ernst Floercken. Director of the University of Halle in Saxony 9000

31 Oct. To James Sinclair[11] of Shadwell. Mariner 500

Lewis Morel of Fleet St. Goldsmith 876

Edward Shewell of Lombard St. Goldsmith 600

17500

14 May 1755. Philip Hale of Basing Lane. Sugar Refiner 500

23 June 1756. Stephen Gardes of Rathbone Place, Gent. 1000

19 May 1758. John Jones of St. Anns, Soho, Gent. 2500

17500

Other legacies included:

£1,000 to the Royal Society of Musicians.

£500 to James Hunter.[12]

£600 for his monument in Westminster Abbey.

£300 each to the five orphan children of his cousin Georg Taust, Pastor of Giebichenstein.

[10] Was left £500 in the will.
[11] Died in 1789 *aetat*. 85, was a senior master in the Navy.
[12] The scarlet-dyer of Old Ford.

£ 300 each to his cousins Christiana Susanna Handelin, and Rachel Sophia; Thomas Harris[13] of Lincoln's Inn Fields; the widow of his cousin Magister Christian Roth.

£ 200 each to Dr. Morell; George Amyand; Reiche, Secretary of Affairs of Hanover.

£ 100 each to John Hetherington, of the Middle Temple; Matthew Dubourg, the violinist; Newburgh Hamilton; Mrs. Palmer, widow, of Chelsea; Thomas Bramwell, his servant.

Fifty guineas each to Benjamin Martyn, of New Bond Street; John Cowland, apothecary; John Belcher, surgeon; Mrs. Mayne, widow, of Kensington; Mrs. Downalan,[14] of Charles Street, Hanover Square.

The will and codicils are in Schoelcher and Rockstro in full.

---

[13] Of the Salisbury family and a master in Chancery.
[14] Or Donellan: an Irishwoman and an intimate of Mrs. Delany.

Appendix F

THE PROBLEM OF PLAGIARISM

THERE ARE TWO considerable books which set with admirable clarity two different points of view concerning Handel's loans from other composers. One is *The Indebtedness of Handel to Works by other Composers* by Sedley Taylor (Cambridge, 1906); the other—in counterblast—*Handel and his Orbit* by Percy Robinson (London, 1908). The passages in Handel (detailed in Sedley Taylor) which appear to refer to music by Muffat (1690–1770), Habermann (1706–83), Clari (1669–1740) and Graun (1711–1759) are of no great significance except in so far as they show Handel's awareness of more or less contemporary publications. To employ other people's thematic material was a usual practice, as Bach often enough indicates; indeed, when Handel was a boy Zachau invariably gave him themes from other composers on which to work. Where Handel's "borrowings" were obvious his contemporaries noted the fact without censure.

"And here it may be noted that the chorus in Mr. Handel's oratorio of *Samson* 'Hear, Jacob's God' is taken from that in [Carissimi's] *Jephtha*, 'Plorate filiae Israel.' " (Hawkins, iii. 92.)

"Handel is supposed to have availed himself of Clari's subjects, and sometimes more, in the choruses of Theodora." (Burney, *History*, iii. 36.)

"In this work [by Turini] there is a canon, upon the subject of which Handel has composed one of his finest instrumental fugues; but, *according to his usual practice* [my italics —P.M.Y.], whenever he adopted another man's thought, he has enlivened and embellished this theme, like a man of true genius, with a counter subject, and shewed that he saw farther into its latent fertility than the original inventor." (Burney, *History*, iii. 521.)

So far so good. But when we come to *Israel in Egypt* we discover that most of the work owes to a Magnificat attributed to one Erba and to a Serenata by Stradella. This means that, if we accept the Sedley Taylor ruling, *Israel in Egypt* should be announced as by Stradella and Erba (edited and arranged by Handel). With regard to the *Dettingen Te Deum* the attribution should be "Urio, arr. Handel." Mr. Robinson, however, suggests, by brilliant reasoning, that Erba, Stradella and Urio were not the composers of the works ascribed to them, but Handel himself. Readers of detective fiction would enjoy following the deductions by which Mr. Robinson proves that one work was written at the house of Benedetto Erba, an Arcadian, that one was simply mis-attributed to the shadowy Stradella and that one was written at Urio on Lake Como: that all, in fact, were really by Handel. Further interesting observations on these works are made by Dr. J. S. Hall.[1]

To revert to the more orthodox doctrine of borrowing, we find Professor Edward J. Dent suggesting that, as Handel used other people's music more intensively after 1737, he needed thematic stimulus of this order on account of the paralysis which had affected the state of his mind. This led speculation up an unpleasant avenue. That form of paralysis which has the direst effect on the mind is syphilitic paralysis. This would have blunted Handel's moral sense and accounted for large-scale depredation of other men's thoughts to an unprecedented degree. Moreover, Handel went to recuperate at Aix-la-Chapelle, which was the European centre for the treatment (such as it was in those days) of venereal disease. Fortunately for Handel's reputation, he did not decline into general paralysis of the insane, which would certainly have been the case had he contracted the French pox. He suffered on two occasions a severe cerebral thrombosis, and recovered in quick time because of efficient vascularity. Such recovery would have left his mentality unimpaired. His "maggots" and his moroseness should therefore not be exaggerated. Since it is the fashion of the day to associate genius with either homosexuality or venereal disease, it had better be stated that there is no particle of evidence to suggest that Handel was tainted by either. Examination of what evidence there is in respect of Handel's physical and mental health has led Dr. Eliot Slater, of the National Hospital for Nervous

[1] See *The Problem of Handel: Latin Church Music*, in *Musical Times*, April 1959.

Diseases, to the conclusion that Handel was a cyclothymic personality—with a fair, but not abnormal, range of mood changes.[2]

[2] "Contributions to a Pathography of the Musicians: 2. Organic and Psychotic Disorders," Eliot Slater and Alfred Meyer, in *Confinia Psychiatrica*, vol. iii, No. 3, pp. 129–145. See also, "Mr. Handel, his health," James S. Hall, F.R.G.S., in St. Mary's Hospital Gazette (London April–May 1960).

Index

HANDEL

Handel, sullen and then suddenly gay, "bursting out of a black cloud"; composing his masterworks swiftly, furiously (two or three weeks for an oratorio); Handel in the royal court, severe at rehearsal, silencing the audience whispers, angry at the prince for coming late; Handel walking in the park, muttering to himself about a charity boy entrusted to his care who absconded; Handel, never married, in love with the charming and brilliant actress, Mrs. Cibber; Handel, famous, idolized, tormented.

We see him here as his contemporaries must have seen him, but, thanks to the insights of modern scholarship, our view of this great, puzzling spirit is now clearer.

Combining biography and musicology of a high order, a distinguished British critic draws a larger-than-life portrait of the composer whose personality has long been such a vexing subject for biographers. Mr. Young flinches from no detail, however bizarre, as he delves into the illness and the strange moods that beset the German-turned-Englishman who created the sublimities of the *Messiah, Israel in Egypt,* and other monuments of music.

Percy M. Young, Mus.D. (Trinity College, Dublin), is a composer as well as a critic. He is the author of The Oratorios of Handel, Vaughan Williams, A Critical Dictionary of Composers and Their Music, The Story of Song, and Instrumental Music.

COLLIER BOOKS
PRINTED IN U.S.A.